Praise for
A Day for Leadership

"Patrick's book is a compelling read. I appreciate how he distills leadership lessons from D-Day into practical insights that can strengthen any team. His perspective is engaging and immediately applicable. As a lifelong learner, I particularly enjoyed his historical evidence, showing how we have always been stronger together in our nation's most pivotal moments."

—Fred Perpall, 67th President of the USGA
and CEO of The Beck Group

"Patrick Ungashick has masterfully woven the most historic event of the 20th century—the 1944 D-Day invasion—into lessons in strategy development and leadership for today's executives and the teams they lead. Utilizing the intricate planning by the D-Day Allied commanders as his standard, Patrick has delivered his readers a well-written series of case studies for developing and executing winning business strategies. A must-read for senior leadership teams of corporations, universities, and nonprofits alike."

—Alec Taylor, chairman and CEO, retired, Foster Grant

"*A Day for Leadership* offers a gripping exploration of the decisions made by leaders on both sides of World War II leading up to D-Day, one of history's most consequential events. Through vivid storytelling and detailed case studies, the book examines the leadership strategies, tough choices, and critical moments that shaped the invasion and its outcome. What sets this book apart is its practical relevance: It's a powerful tool for refining leadership skills in high-stakes situations."

—Oneida DeLuca, owner, Birchwood Consulting

"*A Day of Leadership* does a remarkable job of connecting leadership theories with lessons from the most historic time in human history: World War II and D-Day. The author's instructive and wise approach to these case studies show that, from the battlefield to sports to business, the art of leadership is as unique as each leader's DNA. However, the examples also help us understand that the leadership styles that achieved a winning culture are fragile and must be monitored and amended to meet challenging moments in our ever-changing and highly competitive world."

—John Rowady, president and CEO, rEvolution

"In *A Day for Leadership*, Patrick Ungashick unveils deeply personal and lesser-known stories that offer powerful lessons for today's leaders. Through compelling narratives, Patrick explores the actions of both celebrated figures and those overlooked by history, highlighting moments of remarkable triumph and devastating failure. By examining the pivotal decisions made before, during, and after Operation Overlord—decisions that reshaped the course of history—readers are invited to draw profound parallels to the challenges faced within their own organizations. Complemented by thought-provoking case studies and practical exercises, *A Day for Leadership* is a timeless resource for current and aspiring leaders, offering insights that will inspire and guide for years to come."

—PJ Bain, CEO, Prime Revenue

"Patrick Ungashick's book *A Day for Leadership* is an extraordinarily valuable teaching tool and an exceptional book for any organization or anyone in a position of responsibility—civilian or military. Using various D-Day case studies, Patrick weaves expert teaching points into each cited event. If you run a business or run an army, this is a 'must' book for both you and your people. The key points of building a culture and delegation of complex requirements are as valid today as they were in 1944. Read this book and implement the points Patrick makes—you and your organization will be much better for the experience."

—Col. (Ret.) Keith M. Nightingale, author,
The Human Face of D-Day

"Compelling. Fascinating. Enthralling. As someone who is unfamiliar with the D-Day history, the gripping narrative reveals timeless leadership lessons that resonate powerfully with today's executives and teams."

—Craig Wood, CEO, Premier International

"This is an incredible and interesting read that provides not only the fascinating stories of D-Day and the decisions—both good and bad—that were made around that fateful day, but, more importantly, how organizations can use these lessons to create their own success 'in the heat of battle.' Patrick provides a solid blueprint and outline for thinking through your own strategic decisions in the context of one of the most consequential events of recent history. All my clients will be receiving a copy of the book!"

—Larry Hart, executive coach, Knowledge Experience Value LLC

"Amazing stories that contain real-world lessons for business owners and managers. I can't wait to share this with my company's team."

—Murphy Panagiotou, cofounder and president, Infinity Energy

"Pleasurable read. Interesting post-mortem presentations with crosswalk analysis to today's business challenges. Enjoy the history, ponder the alternate futures, then assess the applicability for current business use cases."

—Rear Admiral (Ret.) Robert P. Wright

"Patrick's unique approach to analyzing history while dissecting the leadership styles, decisions, and moments producing the historic narrative of D-day was brilliant. Not since the 1949 film *Twelve O'Clock High* and the leadership critiques that followed has there been a source as authentic as *A Day for Leadership* for assisting today's business leaders on how to develop their team culture. I look forward to using this book and its enlightening case studies with my Vistage Members."

—Pat Barron, group chair and executive coach,
Vistage International

"I thoroughly enjoyed *A Day For Leadership*. I am exclusively a nonfiction reader who likes serious tomes. This filled the bill. A great read, illustrating historical consequences and impacts from decisions that are hard to imagine having to make. I really enjoyed the 'workshop' tools at the end of each section. I plan to share this with my senior colleagues."

—Steve Peplin, CEO, Talan Products

"I really liked what I read and found that the more I progressed through the pages, the more I wanted to continue. The stories coupled with the 'For you History Buffs' breakouts really addressed how D-Day was more than just a well-planned invasion. I'll be re-reading this book with the idea of starting some of the leadership exercises right away. This is an excellent sampling in helping one understand what goes into great leadership: the tried-and-true steps already in place or being developed that play a huge role in making effective decisions. I'm convinced that whoever reads and practices the lessons revealed in this book will be a better leader and make better decisions."

—Pat Kiernan, president, K-Con Inc.

"With the backdrop of WWII and specifically the strategies, planning, and execution of D-Day, Patrick Ungashick provides an expert framework for today's business executive. Utilizing clear communication, strategic planning, visionary leadership, and the benefit of hindsight, Patrick has recreated the moments of truth for historic leaders that have many revelations for leaders of today."

—Dan Rootenberg, CEO and cofounder, Spear

A DAY FOR LEADERSHIP

A DAY FOR LEADERSHIP

BUSINESS INSIGHTS FOR TODAY'S EXECUTIVES AND TEAMS FROM THE D-DAY BATTLE

PATRICK A. UNGASHICK

FAST
COMPANY
Press

Fast Company Press
New York, New York
www.fastcompanypress.com

This work is being published under the Fast Company Press imprint by an exclusive arrangement with *Fast Company*. *Fast Company* and the *Fast Company* logo are registered trademarks of Mansueto Ventures, LLC. The Fast Company Press logo is a wholly owned trademark of Mansueto Ventures, LLC.

Distributed by Greenleaf Book Group

For ordering information or special discounts for bulk purchases, please contact Greenleaf Book Group at PO Box 91869, Austin, TX 78709, 512.891.6100.

Design and composition by Greenleaf Book Group and Jonathan Lewis
Cover design by Greenleaf Book Group and Jonathan Lewis
Map illustrations by David Borrink
Grateful acknowledgment is made to the following for permission to reproduce copyrighted material: Society of the First Infantry Division: From "Clarence R. Huebner Lieutenant General USA (Retired) 1888 – 1972" by Arthur Chaitt from the *Bridgehead Sentinel*, Spring 1973. Copyright (c) 1973. All rights reserved.

Grateful acknowledgment is also made to:
University of Texas at El Paso Library Special Collections Department, MS307, Terry de la Mesa Allen papers, for the use of the image of US General Terry de la Mesa Allen
Colonel Robert R. McCormick Research Center, First Division Museum at Cantigny Park for the use of the image of US General Clarence Huebner

Publisher's Cataloging-in-Publication data is available.

Print ISBN: 978-1-63908-124-0

eBook ISBN: 978-1-63908-125-7

To offset the number of trees consumed in the printing of our books, Greenleaf donates a portion of the proceeds from each printing to the Arbor Day Foundation. Greenleaf Book Group has replaced over 50,000 trees since 2007.

Printed in the United States of America on acid-free paper

25 26 27 28 29 30 31 32   10 9 8 7 6 5 4 3 2 1

First Edition

"Leadership and learning are indispensable to each other."

—John F. Kennedy, 35th president of
the United States and World War II veteran

Contents

Introduction

On Tuesday, June 6, 1944, the pivotal operation that would decide the outcome of humanity's largest war commenced. On that day, forever known as D-Day, about 156,000 American, British, and Canadian soldiers with 20,000 vehicles invaded the Normandy coast in German-occupied France, transported and escorted by a seaborne fleet of 7,000 ships and seacraft and an airborne armada of 11,000 planes. Within a month, more than one million soldiers representing those three Allied nations, plus a dozen others, stood ashore in France, engaged in a vast struggle that ten months later achieved the final downfall of Germany's heinous Nazi regime. D-Day was the greatest combined amphibious-airborne invasion in history and the most complex military operation ever executed. The day was also a rare example of the course of humanity visibly shifting during a twenty-four-hour period.

The Battle of Normandy that began on D-Day did more than determine World War II's conclusion in Europe. Its outcome immediately impacted the lives of hundreds of millions of people, shaped the future for billions across subsequent generations, and defined political, economic, and cultural realities that remain visible around the planet today. Yet despite the battle's immense scope, its final resolution came down to the decisions and actions of a remarkably few leaders who rose to the occasion in the required moment—or failed to. On D-Day, and during the days leading up to and immediately following the June 6 invasion, the quality and effectiveness of leadership determined the battle's outcome, as much as the size of the armies or the potency of their armaments. These D-Day leaders' military decisions and actions have been extensively studied by historians and popularized in the media. But I believe they remain surprisingly unexamined in light of the lessons they offer to present-day business executives and teams.

An American historian once observed that we study the past to "gain access to the laboratory of human experience."[1] Within the human experience, no laboratory is as deep and vast as World War II. Generally measured as occurring from 1939 to 1945, World War II was the most prodigious event in history in terms of its impact on human civilization. An estimated 60 million people were killed during the war—an average of 27,000 people per day without interruption for almost six years. Hundreds of millions more were injured, maimed, imprisoned, assaulted, or displaced. Civilians—not soldiers—suffered in greater quantity as victims of genocide, carpet-bombings, sieges, enslavement, mass starvation, and disease. Geographically, the war spanned the globe, bringing conflict to nearly every land and sea. The war was humanity's foremost epoch not only because of its unmatched violence, suffering, and oppression. It also reshaped the globe's political, cultural, and economic landscape, and continues to influence world affairs; one is hard-pressed to find a current geopolitical dispute or hotspot that cannot trace some roots back to World War II.

The author John Updike expressed the event as "a vast imagining of a primal time when good and evil contended for the planet, a tale of Troy whose angles are infinite and whose central figures never fail to amaze us with their size, their theatricality, their sweep."[2] Atop the list of central figures were the war's political and military leaders. World War II produced more leaders—both villainous and heroic—than any other period in human history, for leaders are born out of adversity, not tranquility. World War II saw the rise of despots such as Hitler, Stalin, and Tojo. Thankfully, the period also witnessed moments of valor from leaders such as Churchill, Roosevelt, Gandhi, and Eisenhower. Countless men and women, many unknown and irrevocably lost to history, bore the mantle of leadership during the war, whether intentionally or by circumstance. The Pulitzer Prize–winning journalist and historian Rick Atkinson has described World War II as "bottomless" in its infinite quantity of human stories. To his point, the conflict also harbors a bottomless supply of leadership demonstrations.

Even though the war occurred relatively recently, as a leadership laboratory it remains largely unexplored, especially by today's business executives and managers. The military commanders of World War II's great campaigns exhibited leadership under extreme circumstances and adversity, facing potential consequences of a magnitude unfathomable today. Their efforts and outcomes offer a unique opportunity for present-day executives and teams to study and emulate.

Consider the skills and abilities modern business leaders and managers need to be effective: defining strategic goals, solving problems, communicating effectively, fostering team alignment, evaluating individual and organizational performance, and forecasting change. Leaders lacking any of these skills may experience limited success if not outright failure in today's intensely competitive environment.

World War II's leaders had to possess the same skills and abilities but apply them on a colossal stage and scale. They had to set strategic goals and solve problems of staggering and unprecedented ethical, operational, technical, economic, and cultural complexity. Their communication skills could (and often did) determine battlefield victory or defeat. They had to assemble, train, and manage teams ranging from small units up to organizations larger than most of today's corporations. (For example, each of the ninety-one US Army divisions had more than fourteen thousand personnel.) They had to navigate change on an extraordinary range of issues, usually with human lives forfeited when they erred. If World War II produced America's "greatest generation," as journalist and author Tom Brokaw suggested, it arguably produced the greatest leadership generation the world has seen and may ever see.

This book's purpose is to present and examine leadership moments that both entertain and educate today's business owners, executives, and managers. Our leadership laboratory will be one of the most famous and important battles of World War II—the Allied invasion of Normandy, France, code-named Operation Overlord.[3] The Battle of Normandy began on D-Day and lasted almost one hundred days, involved nearly three million combat troops, and ultimately decided the war's outcome in western Europe. D-Day and the Normandy campaign also represented the last chance for Adolf Hitler and Nazi Germany to salvage anything short of total defeat and annihilation.

For You History Buffs: What the "D" in D-Day Means

The "D" in "D-Day" is only a placeholder. When preparing a military operation such as an amphibious invasion, planners initially could not know exactly what date the operation would begin, due to factors such as weather, logistics, the enemy's actions, etc. Therefore, during the war, Allied leaders used the phrase D-Day to mark the operation's kickoff day (and "H-Hour" to indicate the start hour on that day). From there, planners could schedule the operation by assigning deadlines or objectives relative to that D-Day. For example, if the battle plan mandated that a certain town be captured seven days after the operation's launch, they assigned the deadline D+7. A minus sign was used for milestones or deadlines prior to the launch date.

During World War II, military planners used the term D-Day for many different operations. Today, however, the term has become widely accepted to refer specifically to the start of Operation Overlord, the invasion of northwestern France on June 6, 1944.

Leadership and D-Day

This book is not a military history, but rather a detailed examination of a handful of D-Day leadership moments selected with an eye toward what business leaders can learn from them. Some of the case studies demonstrate effective leadership, and some are tales of failure. Some of the case studies involve better-known elements of the D-Day epic, and others present less-familiar leaders and moments. At the conclusion of each case study, analysis and discussion questions help readers and business teams evaluate and apply these stories to their specific organizations. My hope is you will be captivated as a reader and inspired as a leader.

Most of the leaders at the center of the case studies are senior military officers because their decisions and actions offer lessons applicable to the challenges that business owners, executives, and managers face. This is not to diminish the pivotal role that junior officers and enlisted personnel played during the campaign, nor is it to overlook the extraordinary displays of individual bravery that occurred on the battlefield. While courage is undoubtedly a leadership virtue, the modern business executive thankfully does not have to charge machine gun nests and navigate minefields—at least not literally. The officers I discuss are white males, as the door to senior military leadership was still closed for most women and people of color in the 1930s and '40s.

For You History Buffs: Diversity and D-Day

Women and people of color played an immense role during the war, particularly for the Allied nations. In the US alone, more than 350,000 women and one million African Americans served in uniform during World War II. During Operation Overlord, the Allied victory would have been less certain and more costly without their under-sung contributions. Specifically on D-Day, of the nearly 60,000 US soldiers who landed on Omaha and Utah Beaches, an estimated 2,000 were African American.[4]

While I am neither a professional historian nor a leadership expert, much of my life's passion and experience lie at the intersection of history and leadership. My role in this book is not to supply new historical narratives or interpretations, as does the historian. Nor is my role to propose innovative business leadership methods, as does the management guru.

Rather, my charge is to extract from the historical record relevant leadership stories and present their value and application within the modern business environment.

As a lifelong student of history and particularly World War II, I have read hundreds of published studies of the war, and spent countless hours immersed in unpublished sources such as journals, unit histories, oral archives, and after-action reports. It has been my honor to speak with veterans and be a guest at divisional reunions. I have stood at low tide on the Norman bluffs overlooking crescent-shaped Omaha Beach, feeling horror for the first waves of soldiers from the 16th and 116th US infantry regiments who, starting at 6:36 a.m. on June 6, 1944, crossed exposed fields of surf and sand against withering German fire, with three out of four men falling either killed or wounded. I have also stood two oceans away on a small memorial floating atop the dark blue waters of Pearl Harbor, straddling the submerged remains of the battleship USS *Arizona*, a tomb for 1,200 American sailors killed aboard the 29,000-ton warship during the Japanese attack at Pearl Harbor on that infamous Sunday morning in late 1941. Standing at these hallowed sites connects a person in an intensely intimate way to the events that unfolded there, and inspires a heightened appreciation for the leaders and service members who sacrificed there.

As both a business owner and a consultant to other business leaders, for more than thirty years I have sat in the room with company heads as they set strategic goals, analyzed and solved problems, led teams, and forecasted change—sometimes successfully, sometimes not. My professional capacity as an exit strategist affords me the opportunity to witness business owners and executives confronting difficult decisions that do not merely impact the company's monthly sales goals or annual profits, but rather determine the organization's survival on a long-term basis. The companies I have worked with range in size from revenues measured in the millions to billions and represent a wide range of industries, yet their leadership issues transcend size and sector.

A Day for Leadership's Case Studies

This book is written for business owners, executives, leaders, and managers. The core content consists of case studies providing readers with insights and lessons relevant to real-world leadership roles and responsibilities. Case studies are stories told with a business purpose, and as many of us will agree, "a great story beats a boring business discussion every day."[5] I encourage leadership and management teams to approach these stories as group exercises. Case studies unlock conversations and foster individual and team development. They can—

1. **Enhance problem-solving skills.** Case studies present real-life challenges. By dissecting various elements of a case study, teams can explore multiple perspectives and consider diverse solutions, ultimately improving their problem-solving capabilities.

2. **Apply theoretical knowledge.** Applying theoretical knowledge to real-world scenarios is crucial for effective leadership and management. Case studies bridge the gap between theory and practice.

3. **Improve decision-making.** By analyzing other leaders' decisions, understanding the outcomes, and evaluating alternative approaches, teams learn to make more informed and effective decisions.

4. **Promote learning from successes and failures.** Case studies can highlight both effective and inadequate leadership. Analyzing cases allows teams to learn from others' experiences, understanding what worked, what didn't, and why, ultimately helping leaders avoid common pitfalls and replicate successful strategies.

5. **Encourage collaborative learning.** Discussing case studies in a team setting encourages collaboration and knowledge sharing. Team members bring diverse perspectives and experiences to the table, enriching the discussion, leading to more comprehensive insights and strengthening relationships within the team.

6. **Develop communication skills.** Effective communication is a critical skill for any leader and team. Discussing case studies requires team members to articulate their thoughts, present arguments, and persuade others of their viewpoints.

7. **Build a learning organization.** Incorporating case study discussions into regular leadership development helps build a learning organization that is more adaptable, resilient, and better equipped to navigate the complexities of the modern business environment.

Consider using this book as resource material to conduct a leadership retreat, exploring the case studies over one or two days. Alternatively, your team could approach the case studies one at a time, either on a stand-alone basis or by adding them on to regularly scheduled meetings. To facilitate individual and group learning, each case study includes a section called "Leadership Insights," which unpacks the business lessons embedded within the historical events, and a set of suggested questions and conversation starters called "Leadership Exercises" to spark critical thinking and group discussion.

The book's case studies are presented in approximate order consistent with Operation Overlord's chronology. Therefore, readers will benefit from touring the case studies in the sequence laid out in this book. However, each case study focuses on a primary theme, such as effective decision-making, adapting to change, or selecting strategy. If you and your team prefer to explore a specific theme, feel free to advance directly to that case study after completing this introductory chapter. Each case study opens with the necessary historical context, giving you and your team the freedom to jump around. If you are hungry for more of the history of the D-Day campaign, within each chapter I have included special segments titled "For You History Buffs." You will also find additional historical information in the Notes section at the back of the book.

To create superior case study experiences for you and your team, check out the following instructions.

How to Use These Case Studies with Your Business Team

Case study exercises are a powerful tool for business teams, creating a unique set of experiences that enhance problem-solving, decision-making, and strategic thinking. By learning from real-world stories, leadership and management teams can apply theoretical knowledge, improve communication, foster innovation, and build a culture of continuous learning.

Processing case studies effectively requires a structured approach to ensure thorough analysis and insightful discussions. For teams to maximize the benefits of case study analysis, consider following these steps:

1. Choose a relevant and impactful case study. From this book, consider taking the case studies in sequence. Or if you wish to skip around, read the brief Introduction at the start of each case study to identify its specific issue or lesson. Select one that addresses a current need or situation.

2. Instruct your team members to independently read the case study by a certain deadline. On average, a case study can be read in about thirty minutes. Team members should read the case study carefully, noting key facts, figures, and narratives. Encourage them to prepare their thoughts around the critical issues, important decisions, outcomes, and any surprising elements.

3. If you are the team leader, after reading the case study, review the Leadership Exercises. They provide you and your team with questions and conversation-starters to help digest the material and discuss how it may apply to your team, company, or organization. Feel free to prepare additional questions to supplement the Leadership Exercises presented in the book.

4. Schedule your team's group discussion. Select an environment conducive to distraction-free discussion. To start, consider allocating forty-five minutes to one hour per study, but it is possible to spend more or less time with each. Case studies are intended to immerse your team in real-world leadership situations and create vibrant discussion, debate, and collaboration. Your team might fully process

continued

and extract value from one case study rather quickly, while another might uncover issues and open discussions that last far longer. Also, because the case studies typically include between five and seven Leadership Exercises, you can limit the time that your team spends on a case study by exploring only a portion of the Leadership Exercises during your session.

5. Conduct the exercise. Open with a review of the D-Day story told in the case study. Then pivot into a discussion of the business issues presented in the case, following the Leadership Exercises. Focus on what worked, what didn't, and why. Encourage candid discussion and create a safe place for different points of view or disagreement. Seek participation from every team member. Summarize the main takeaways from the discussion.

6. Create and implement a plan for applying any lessons learned. Case studies are intended to uncover practical learnings for your team and company. Identify specific steps for applying the insights gained to your team's current challenges or strategic goals. Assign responsibilities and timelines for implementation if applicable. Distribute a written summary to relevant stakeholders within the organization to share knowledge and foster a culture of learning.

7. Monitor results and promote additional learning. Follow up with team members to ensure the implementation of action plans and continuous learning. Regularly check the progress of any action plans or strategies developed during the discussion. Evaluate the effectiveness of the implemented strategies and discuss any adjustments needed. Finally, encourage team members to reflect on their learning experiences and continue discussing new case studies.

To engage this author's company to lead and facilitate an in-person leadership retreat for your team, either at your facility or at a destination location such as Normandy, see the About the Author section.

Further Points

Two final introductory points. First, in approaching this project I did not compose a list of leadership skills and principles and then plunge into the historical record looking for events and people displaying those skills and principles in action. That approach would have demanded that I filter the historical narrative to fit a predetermined leadership menu.

Instead, my process started with the history itself. Diving into the D-Day story, I let the actual events reveal captivating and meaningful leadership lessons. I was surprised on multiple occasions. Some of the more widely regarded D-Day events and heroes that I had initially expected to merit case studies failed to offer sufficient applicability for business leaders. Other moments that I might never have considered leapt out as stories that business leaders need to hear. The result is a more genuine business leadership tour of D-Day. However, because I let history be the guide, there are leadership skills and principles not specifically explored within this book. I believe that is a small sacrifice to make in exchange for a collection of case studies that authentically and powerfully demonstrate those leadership lessons presented here.

Second, this book is not a complete narrative of Operation Overlord and D-Day. The book explores specific historical episodes pulled from the overall D-Day saga, extracted for their illustrative value to modern business leaders. If you are not familiar with the story of D-Day, I encourage you to explore beyond this book. D-Day is a gripping tale, in the words of one historian, "the decisive chapter of a twentieth-century Iliad."[6] To assist you, I have provided a suggested reading list at the back of this book.

Before we dive into the first case study, I will set the historical stage for the wartime events that led to D-Day.

Setting the Stage for D-Day

By the spring of 1944, about four a half years after starting the war in Europe, Nazi Germany's armies were falling back on all fronts, suffering irreplaceable losses of men and matériel. Its overmatched air force was being shot out of the skies and starved for fuel. Its navy had dwindled to a few scattered warships hiding in distant anchorages and a fleet of obsolete submarines. Its cities were being bombed around the clock, with thousands of civilians wounded or dying each day and night. Yet Nazi dictator Adolf Hitler still saw a path to victory.

Hitler believed the coalition aligned against Germany between the Communist Soviet Union (modern Russia) and the Western democratic Allies, led by the United States and Great Britain, was unsustainable and would eventually collapse.[7] (The Western Allies on D-Day were led by the United States, Great Britain, and Canada, joined by forces representing France, Belgium, Norway, Poland, Luxembourg, Greece, Czechoslovakia, New Zealand, and Australia. Throughout this book the term "Allies" will refer to the combined effort of these nations, excluding the Soviet Union.)

Hitler publicly welcomed the Allies' invasion of western Europe that would become D-Day, because he believed his forces would finally defeat the US and British to his west. In so doing, the Nazi dictator believed he would force a rupture between the politically incompatible democracies and Communists. After repelling his American and British enemies in the west, Hitler then could turn all his forces east, defeat the Communists in Soviet Russia, and win the war.

Hitler's plan was desperate but not as fanciful as it may seem. In early 1944 the Western Allies held the momentum, but Hitler still held nearly the entire European continent. If the Allies could not successfully invade the mainland and defeat Germany, they could not win the war. Yet Allied success in an invasion of western Europe was by no means assured. Amphibious invasions were (and remain) among the most difficult and risky of military operations. Hitler knew this firsthand. Earlier in the war his armies had conquered continental Europe with devastating speed, but subsequently Hitler had been unable to bring Britain to its knees because he lacked the means to cross the English Channel—a stretch of sea (twenty miles wide at its narrowest) that has served as Britain's protective moat for a thousand years. In another example, about two years before D-Day, a combined British and Canadian amphibious raid on the German-occupied French port of Dieppe ended in humiliating defeat for the Allies.[8]

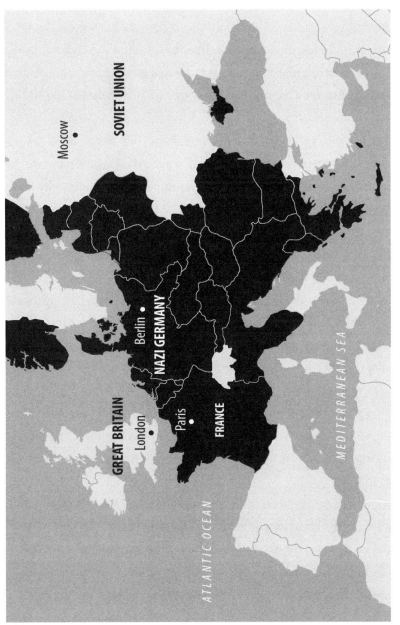

Nazi-occupied Europe as of June 1944, shortly before D-Day.

During 1942 and 1943, the Allies did achieve several amphibious successes against the Germans and their Italian Axis partners in North Africa, Sicily, and Salerno.[9] However, those victories had not come easily, even though the Allied invaders had outnumbered the Axis defenders in each battle. Also, those sea-launched invasions had not faced a heavily fortified coastline like the vaunted Atlantic Wall, the extensive network of defenses Germany had constructed along much of western Europe's coastline to repel the Allied attack that everybody knew was coming.

For Operation Overlord, the Americans and British held several strategic advantages: chiefly, near-total supremacy in the air and on the sea, and highly trained and superbly equipped land armies. However, the Germans initially outnumbered the Allies on the ground in the western European theater. Also, once the invasion began, the Germans would hold the advantage of fighting on the defense, often from prepared fortifications and lines.

Furthermore, those fresh and well-equipped Allied troops were useless while they sat in England. The constrained capacity of Allied transport shipping and limited beachfront space meant that during the first days and weeks of the invasion, the Germans—with their advantage of already being on land—could win the "Battle of the Buildup" by moving more troops and tanks into the immediate invasion area at a faster pace than the Allies could bring their forces ashore. Should this occur, the Germans might overwhelm and defeat the invasion while in its infancy.

Another issue seemed to favor the Germans. The Western Allies had a healthy apprehension about engaging Nazi Germany's land armies in combat. By that point in the war, the Germans had earned a reputation, soldier-for-soldier and tank-for-tank, as being the superior ground-fighting force.[10] After more than four years of war and having suffered millions of military casualties, the Germans were forced to station lesser-quality troops on the Atlantic Wall: older men, teenage boys, injured veterans, and troops conscripted into service from conquered lands such as Poland and Russia. However, the German forces in France included a core of veterans hardened by years of fighting in the east against Soviet Russia. In contrast, most of the invading Allied soldiers had never been in combat. For all these reasons, Allied political and military leaders were right to feel unsettled about their prospects for victory.

If the Western Allies were to suffer an invasion defeat and be expelled from the European continent for a second time, the consequences would have been severe, far-reaching, and perhaps irreparable. One can speculate about the repercussions of an Allied defeat on D-Day. Troop morale likely would have been severely shaken. Civilian populations might have questioned the wisdom of continuing the war against Germany, especially with the fanatical Empire of Japan on the other side of the globe still undefeated. The operation's senior American and British military leaders likely would have been sacked.[11] Elected leaders such as US President Franklin Roosevelt and British Prime Minister Winston Churchill would have faced serious challenges to their continued service in office. (During a private lunch only a few weeks before the invasion, Churchill tearfully confided to the invasion's supreme commander, US General Dwight D. Eisenhower, that "I am in this thing with you to the end, and if it fails we will go down together.")[12]

A defeat would need to be operationally scrutinized from top to bottom, a postmortem that would have taken months, by which time unfavorable fall and winter weather conditions would prevent the Allies from attempting another invasion in 1944. If the Allies lost, it's highly unlikely they could have mustered the leadership, resources, and resolve to launch another invasion for a year and perhaps longer. This delay could provide Hitler with exactly the time he needed to fully concentrate his forces against Soviet Russia, and possibly snatch victory from the jaws of defeat.

General Eisenhower,[13] knowing what was on the line, accurately stated, "We cannot afford to fail."[14] There was no Allied contingency plan to D-Day. Overlord was an-all-or-nothing venture, with the war's outcome in western Europe and much of the world on the line. Churchill strongly opposed Overlord up until the last minute for fear of catastrophic Allied losses, but still acknowledged that "unless we can land overwhelming forces and beat the Nazi in battle in France, Hitler will never be defeated."[15]

For You History Buffs: No Escape Plan on D-Day

Operation Overlord risked everything for the Allies. There was no backup or alternative plan. If the beach assaults failed, there were no contingencies or resources in place to evacuate the paratroopers and soldiers already on shore. At one point in mid-morning on D-Day, the American attack at Omaha Beach appeared in danger of suffering a disastrous defeat. Consequently, US Army General Omar Bradley briefly considered a halt to landing any further troops. However, he chose to continue, in part because there was neither plan nor means to rescue the besieged American troops pinned down on the beach.

Hitler too knew the stakes. In March of 1944, less than three months before D-Day, Hitler warned his senior military leaders that "the destruction of the enemy's landing attempt means more than a purely local decision on the Western Front. It is the sole decisive factor in the whole conduct of the war, and hence in its final result."[16]

If the Western Allies could not win on D-Day, then they could never win World War II. Or, as we know now with the benefit of hindsight, if D-Day had failed, then hideous Nazi Germany might still have been defeated, but only by the Soviet Russians rolling into Europe from the east. This would have left the Communist Soviet Union dominating most of the European continent, in effect merely swapping one totalitarian regime for another. Therefore, on June 6, 1944, the fate of much of the world would be decided.

Against this strategic situation, let us examine our leadership case studies.

For You History Buffs: The Scale of Overlord

Overlord was the most complex military operation in history. More than sixteen million tons of Allied supplies from a 700,000-item inventory list had to be ordered, produced, transported, and stockpiled in preparation. Allied equipment piling up in England required eighteen million square feet of covered storage and thirty-five million of open storage.[17] More than two million soldiers barracked in over eleven hundred camps spread across the English and Welsh countryside.

D-Day's combined airborne and seaborne assault—the largest in history and likely to forever remain so—was choreographed over thousands of miles and timed to precise five-minute intervals. Thousands of ships and planes transported tens of thousands of paratroopers, infantry, engineers, machine gunners, tankers, medics, nurses, radio operators, typists, news reporters, and chaplains across the sea and through the air to five beaches on the Normandy coast code-named (from west to east) Utah, Omaha, Gold, Juno, and Sword. This unprecedented logistical organization and deployment of men and women, machines, and matériel was planned and executed without a single computer.[18] All the while, the operation's details had to be kept secret from the ever-watchful Germans. From an operational standpoint, one prominent historian has described Overlord as "the greatest organizational achievement of World War II, a feat of staff work that has dazzled history, a monument to the imagination and brilliance of thousands of British and American planners and logisticians which may never be surpassed in war."[19]

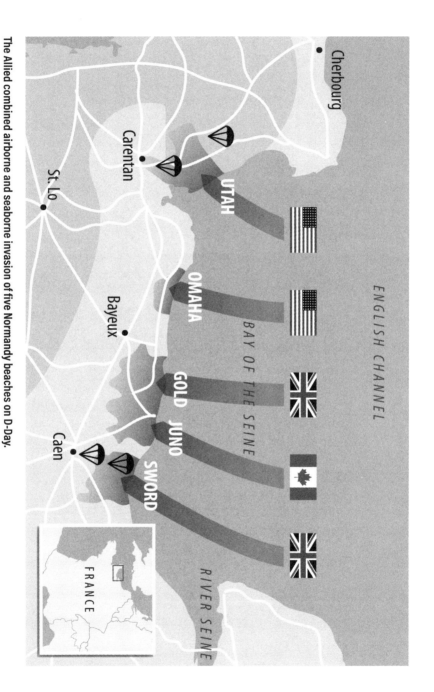

The Allied combined airborne and seaborne invasion of five Normandy beaches on D-Day.

Readying the Big Red One

CREATING ELITE CULTURE

"Culture isn't just one aspect of the game. It is the game."
—Louis V. Gerstner Jr., former CEO of IBM

"Everybody hated him! Absolutely hated him!"
—US Army Captain Joseph Dawson, referring to General Clarence Huebner, Commander of the US 1st Infantry Division on D-Day

In the early evening of Tuesday, June 6, 1944, General Clarence R. Huebner, commander of the US 1st Infantry Division, stepped from a thirty-six-foot Higgins boat onto perhaps the most famous stretch of sand in American history, at the time known to Norman locals as the *Plage d'Or* (Golden Beach), but from that day forward forever rechristened Omaha. Twelve hours earlier, the first waves of American soldiers under Huebner's command[1] had landed on the crescent-shaped beach to open one of the bloodiest and most pivotal days in American history.

A hellish scene greeted the fifty-five-year-old general. Sporadic artillery and sniper fire still targeted the beach. The ruined bodies of young American servicemen lay where they died in the sand, huddled against the seawall, or rolling in the surf, some clustered two or three deep. Medics triaged the wounded, many of whom were calling out in pain. Long lines of soldiers filed past Huebner, struggling through the surf, scaling the Norman bluffs while warily snaking between minefields on narrow pathways marked by strips of white tape. Tanks, trucks, and half-tracks motored up the beach, taking particular care to avoid running over the dead. In the distance, the staccato of machine guns and crackle of rifles could be heard as survivors of Omaha pushed inland. The terrible beachscape gave evidence that Huebner's superbly prepared 1st Division had prevailed—at awful cost. While D-Day was coming to a close, for Huebner, Operation Overlord and the Battle of Normandy had just begun.

Operation Overlord's senior leaders, starting at the top with Supreme Commander General Dwight D. Eisenhower, had specifically assigned Omaha Beach on D-Day to Huebner's 1st Infantry Division, also known as the Big Red One in reference to the division's distinct shoulder patch with a red number one. The Big Red One was America's foremost division in name and fame, having already spearheaded two Allied amphibious invasions earlier in the war. Eisenhower would entrust only the elite Big Red One with Omaha Beach, the most heavily defended and isolated of D-Day's five target beaches. And the Big Red One could only be entrusted to Clarence Huebner, even though Huebner had not led the division during its prior wartime victories, and just ten months earlier was widely despised by the 1st Division's soldiers.

Before Huebner, General Terry de la Mesa Allen had been handpicked to lead the Big Red One. Revered by his troops, Allen molded the 1st into America's proudest and most accomplished division. Shockingly, however, Allen had been fired for escalating disciplinary problems within his division, the byproduct of a defiant culture. Thus, Huebner assumed command over fourteen thousand hardened veterans stunned by the dismissal of their beloved commander, embittered over leading their third amphibious invasion of the war while most other US Army divisions had yet to see combat, and too culturally insulated to trust outsiders.

Few characteristics of a company or team have a greater impact on across-the-board results than culture. It is an enterprise's DNA, the collection of values and beliefs that define and govern its relationships and behaviors. The right culture propels sustained business growth and excellence. The wrong culture weakens or destroys an organization.

This case study explores how Huebner, following in the footsteps of a venerated leader, reshaped the division's cavalier culture into one befitting its elite reputation and illustrates the close tie between behavior and culture and how to extract elite performance from an organization.

As you read the case study, consider the following questions, each of which will be explored in the exercises following the story:

- How well defined is your organization's ideal culture?
- What is the relationship between culture and behavior?
- What actions can leaders take to positively influence a team or company culture?

The Case Study: Readying the Big Red One

Terry de la Mesa Allen had military service and command in his blood. His grandfather had served in the Union Army during the American Civil War. His father was an artillery officer in the US Army. Thus, Allen grew up on military posts, learning from soldiers how to ride horses, gamble, cuss, smoke, and drink. From an early age, Terry Allen displayed a magnetic personality—an unusual mix of maverick self-confidence to the point of swagger tempered by approachability, warmth, and sincerity. In 1907, Allen entered West Point, only to flunk out his senior year after earning too few passing grades and too many demerits. Undeterred, Allen graduated from another university and secured commission as an Army lieutenant in 1912.

After America entered World War I in 1917, Allen was desperate to get into the action. He got himself assigned to a supply unit heading for France. Once he arrived, Allen snuck into the graduation line of a group of infantry officers soon to receive combat commands. Finally in the fight, Allen proved to be a fearless warrior. He was wounded four times. On one occasion, Allen was carried unconscious from the fray but recovered to lead his men in the next attack. He was promptly shot through the jaw, shattering his back teeth, but only after breaking his wrist punching a German machine gunner.

Allen was an audacious battlefield leader, shunning conventional tactics to maximize surprise and keep his enemies off balance. In one engagement in the Argonne, Allen disobeyed orders and launched an unconventional night assault against a heavily defended German position; but fortunately for him and his soldiers, the night attack succeeded. "We took the position with a loss of twenty killed," Allen would later report, "and if we'd done it by day we would have lost three hundred."[2]

Allen stayed in the Army after the war. He attended the prestigious Army Command and General Staff College, where he graduated near the bottom of his class. While there, Allen came under the attention of George C. Marshall, who would later become the chairman of the US Chiefs of Staff, the top American military leader of World War II. Marshall liked Allen's combative spirit and wrote that Allen "had a dubious future in peacetime but should be entrusted with a division in time of war."[3]

When World War II came, Marshall followed through on his pledge. In the summer of 1942, with the US racing to field dozens of new army divisions,[4] Allen was assigned command of the Big Red One, leapfrogging over hundreds of officers with greater seniority. But the US Army needed combat leaders, and Marshall recognized Allen would get the Big Red One ready for war. General Theodore Roosevelt Jr., the eldest son of President Theodore Roosevelt—and, like Allen, a hard-fighting, hard-drinking combat veteran of World War I—was appointed Allen's assistant division commander.

The Unconventional Leader

Allen was a soldier's soldier. He was as comfortable with the division's lowest-ranking privates as with senior staff officers, slapping backs, telling jokes, playing cards and dice, and sharing stories. Allen did not participate in the creature comforts that generals often enjoyed and instead avoided showy uniforms or insignia, declined to eat special fare, and spurned a cot in favor of a sleeping bag laid across the bare ground. He did participate in hard training and hard drinking. His men came to not just respect their leader but also revere him.

Within the division he was universally referred to as just "Terry" and the men often addressed him so. In return, Allen spoke of 1st Division soldiers as "his boys." Allen paid little attention to traditional military discipline and formalities, emphasizing camaraderie over conformity to foster an elite culture within his division. "By some subtle yet predictable chemistry, the division gradually [assumed] the personality and characteristics of its commander," as one of his officers later recalled.[5] Under Allen, the Big Red One, despite not yet having fired a weapon in anger in this war, arrived at its first combat engagements "proud, self-absorbed, and ornery."[6]

The Big Red One became the first Army division sent to Europe, arriving in England in the summer of 1942 to commence the planned buildup of forces earmarked to invade German-occupied continental Europe. However, British and American forces were still too weak to tackle Europe head-on, so Allen, Roosevelt, and the Big Red One loaded onto combat transports and shipped to North Africa, where they would spearhead Operation Torch. During the North Africa campaign, Allen's Big Red One cemented is reputation as America's toughest division, handing defeats to enemy forces from Vichy France,[7] Italy, and Germany. At the Battle of El Guettar in Tunisia, the Big Red One vanquished the veteran German 10th Armored Division in "the first solid, indisputable defeat we [America] inflicted on the German army in the war."[8]

For You History Buffs: Why Did the Allies Attack in North Africa?

Shortly after the US entered World War II in December of 1941, British and American leaders hotly debated when the two nations would invade the European continent and take the war directly to Nazi Germany. The Americans wanted to invade as soon as possible, whereas the British urged patience to build up their combined forces.

As the disagreement dragged on, US President Franklin D. Roosevelt became increasingly sensitive to the fact that American and British armies in Europe sat idle, while their ally Soviet Russia suffered millions of casualties in titanic land battles against German invaders. Consequently, Roosevelt overruled his military advisors and agreed to postpone invading Europe, instead joining British Prime Minister Winston Churchill's strategy of attacking Germany and Italian forces in North Africa and the Mediterranean.

Allen's aggressive spirit drew him to action, but he did not suffer bloodlust nor seek personal fame. A devout Catholic, before every engagement he prayed for the safety of his men. "Do your job," he told his boys. "We don't want dead heroes. We're not out for glory. We're here to do a dirty, stinking job."[9]

Allen and the division's notoriety spread. Fellow Allied commanders, the media, and the American public took notice of the "Fighting First" and its bold commander. One newspaper correspondent wrote, "Never in my life have I seen a man so worshipped as Terry."[10] US General George S. Patton, initially Allen's boss during Operation Torch, publicly proclaimed that the Big Red One's "valorous exploits have brought undying fame."[11] Even America's allies noticed Allen's dynamic leadership, as one British general called Allen "the finest divisional commander he had seen in two wars."[12]

However, the organizational swagger and elite spirit that fueled the 1st Division's battlefield prowess was causing problems. Allen's emphasis on unit loyalty and esprit de corps morphed into an air of superiority, an us-versus-them attitude, and antagonism toward anybody not wearing a red number one on their shoulder. Soldiers from other units took to derisively calling the 1st Division the "Holy First." Somewhere along the way a saying began that the US Army merely consisted of "the Big Red One and eight million replacements."[13]

The 1st Division's toughness spilled over into unruliness. Allen and his officers failed to comply with dress code regulations, a serious issue for spit-and-polish Patton, who expected officers to be in uniform complete with necktie and steel helmet. Instead, Allen "wore a funny old green uniform and his orderly had sewn creases into his trousers but they had long since bagged out. The aluminum stars he wore had been taken from an Italian private and were stitched to his shirt."[14] The 1st Division also grew lax in saluting. During an inspection trip, one of General Eisenhower's aides noticed that the Big Red One failed to properly salute as Eisenhower's staff car drove by, despite its adornment of flags featuring the general's four-star rank.

In April of 1943, Allen and the 1st Division received a new boss—General Omar Bradley—a West Point graduate. Proper, soft-spoken, detached, and not one to countenance excessive drinking, Bradley quickly took notice of the 1st Division's cocky attitude and rebellious behavior. "Under Allen, the 1st Division had become increasingly temperamental, disdainful of both regulations and senior commanders," Bradley wrote in his memoirs after the war. "It thought itself exempted from the need of discipline by virtue of its months on the line. And it believed itself to be the only division carrying its share of the war."[15]

Allen's behavior suggested rules did not apply to the Big Red One. The division's mess halls enjoyed a consistent supply of fresh beef despite regulations prohibiting American troops from eating the local stocks. Allen's troops stole supplies—a widespread practice to some degree in most armies, but the thievery was so flagrant that one supply officer pleaded with Bradley, "Please get General Terry de la Mesa Allen under control!"[16]

American senior commanders outside the Big Red One increasingly disliked what they saw. Patton wrote in his diary that Allen "thinks the 1st Division is the only unit in the show."[17] Bradley later recalled that he warned Allen, "'We'll all play by the same ground rules. . . . Whatever the patch we wear on our sleeve.' I'm afraid Allen gave little notice to my admonition."[18]

On the battlefield, Allen's independent-mindedness did not always produce positive results. On the night of May 5, 1943, a restless Allen launched a signature night attack against German forces at the Tine River in Tunisia. He gave the order despite opposition from his assistant commander Roosevelt and others, and in violation of instructions from Bradley to sit tight. The assault failed badly; Allen's men suffered almost three hundred casualties for little return. Eisenhower and Bradley visited the 1st Division headquarters the following afternoon, waking an exhausted Allen only to hear him deliver a half-coherent report full of excuses.[19] Bradley fumed over Allen's attack decision, "a foolish one and undertaken without authorization."[20]

The division's misbehavior deteriorated beyond poor dress code, lax saluting, and pilfered supplies. Several weeks after the Tine River debacle, the Big Red One was assigned to a rest camp outside the Algerian city of Oran, a city they had liberated the previous November. The Fighting First was weary, having spent 112 of the previous 132 days in combat, significantly more than any other outfit. They were also in a quarrelsome mood, for the men had expected to rotate home, having done their part in the war. However, Oran would provide no rest and relaxation for the 1st Division, for the town (and its bars and brothels) was only open to rear-area troops—"typewriter commandos" according to the Big Red One. Allen, intolerant of any slight against his men, defiantly issued passes and shuttled troops into Oran by the truckload.

Roosevelt, who allegedly once told Bradley that the 1st Division "gets along a helluva lot better with the Krauts up front than we do with your people here in the rear," threw gasoline on the fire.[21] He teased the 1st Division soldiers to "go back to Oran and beat up every MP [military police] in town."[22] In what would later be called the "Second Battle of Oran," the Holy First trashed bars, looted wine shops, and brawled with fists and brass knuckles against any noncombat American troops they found wearing brown-and-green striped campaign ribbons, unearned in the eyes of combat veterans from the Big Red One.

For Bradley this was the final straw. The incident "convinced me that Terry Allen was not fit to command and I was determined to remove him and Teddy Roosevelt from the division."[23] However, Allen's Big Red One had become indispensable. When Patton learned that the Big Red One might be left out of Operation Husky, the upcoming Allied invasion of Sicily, he exploded in opposition. "I want those sons-of-bitches. I won't go without them!"[24]

For the second time in the war, the 1st Infantry Division led an American amphibious assault. In the predawn hours on July 10, 1943, the Big Red One landed near the Sicilian town of Gela. Enduring three days of furious German and Italian counterattacks, the Fighting First held on and eventually turned the tide. Even Bradley acknowledged that Terry Allen and Big Red One had saved the day.

Meanwhile, Bradley lined up his cards against Allen. Patton's opposition to firing Allen had cooled, at least partially because Allen occupied too much of the spotlight.[25] Eisenhower also finally consented to removing Allen after seeing the Big Red One commander's physical and mental exhaustion. On the evening of August 7, Allen's divisional headquarters received three telegrams from Bradley. The first two unceremoniously announced the firing of Allen and Roosevelt from command. After reading his dismissal notice, Allen "said nothing for a while, and then burst into tears."[26] The third telegram informed the 1st Division their new commander would be General Clarence R. Huebner.

Allen handled his dismissal with dignity. He personally escorted Huebner to meet the division's senior officers, instructing each to extend to Huebner their respect. Allen wrote Marshall, thanking the US Chief of Staff for the opportunity to command the 1st Division over the previous fifteen months. Unsurprisingly, Allen never wavered from crediting the division's battlefield accomplishments to his soldiers rather than himself. He wrote his wife: "The accomplishments of the 1st Division would have been equally as good under almost anyone else."[27]

But Allen and Roosevelt's firing hit the men of the 1st Division like a bombshell. Both leaders were revered and admired. The terminations seemed unjustified, a capricious attack on the Big Red One by the Army's top brass. After all, Allen had never lost a major battle he commanded in either World War and he'd made the Big Red One America's most accomplished division.

General Clarence Huebner Takes Command

The outrage compounded when the 1st Division soldiers learned what their future had in store. First, they had a new and unknown commander in General Clarence Huebner. Second, the Fighting First was shipping back to England to prepare for the most dangerous amphibious operation yet, the invasion of continental Europe—Operation Overlord. The news caused "a lot of trouble among the soldiers, a lot of unrest and anger," recalled one junior officer at the time. "The hope of going back to the States . . . died hard. If we didn't go home this time, we wouldn't go home until the end of the war."[28]

Huebner inherited a powder keg. He assumed leadership over fourteen thousand armed combat veterans incensed over the wrongful firing of their beloved leader, deeply distrustful of outsiders, and self-pitying that they were to risk their lives yet again when so many other divisions had yet to see any fighting.[29] First impressions of Clarence Huebner did not set the division at ease. Short, plain faced with thin, graying hair, the fifty-five-year-old, no-nonsense Huebner lacked Allen's moxie. Rumors spread that the new division commander was a career desk officer, given the Big Red One command in a nod to his long Army service but wholly unqualified for the job.

Huebner was no honorary appointee and certainly no outsider. He'd been an inaugural member of the 1st Infantry Division when it was formed more than twenty-five years earlier in World War I and had served longer in the unit than Allen. During World War I, Huebner led Big Red One combat forces for eighteen months, eventually becoming one of the youngest regimental commanders in the US Army. Twice wounded in combat, he was awarded for gallantry two Distinguished Service Crosses, an Army Distinguished Service Medal, and a Silver Star.

After World War I, Huebner remained in the Army, spending several years at the Army Command and General Staff School, where he established a reputation for being a "flinty disciplinarian."[30] In mid-1943 with World War II well underway, Huebner was sent to the Mediterranean theater, where Eisenhower, Patton, and Bradley jumped at the opportunity to turn over to him the problematic but indispensable Fighting First.

Huebner's challenge was clear. At stake were the lives of thousands of soldiers and the potential success or failure of Operation Overlord, the most important battle of the war. He must take the most accomplished, prideful, and distrusting division in the US Army and remake its wayward culture, without dulling its warrior spirit or the unit's cohesion. He must ready the rebellious Big Red One for Omaha Beach.

Inheriting a Disgruntled Team

At the start, Bradley advised Huebner to clean house at the top, believing the division's senior officers were contaminated by Allen and unlikely to follow Huebner. But Huebner declined, retaining the disgruntled leadership until he could evaluate what he had to work with. For his first step, Huebner would teach America's preeminent combat division how to salute.

Huebner opened his tenure by hosting one-on-one lunches with his new senior staff. At the end of each meal, Huebner informed his subordinate that he was displeased with how the division saluted, and then instructed that officer to execute a proper military salute to Huebner and a pair of MPs. If the officer's salute was not satisfactory, Huebner delivered a "beautiful chewing out" and immediately instructed the offender on the proper form. Then, Huebner gave that officer twenty-four hours to instruct his own staff and soldiers on the proper saluting method.

In between lunches, Huebner toured the division, issuing preprinted delinquency notices fining any soldier who incorrectly saluted in his presence. The notice ordered the offending soldier's unit commanders to report to Huebner and explain why one of their soldiers did not know how to properly salute. Then, they too were tested on the spot. If they failed, they were fined and their respective commander was ordered to report to Huebner to answer for the deficiency and demonstrate the proper salute, and so on up the line.

While confronting substandard saluting, Huebner addressed any violations of rules and regulations. After more than three decades in the military, including a stint as an infantry school instructor, Huebner knew the Army's book inside and out, and he threw it at them. He reprimanded officers and enlisted men alike for not shaving. He cut off personal use of the division's motor pool. He turned evening meals with his officers into lectures on everything from saluting to dress code to the importance of daily weapons inspections. Previously under Allen, the mess hall had been a joyful affair full of laughter and questionably sourced steaks. Under Huebner, "The dinner time ritual came to resemble a death march," in one officer's words.[31]

The remedial saluting drills and seemingly petty rebukes drove the division into a rage. One officer with the Big Red One later reported that "Everybody hated him! Absolutely hated him!"[32] Soldiers vowed to personally address their grievances with Huebner after the war, once out of uniform. The division concluded Huebner was either crazy or just full of "stateside chickenshit."[33] Huebner himself later acknowledged, "I got the reputation for being an unreasonable and mean old bastard."[34]

Monitoring the leadership succession, Bradley understood "Huebner knew what he was doing," Bradley later wrote, "however unpopular his tactics might be. From the outset he was determined to show the Division that he was boss, that while the 1st might be the best division in the US Army—it nevertheless was a part of the Army, a fact it sometimes forgot."[35]

Retraining the Disorderly Division

As if teaching Big Red One how to salute was not sufficiently degrading to the cocky combat veterans, Huebner next turned his sights on teaching them how to shoot. After reviewing the division's recent battle reports, Huebner suspected the soldiers were not properly using their rifles in combat, instead relying too heavily on artillery support. If true, this reduced combat effectiveness and in turn increased casualties. Offering the first glimpse that he was neither crazy nor full of bird excrement, Huebner ordered his officers to pull ammunition expenditure data from the unit's recent combat. The figures confirmed that 1st Division soldiers were not maximizing use of small arms weapons. Suspecting the underlying reason was lack of confidence, Huebner ordered a check of every man's training record and discovered that more than two thousand soldiers in the Fighting First had never qualified to fire the rifle.

Huebner devised a novel response. He decreed that only soldiers rated as expert shots could serve in a Big Red One rifle company. In most US Army divisions, assignment to a rifle company was to be avoided due to the increased danger and physical demands. But Terry Allen had instilled a warrior culture that elevated rifle company membership into an elite service within the Fighting First. Thus, thousands of disgruntled 1st Division soldiers showed up for basic rifle training. Arriving at hastily improvised practice ranges in the middle of Sicily, they met their new rifle instructor—none other than Huebner himself.

Huebner was a ringer, having first learned to shoot growing up on a Kansas wheat farm and becoming an expert marksman in the Army. He was also an excellent teacher. Huebner personally supervised every aspect of rifle training. He taught proper positions and firing techniques, including a squatting position of his invention. If Huebner encountered a soldier using an improper technique, after teaching the correct form he located the soldier's immediate commander and asked if that man knew the proper technique. If that man knew it, Huebner asked why that leader had not properly trained his unit on it, and how the situation would be rectified. If that man did not know the proper technique, Huebner would teach it, and proceed up the chain of command to make the same inquiry of the next leader, and so on. Within a short time, the Big Red One's sergeants, lieutenants, captains, and majors adopted a serious interest in marksmanship training for their men, and many improved their skills as well.

Huebner was hands-on with all 1st Division training, starting with these rifle qualifications and later continuing into the division's extensive preparations for D-Day. He understood the job of nearly every soldier in the division because at some point he had held that job himself. While leading one anti-tank training exercise, Huebner climbed into a trench and coolly let a tank drive over him. "The old man surely knows his business," admitted one veteran while watching his commanding general climb out of the ditch.[36]

Huebner was at heart a teacher and sought to build his troops up rather than tear anyone down. The 1st Division lacked discipline, which Huebner understood was important not simply for the sake of conformity, but because discipline increased combat effectiveness and reduced casualties. The Big Red One would occupy the lead position at Omaha Beach in America's most important and perilous military attack of the war, and Huebner must get them ready. Under his driving leadership, the 1st Division, reputationally the best US Army division, begrudgingly began to salute like it, shoot like it, and behave like it.

Huebner gradually created allies and converts, particularly among the officers closest to him. They had received their share of tongue-lashings and fines, but they also saw Huebner's competence, patience, and a sense of humor that balanced his cool demeanor. At one moment during the saluting hysterics, Huebner yelled at General Clift Andrus, the Big Red One's head of artillery, because a major serving under Andrus had saluted Huebner crookedly. Andrus laughed and explained the major in question was an excellent officer but was nursing a broken hand. Huebner "grinned, joined in the laugher, and shook his head at his own ignorance."[37]

Colonel Stanhope Mason served as Huebner's chief of staff. Shortly after Huebner assumed command, Mason approached his new boss about their respective leadership roles. Under the idolized Terry Allen, Mason had been left to play the division's bad cop, a part he did not enjoy. When Mason asked Huebner who would fulfill that role going forward, Huebner replied, "Stan, somebody in this outfit's got to be an SOB." Mason later recalled, "I thought I caught just a little gleam in his eye the way he put it to me, so I got just a little bit on the impudent side and said, 'General, I have been it for a long time. How about you being it for a while?' He turned around and laughed and said, 'That's a fine idea, Stan. That's the way we'll work it from here on in. I'll run them down and, if they're worth picking up, you pick them up again.'" Mason admitted that "from that time on there was no question that the Old Man had me in his pocket."[38]

The saluting drills and marksmanship qualifications changed the division's behavior, which in turn transformed the division's culture. After the war a Huebner staff officer remembered during the saluting exercises, "I saw officers of all grades going through the hand-salute routine, sometimes once, sometimes three or more times with a giant MP stationed at the entrance of the Headquarters. . . . Even though this seemed to us at the time a bit eccentric way to run the railroad, it exemplified the General's determination that in details, as well as in the free and easy business of campaigning, we were to be *numero uno*."[39]

Huebner had ignored the suggestion to replace the division's senior staff, and eventually he converted Allen's former team into his team. After the war, one officer who served under both generals recalled that "I asked him why he had not fired all of us because of our unreasonable attitude toward him when he first assumed command. I shall never forget his response. He chuckled and ducked his head forward with that little puckish squint which was so endearing. 'Hell, I knew you would all come around in good time. I wasn't about to get rid of the best damn staff in the best damn division in the Army.'"[40]

Coach Prepares His Units for D-Day

Somewhere along the way, somebody bestowed upon Huebner the nickname "Coach." It stuck. The Big Red One called him Coach for the rest of the war and after.

In November of 1943, Huebner returned the Big Red One to England to train for D-Day. Working from his headquarters in Dorset, Coach supervised a grueling program over the next six months. Twenty-five-mile road marches wearing full combat gear to be completed in under ten hours. Constant combat drills. Battlefield medicine techniques. Stripping and cleaning weapons while blindfolded. Emergency gas mask procedures. Driven by Huebner, the "men worked as they never had worked before," according to one veteran's account. "They trained as an army had never trained for any other war."[41]

About three months prior to D-Day, Coach introduced amphibious training into the schedule. The Big Red One practiced loading onto landing craft and unloading via cargo nets and ramps so often that one soldier remarked, "I wasn't sure if I was in the Army or Navy."[42] They participated in mock invasions, rushing onto beaches selected to replicate Omaha's terrain while live gunfire whistled and exploded overhead.

Huebner was not satisfied with ensuring each of the fourteen thousand Big Red One enlisted men and officers was ready to carry out their own assignments. He wanted them prepared to carry out others' if needed. So he had his men cross-train in other functional areas or leadership roles, so that on the beach the inevitable combat casualties and battlefield confusion would not cripple team effectiveness. Riflemen, machine gunners, and mortarmen practiced with the others' equipment. Infantry trained in engineering procedures and engineers trained in infantry tactics.[43] Sergeants prepared to lead platoons should their lieutenants be wounded or killed, and lieutenants prepped to lead companies should their captains fall. Battalion commanders worked with one another's executive teams so that if one battalion leader was lost, another could readily move over to take his place.

Six days per week the Big Red One engaged in continuous and demanding invasion preparations. On the seventh day the division rested, taking well-deserved and desperately needed breaks, usually enjoying

English hospitality and pubs. While the Fighting First maintained its reputation as an aggressively festive outfit, disciplinary issues were few, the previous troubles in North Africa and Sicily left behind.

In early May 1944, with D-Day fast approaching, the Big Red One and other Allied divisions sequestered in marshaling areas for operational security. Sealed off from outside communications, the 1st Infantry Division learned their specific invasion target, a four-mile sandy stretch of curved coastline nestled between the small Norman villages of Colleville-sur-Mer and Vierville-sur-Mer. Huebner's men scrutinized hundreds of aerial reconnaissance photographs of Omaha Beach and its extensive defenses. They studied a ten-foot-long scale model so detailed it accurately depicted individual buildings and trees. A model train enthusiast would have been envious if only the miniature's purpose was not so somber.

By June 3, Huebner and his division completed loading onto nearly three hundred ships and landing craft, waiting to sail to Normandy from the English harbors of Weymouth, Poole, and Portland once the invasion order was issued.[44] Training was over. Preparations were complete. The Big Red One was ready.

For You History Buffs: The Assault on Omaha and *Saving Private Ryan*

Huebner's plan for assaulting Omaha Beach was to attack up through five natural gullies (or "draws") that cut pathways between the two-hundred-foot-tall (sixty-meter) bluffs that overlook the beach. Of course, the German defenders anticipated this, and they turned each draw into a kill zone defended by concrete pillboxes, mortars, machine guns, barbed wire, and minefields. On D-Day, this German resistance at the draws initially proved too difficult to overcome. Huebner's troops improvised by climbing the bluffs while under heavy fire as depicted in the famous twenty-four-minute Omaha Beach combat scene from the movie *Saving Private Ryan*.

Leadership Insights

At the start of World War II, the US Army lacked most of what it would need to achieve victory: scale, modern equipment, and combat experience. Terry Allen was assigned command of the 1st Infantry Division and ordered to ready it for a war that the broader US Army was unready to fight. Allen, drawing from his own personality, gave the division what few could at the time: confidence, fortitude, and guts. He inspired a winning culture founded on the unit's elite history and brand, and genuine two-way devotion between him and his boys. Without Allen's imprint, it's unlikely the division would have performed as well as it did.

Yet as the Big Red One's accomplishments grew, the spotlight on Allen and the unit intensified. Those outside the 1st Division observed that the esprit de corps that Allen cultivated to inspire combat effectiveness had blossomed into an organizational culture of detachment and arrogance.

The noted leadership author Simon Sinek once said that "leadership is absolutely about inspiring action, but it is also about guarding against mis-action." Within the Big Red One, there were too few guards against mis-action. Allen permitted his unit's internal loyalties to twist into lack of respect toward those external to the team, such that outsiders became unworthy of a salute or the right to wear the same uniform campaign ribbon.

Allen's top priority was his division, at the expense of other considerations. Behaviors that Eisenhower and Bradley considered mis-actions Allen promoted as meeting his team's needs: pilfering supplies to secure scarce equipment, killing livestock to fill mess halls with superior food, and trashing bars to blow off steam. Allen's zeal to provide for his division did not stop at tolerating raucous behavior in the rear areas. In combat, Allen selectively obeyed orders based on what course of action maximized outcomes for the division with less regard for the broad battlefield picture.

A Leader's "First Team"

To apply a business concept, Allen lost sight of his First Team. The author and speaker Patrick Lencioni introduces the concept of the "First Team" in his popular leadership book *The Five Dysfunctions of a Team*. The First Team concept seems straightforward—leaders must give higher priority to the team they are on rather than the team they lead.

However, this simple premise is often overlooked or violated by well-meaning leaders and managers, who place greater priority on the team they lead rather than the team they are on. This can happen for understandable reasons. For example, you probably have hired or promoted many of the people on your team, strive to see them succeed, and care about them as colleagues and individuals. You go to bat for them and protect their backs. However, under the First Team premise, your organization's greater goals must command your focus and concern, above the needs of the team you lead.

A team populated by leaders and managers who each place higher priority on their individual department, branch, or division is a team that lacks alignment around shared responsibilities and accountabilities. That team is like a collection of individual boat captains all leading their vessels in separate directions with little regard to the needs and directives of the entire fleet. The First Team concept does not suggest that leaders and managers should refrain from passionately championing the needs of the teams they lead. But it requires high-performing executives to maintain a holistic understanding of their broader organization's objectives and, where necessary, to forfeit or pause pursuits that may benefit the team they lead but are inconsistent with the needs of the team they are on.

First Team's members share responsibility and embrace accountability over the wider enterprise's objectives. They collaboratively weigh and allocate resources to meet the enterprise's highest needs, avoiding divisive resource tug-of-wars. In a healthy First Team, members challenge one another, ask tough questions, and demand maximum effort from one another, confident and trusting that the team's members share a commitment to the greater organization.

General Allen lost sight of his First Team. He obsessed over the interests of the team he led, the Big Red One, and paid insufficient attention to how his actions and decisions impacted the team he was on, the US Army in North Africa and Sicily. In the beginning, Allen's misplaced priorities produced wayward behaviors that were easily overlooked. But as the war expanded, the stage got bigger and the spotlight grew brighter; everyone from Eisenhower down to the average soldier could see the "Holy First" was not marching in step with the greater good.

When Allen was given the command of the 1st Infantry Division, the objective was to get ready for war. Now America needed the Big Red One ready for the invasion of Europe, the battle that would determine if the war would be won.

Huebner Changes Behavior to Change Culture

Allen and Roosevelt's dismissal opened the door for Huebner, who had to bring the Big Red One back into good stead and prepare it for a burden that the Fighting First was best qualified to carry, leading the American landing on Omaha Beach.

The word "culture" rarely shows up in wartime communications. These mid-twentieth-century military leaders described the 1st Division's problem as a lack of "discipline," primarily manifest as the serious and ongoing refusal to follow regulations and orders. Yet the root cause for the division's lack of compliance was a culture that interpreted elite combat performance as an excusal from professional behavior.

To drive cultural change, Huebner demanded behavioral change. He began with two activities core to the daily experience of an infantry soldier: saluting and shooting. By requiring that every divisional officer and soldier observe the formal courtesy of a salute and deliver it correctly,

Huebner created behavior that continuously displayed and reinforced professionalism and respect.

Saluting is a military courtesy, but shooting is a military necessity. Discovery of the division's subpar rifle competency gave Huebner the opportunity to expand his demand for professional behavior, break down the unit's cockiness, and elevate their skills. Stipulating that serving in a Big Red One rifle company required expert marksmanship qualifications cleverly turned the division's warrior spirit and conceit against itself. The soldiers could not tolerate being removed from their rifle companies and would not tolerate being graded as anything short of the best.

In his campaign to elevate the division's culture, Huebner possessed a tool set typically not available to modern business executives: burly MPs, monetary fines, and a human relations environment where a supervisor can "beautifully chew out" subordinates without threat of legal action. While Huebner's tools were different, his tactics and process are applicable to molding elite culture in today's business organizations. He began with a clear vision of the culture he sought to create. From there Huebner—

1. **Built a leadership team that embraced the desired culture.** Huebner gave the incumbent team an initial trial but was committed to replacing anybody who would not adapt. "Rather than make a clean sweep and get everybody off the slate," he later explained, "I'd get rid of only those who weren't doing the job right. The rest must be pretty good—based on the Division's record—and I didn't want to lose those people."[45]

2. **Communicated expectations and relentlessly followed up.** Starting on his first day, Huebner announced the new behavioral standards—in jarring fashion. He required his leaders to take responsibility for learning and teaching new behaviors to their respective teams, usually within twenty-four hours.

3. **Led by example.** Huebner presented the Big Red One with a

role model of an accomplished combat leader who acted with elite discipline and respectability. The new general shattered their paradigm that elite performance and professionalism were incompatible values.

Allen had readied the once-green division for war, instilling a culture of elite confidence and high morale. Huebner had readied the now-veteran division for D-Day, elevating the unit's culture to include elite professionalism. Huebner was the leader the Big Red One needed on June 6, 1944. "His emphasis on discipline and training, coupled with his keen sense of tactics, made the 1st Division the unbeatable team that it was when we went into Normandy," recalled one veteran after the war. "He was a great man and a great leader."[46]

Leadership Exercises

The following exercises revisit and expand on the historical events associated with "Readying the Big Red One," and present leadership learning opportunities for individuals and teams to explore.

Exercise #1

Terry Allen and Clarence Huebner each contributed to an elite culture within the Big Red One. Allen bestowed military spirit and élan, propelling the division to its initial successes in the war. However, he failed to see how his personal rebelliousness and the division's pride undermined coexistence with a rapidly expanding US Army. Huebner recognized the need to layer elite professionalism and self-discipline into the division's cultural ethos. After reviewing the case study, consider the following questions:

- What was the most interesting or surprising aspect within the story?

- What potential lessons does the case study offer to our team or organization?
- How effectively do we define our culture and promote the desired mindset, values, and behaviors?
- In what ways are we pleased with our organization's culture? Are there any elements to our organization's culture that we would change?

Exercise #2

Allen's priorities clashed with the needs of his First Team, the US Army senior command in the Mediterranean theater. The First Team concept does not devalue leaders' sense of commitment to their teams; it requires leaders to place higher priority on the needs of the teams on which they serve, which is usually the greater enterprise.

- How can leaders and managers balance prioritizing the needs and objectives of the team they are on while supporting and focusing on the teams they lead? What are the signs that there might be an imbalance or lack of alignment? Do our individual or team-level priorities and objectives align with our company-wide needs and objectives?
- Do we allocate resources (budget, people, etc.) in a collaborative manner, keeping focus on the greater good? Are there ways that our resource allocation discussions and decisions can be improved?

Exercise #3

Huebner embarked upon a plan to shape the Big Red One's culture by demanding immediate and universal changes to its behavior. Business executives possess less authoritarian power than military leaders, yet still need to shape and sustain a desired culture for their teams and enterprises.

- What is the relationship between behavior and culture?
- What are some of the tools or methods business leaders have at their disposal to positively influence culture? Which do we use? Are there other tools or methods that we should consider using?
- Are our company's values clearly understood and embodied by all employees?

Exercise #4

Allen and Huebner brought utterly different leadership styles to their command. Allen focused on team loyalty and morale, operated informally with selective attention paid to regulations and procedures, and delegated details to his direct reports with little supervision. Huebner's style was the total antithesis. He focused on attention to detail, operated formally, complied with regulations and procedures, and closely supervised his subordinates. Both believed their leadership style maximized battlefield results and minimized divisional casualties.

- What are the pros and cons of Allen's and Huebner's leadership styles?
- Is either Allen's or Huebner's approach more applicable or preferable in today's business environment? Are there any types of companies or stages of organizational evolution where certain leadership styles may offer a better fit or be more effective? For example, are there leadership methods better suited to a startup company versus a more mature organization? How about within smaller teams versus larger?
- How well do we as leaders understand our individual leadership styles, identify strengths and weaknesses, and continuously improve our knowledge and skills?

Exercise #5

Huebner's leadership philosophy emphasized that accountability starts at the top. If a team or individual is not performing, Huebner believed the root cause was the leader's lack of clear communication, inadequate training, and/or tolerance of having the wrong people in the position.

- Rank how well we do the following, from most to least effective: (1) clearly and consistently communicate expectations and standards within our organization; (2) adequately train our people for their roles and responsibilities; and (3) put and keep the right people in the right positions.

- What are we doing to be successful in the highest-ranked activity? How can we improve results in the second- or third-ranked activity?

- Are we consistently experiencing underperformance in any area within our organization? What needs to change to address this issue?

Exercise #6

After the war, one of Huebner's former officers asked him "how a gentle guy like him could have been such a mean bastard?" Huebner replied, "Remember when you take over a command, you can start off being an SOB and later become a good guy. But you can never start off being a good guy and later become an SOB."[47]

- What are the pros and cons of Huebner's philosophy and approach? Would his methods (minus the harsh language) apply in today's business environment?

- All leaders and managers eventually must welcome new members to their team, or in some cases are assigned or promoted to lead a new team. At these moments, what steps can leaders take to establish healthy new relationships?

- How do we onboard new employees, associates, or teams (such as in an acquisition)? Is this working sufficiently well, or can we make any improvements?

Epilogue

United States forces, led by the Big Red One, conquered Omaha Beach on D-Day, but at terrible cost. Omaha was the deadliest site on the bloodiest day for US forces in all of World War II. While other American and Allied units and personnel on D-Day acted with valor and made sacrifices that must not be overlooked, the 1st Infantry Division under General Clarence Huebner is rightly credited for leading the victory at Omaha.

For You History Buffs: Omaha Beach Casualties

The exact number of D-Day casualties at Omaha is unknowable, but the most common estimates range from about 2,400 to more than 4,700 killed, wounded, or missing American servicemen. The first waves paid the highest price. In one tragic example, Company A of the 116th Infantry Regiment suffered 212 casualties out of 230 soldiers, including more than 100 killed. The total American casualties on Omaha was about equal to the combined British, Canadian, and American casualties on D-Day's four other beaches.

Most military analysts and historians agree that the Americans could have been defeated at Omaha, or paid a higher price in lost lives, if not for the superb training and magnificent courage of the soldiers who landed there. Just as Bradley acknowledged that the Big Red One under Allen carried the day at Gela in Sicily, he acceded that the division under Huebner again proved its indispensability at Normandy. "Had a less experienced division than the 1st stumbled into this crack resistance, it might easily have been thrown back into the channel,"

Bradley wrote after the war. "Unjust though it was, my choice of the 1st to spearhead the invasion probably saved us at Omaha Beach and a catastrophe on the landings."

The Big Red One gave the United States a victory at Omaha Beach, and in exchange Omaha gave the division its legacy. The division and beach are forever linked in history. The American wartime reporter Don Whitehead noted, "In all its battles in Africa, Sicily, France, Belgium, and Germany, there never was one quite like the battle of Omaha Beach. In that battle alone the Fighting First won a niche among the immortals of American history. Huebner's men smashed the main strength of the Germans and by so doing turned the key that unlocked the door to victory in Europe."[48]

The Fighting First continued combat operations in Europe after D-Day until the last day of the war. In all, the Big Red One spearheaded three amphibious invasions, participated in eight campaigns, and spent 443 days in combat. Sixteen of its soldiers earned the Congressional Medal of Honor during the war, America's highest military award for valor. On D-Day, soldiers from the Fighting First earned three Medals of Honor and fifty-three Distinguished Service Crosses[49] (DSCs)—more than one percent of all US Army DSCs awarded during the entire war.

After their dismissals from the Big Red One, Roosevelt and Allen were reassigned new combat leadership roles, a rare example where US Army division-level leaders nominally dismissed for "rest and recuperation" were put back into action rather than quietly retired or confined to desk jobs. Teddy Roosevelt became the assistant division commander of the US 4th Infantry Division, an inexperienced unit scheduled to land at Utah Beach on D-Day. Eisenhower and Bradley correctly predicted that Roosevelt's infectious courage would bolster the 4th Division's untested troops. Roosevelt went ashore in the first wave, only to discern he and his soldiers were nearly a mile from their intended landing site.[50] Predictably unshaken, Roosevelt is said to have ordered, "We will start the war from right here!" For his actions on D-Day he was awarded the Congressional

Medal of Honor, matching his father in the accomplishment. Five weeks after D-Day, Roosevelt died in his tent of a heart attack. In a letter of condolence to Roosevelt's wife, Patton wrote, "He was one of the bravest men I ever knew."[51]

Terry Allen too soon found new work. Marshall and Eisenhower recognized they could not leave a combat leader of his caliber sitting on the bench, so Allen was given command of the raw US 104th Infantry Division, known as the Timberwolves. Thus, Terry Allen holds the distinction of being the only US Army general in World War II to lead two different divisions in combat. Allen completed his new unit's training in the US and led them to Europe, landing in France several months after D-Day. The Timberwolves came to adore their fiery leader and established a reputation as a hard-fighting outfit, without significant disciplinary problems. The division also picked up a second nickname—the "Nightfighters"— reflecting their prowess in night combat operations. Allen retired from active duty shortly after the war's end. Tragically, Allen's son and only child, Terry de la Mesa Jr., was killed in combat while serving as an officer with the 1st Infantry Division in the Vietnam War. A heartbroken Allen died two years later in 1969.

Clarence Huebner readied the Big Red One for D-Day and then led them to Omaha Beach, where the division carried the day. Huebner served with distinction but not notoriety—many historical D-Day accounts extend him little to no mention. The leadership expert and best-selling author Jim Collins coined the phrase of a Level Five leader, defined as one who possesses "Humility combined with a ferocious will."[52] Among World War II military leaders, few could make a better case of matching this description than Huebner.

In December of 1944, after sixteen months leading the 1st Division, Huebner was promoted to command an Army corps.[53] He smoothly turned over the division's leadership to one of the many former Allen disciples who had initially doubted and distrusted him.

After the war, Coach served for twenty-five years as president of the Society of the 1st Infantry Division, a veterans' organization chartered to "perpetuate the memory of the 1st Infantry Division, US Army, and to honor the service and sacrifice of its soldiers and units," until he passed away in 1972. To this day, the society awards annual "Huebner Scholarships" to help provide a college education to descendants of men and women who have served in the Big Red One.

After Huebner left the 1st Division in December of 1944, General Omar Bradley recorded that the division "missed him almost as much as they did Allen."[54] Almost. In Huebner's final assessment he reflected, "They respected me; they loved General Allen."[55]

‖‖‖

Where to Put the Panzers

SELECTING STRATEGY—PART 1

"The essence of strategy is choosing what not to do."

—Michael Porter, business professor, consultant, and author

"The last out of his door is always right."

—German Field Marshal Erwin Rommel, referring to Adolf Hitler

By late 1943, Adolf Hitler and his German military commanders knew an Allied amphibious invasion somewhere along the coastline of western Europe was imminent. They also knew their only military arm seriously capable of defeating the expected invasion was their powerful *panzer* (tank) force. At the start of Germany's aggressions in 1939 and 1940, the panzer-led German army, supported by a highly trained air force and confident navy, had overrun with apparent ease much of central and western Europe. As German tanks speedily rolled over one country after another, the Allied nations coined a new word in warfare—*blitzkrieg*: "Blitz" (German for lightning) + "Krieg" (war).

However, much had changed after four years of war. The vaunted German air force was a shell of its former self, often outnumbered twenty to one when its planes managed to get into the skies. The navy's few remaining ships posed no major threat to America and Britain—the two largest sea powers on the planet. Germany's only potential hope to stop an Allied invasion and throw it back into the sea was its feared panzers.

The question left for Hitler and his commanders was where to put the panzers. German-occupied western Europe included more than 2,500 miles (4,000 kilometers) of coastline to defend, and there simply were not enough panzer units to defend everywhere. Where to put the panzers to meet and defeat the expected Allied invasion was arguably the most important strategic question German military leaders faced.

No leader or team can accomplish everything all at once. All leaders must pursue important objectives with finite resources. The strategy that leaders select to employ and deploy those resources may make or break achieving the goal or mission. **This case study examines how German military leaders, facing an existential threat with severely constrained resources, failed to select and align around a viable strategy for positioning their tank forces to have any legitimate chance of defeating the invasion.** Their experiences illustrate for business leaders and teams how *not* to debate, adopt, and organize around a common strategy.

As you read the case study, consider the following questions, each of which will be explored in the exercises following the story:

- Currently, what are the most important strategic goals for our team or company?
- Are we aligned as a team around how we will achieve these strategic goals?

- To maximize our focus and resources toward the pursuit of our strategic goals, is there anything we should stop doing or not pursue at this time?

The Case Study: Where to Put the Panzers

By the fall of 1943, German Field Marshal Gerd von Rundstedt was frustrated and worried. For more than two years Rundstedt had presided as the commander-in-chief over German forces in occupied western Europe. Even though he lived comfortably in a Parisian hotel, enjoyed French wine, and tended to a rose garden, Germany's oldest active field marshal still recognized his duty to lead the German defenses in western Europe. Rundstedt's fifty years of military service showed on his hard, lean face, featuring a graying toothbrush mustache framed by prominent marionette lines, set under a pair of eyes whose default gaze seemed to be stern. Those eyes could see that German defenses were woefully inadequate to meet the rising threat of an Allied seaborne invasion somewhere on Europe's western coastline. Determined to draw Berlin's attention to his command's needs, in October of 1943 Rundstedt sent an alarming thirty-page report to his bosses—Adolf Hitler and the German high command.

Rundstedt's report charged that German fortifications in western Europe, including the highly propagandized Atlantic Wall coastal defenses, were more fiction than fact. Additionally, he noted that many German army divisions permanently stationed in western Europe contained inferior-quality equipment and troops.[1] Higher-quality divisions often were temporarily deployed to western Europe to recuperate after combat against Soviet forces. Once rested and re-equipped, these restored units were sent back east. Rundstedt up to that point had tolerated western Europe being used as a convalescent area. But he saw an urgent need for change.

Rundstedt's report recommended expanding construction of coastal fortifications and digging in additional layers of troops at likely invasion sites. Once the Allies launched their seaborne attack on a coast, the primary anti-invasion punch would be delivered by panzer divisions equipped with fearsome tanks such as the Tiger and Panther. The panzers had to be positioned far enough from the beaches to be safe from bombardment by Allied warships but close enough to quickly move forward and strike the invasion, preferably on its first day. Rundstedt's assessment was sound, and his conventional recommendations were consistent with established German military doctrine and recent wartime experiences.[2]

Rundstedt's analysis galvanized Hitler and the German high command into action. First, Hitler wrote a plan to organize the defense of western Europe, called Directive 51.[3] "I can no longer justify," Hitler declared, "the further weakening of the West in favor of other theaters of war. I have therefore decided to strengthen the defenses in the West." Hitler called for "an all-out effort in the construction of fortifications" on the coasts to defeat any invasion before it could gain hold. However, Hitler shared Rundstedt's concern that beachhead fortifications might not be enough to stop the Allies, and he approved Rundstedt's recommendation that a powerful reserve force of panzers must be created and tasked with defeating an invasion. "Should the enemy nevertheless force a landing by concentrating his armed might," Hitler wrote, "he must be hit by the full fury of our counterattack . . . (by) fully mobile general reserves suitable for offensive operations. The counterattack of these units will prevent the enlargement of the beachhead and throw the enemy back into the sea."[4] Ten panzer divisions would be deployed to western Europe to power this furious counterattack against the invasion.[5]

Hitler's second move was to send Field Marshal Erwin Rommel—known to the German public and his Allied adversaries as the Desert Fox—to western Europe. Hitler liked and trusted Rommel, who at fifty-two years old was Germany's youngest field marshal, and its most dashing and popular. The Desert Fox's orders were to conduct a defense inspection tour, ostensibly to verify Rundstedt's findings but also as a stepping stone to adding Rommel to the team tasked with defeating the invasion and turning the war back into Germany's favor.

For weeks the energic and hard-driving Rommel and his small staff spent eighteen-hour days inspecting coastline defenses from Denmark to France, hiking over beaches, crawling through fortifications, and reviewing troops. On the final day of 1943, Rommel issued his own report, which validated Rundstedt's earlier findings and seconded the urgent call for improving German defenses. However, Rommel had different ideas for where to put the panzers. He had spent his wartime career fighting the Western Allies, first the British and then the Americans, and had experienced the suffocating power of Allied air dominance. Consequently, Rommel was convinced that any panzers positioned far from the coast would not reach the beaches in time to counterattack an invasion. Allied air forces, enjoying complete command of the sky, would delay or destroy the panzers before they could arrive. In his report, Rommel suggested an altogether different strategy for deploying the panzers.

> With the coastline held as thinly as it is at present, the enemy probably will succeed in creating bridgeheads at several different points and in achieving a major penetration of our coastal defenses. Once this has happened, it will only be by the rapid intervention of our operational reserves that he will be thrown back into the sea. This requires that these forces should be held *very close* behind the coast defenses. . . . British and American superiority in the air alone has again and again been so effective that all movement of major formations has been rendered completely impossible, both at the front and behind it, by day and by night. I therefore consider an attempt must be made, using every possible expedient, to beat off the enemy landing

on the coast and to fight the battle in the more or less strongly fortified coastal strip.[6]

Rommel recommended breaking with convention. Rather than placing the panzers to the rear, maximizing the area they cover and relying on mobility to conduct coordinated attacks, the Desert Fox wanted to bring the panzers forward, putting them all the way up to the coast, just a few miles behind the water's edge at the most likely invasion beaches. From this position, Rommel's panzers would counterattack an Allied invasion within a few hours of its start, when troops coming ashore would be disorganized, wet, seasick, and still lack heavy weapons such as tanks and anti-tank guns.

For You History Buffs: Seasick Landings in Normandy

One of the underappreciated sufferings inflicted upon troops in an amphibious attack is seasickness. Seaborne soldiers often endure being tossed around for hours or even days before reaching the shore, on small watercraft designed with flat bottoms to permit beach landings but that are consequently highly unstable on the open water.

On D-Day, high winds and rough waves created torturous conditions for Allied soldiers riding to shore, with reports of entire boatloads of men uncontrollably vomiting, leaving them severely weakened and disoriented. Some seasick D-Day survivors later recalled stumbling off their boats, initially unable to fight or even find proper cover. The Germans understood this, which is one reason why Rommel wanted to attack the Allied beach landings within the first few hours.

Rommel's coastal defense strategy was beyond novel. It was heretical, violating armored warfare principles of mobility and concentration of force that propelled Germany to its blitzkrieg victories earlier in the war. Rommel's proposed panzer strategy also ran counter to how he had earned his fame. Rommel forged his reputation in the conquest of France in 1940, charging his tank division over the same Norman countryside that in 1944 would be the target of the Allied invasion. But Rommel believed airpower had changed the nature of warfare, rendering obsolete existing German tactics. "The day of the dashing cut-and-thrust tank attack of the early war years is past and gone," he lamented to one of his staff officers.[7]

For You History Buffs: Rommel and Blitzkrieg

In 1940, Rommel led the 7th Panzer Division in Germany's invasion of France. Applying the then revolutionary blitzkrieg tactics involving large, highly mobile armored units surrounding and overwhelming enemy forces, at one stretch Rommel's division captured more than 100,000 French prisoners and 500 tanks while suffering about 2,500 casualties.

Blitzkrieg means "lightning war" in German. It refers to offensive warfare using mobile combined arms including tanks, artillery, and vehicle-mounted infantry to attack swiftly, overwhelming and surrounding enemy forces with the goal of achieving rapid victory. The term *blitzkrieg* was never officially used by the German military.

During Rommel's inspection tour, he and Rundstedt met several times to discuss anti-invasion preparations.[8] While their opposing ideas for positioning the panzers became a point of contention, Germany's oldest and youngest field marshals shared a professional military approach and authentic sense of duty. Rundstedt disliked Rommel's brash self-confidence and desire for the limelight—in private he referred to Rommel as an "unlicked cub." Yet Rundstedt appreciated Rommel's inexhaustible energy and commitment to elevate preparations against an invasion they both knew was coming and against which their army was not ready. (At the conclusion of a lunch together, Rundstedt confided that "it all looks very black to me.")[9]

Within short order the two men agreed that Rommel's awkward investigative role should be upgraded to permanently command an army group under Rundstedt, assigned to the French and Belgian coastal areas that both leaders considered to be the most likely target for an Allied invasion.

Panzer Group West

About the same time Rommel joined the German team in western Europe, Rundstedt appointed General Leo Geyr von Schweppenburg (commonly referred to as Geyr, pronounced "guy-er") to lead Panzer Group West, a new organization tasked with overseeing training of panzer forces and advising on all panzer matters. Once the Allied invasion started, Panzer Group West, presumably under Geyr, would launch the decisive armored counterattacks that would throw the Allies back into the sea.

Like Rundstedt, Geyr came from a Prussian aristocratic family. He was intelligent, well read, and fluent in several languages.[10] At fifty-seven years old, Geyr's clean, youthful face and warm eyes belied nearly forty years of military service, during which he rose through the ranks to become an expert on the use of tank forces. After he had led German armored units during the invasions of Poland and Soviet Russia earlier in the war, Rundstedt tapped him for this crucial new role in the west.

Rundstedt, a hands-off leader, left to Geyr the details of preparing the panzer strategic reserves against the invasion. However, Geyr had his own ideas for where to put the panzers. Rundstedt wanted the panzers organized into mobile reserves safely set back from the coasts but sufficiently close to counterattack the beachhead on the invasion's first day. Geyr disagreed, believing that defeating the Allies at the water's edge was impossible. Allied air and sea dominance was too great, the coastline was too long, and Germany lacked sufficient forces to cover every potential invasion site. Geyr believed that "in view of the formidable enemy air superiority and the number, caliber, and effectiveness of the naval guns of the combined Anglo-American battle fleets, a landing some place on 1300 kilometers of coastline could not be prevented and would succeed in any case."[11]

Consequently, Geyr condemned as folly Rommel's strategy of defending the coasts. He criticized the Desert Fox's frantic efforts using millions of laborers (including prisoners of war and forced laborers) to build some sixteen thousand concrete bunkers on the beaches and lay more than four million mines in the sand as a fantastic waste of time and resources. "The Atlantic Wall was worth exactly as much as the panzer divisions behind it," Geyr said derisively after the war.[12]

In contrast to both Rundstedt and Rommel, Geyr wanted to put the panzers deeply inland, concentrated near Paris, which was roughly equidistant from the most likely invasion coasts. Sited there, the tank units could safely organize and train. Once the Allies invaded and moved off the beaches and into the European countryside, Geyr's Panzer Group West would launch a single, massive textbook counterattack several days after D-Day. To Geyr, a delayed counterattack was preferable over a foolhardy attempt to defeat the Allies at the shoreline; the extra time would permit the Germans to discern the main invasion site and rally an overwhelming response.

Thus Geyr, Rundstedt, and Rommel each advocated a different solution for where to put the panzers. On one extreme, Geyr advocated placing the panzers into a concentrated mobile reserve, centrally sited inland to identify the invasion and mobilize a massed counterattack likely several days after the invasion. Rundstedt occupied a middle-ground strategy, opting to deploy the panzer divisions sufficiently close to counterattack a beachhead on the first day. On the other extreme, Rommel abandoned traditional doctrine and sought to spread out the panzers immediately behind suspect beaches, pre-positioned to counterattack within a few hours. While many postwar histories portray the panzer controversy as a dispute between Rommel and Rundstedt, Rommel's and Geyr's plans were in greatest philosophical opposition. The two commanders' strategies were "hardly understandable to the other," commented Geyr after the war.[13] The decision on which strategy to employ would influence whether Germany had a legitimate chance to turn back the Allied invasion and stave off total defeat in the war.

For the next five months—literally until the day of the invasion—these German commanders and their staffs debated and argued over where to put the panzers. Rommel doggedly drove the issue, for his coastal defense strategy most radically challenged the status quo. Rommel met with Rundstedt, Geyr, and any other senior German officer whose ear he could bend to convert them to his way of thinking. He laid out his case in a constant stream of letters and reports. He tasked his staff with lobbying their peers at other German commands. Rommel's persistence, while partially fueled by an egotistical need to be right, was rooted in an absolute conviction that only his coastal defense strategy could produce German victory. One of his wartime aides would later write,

> Rommel's ideas were fundamentally influenced by the vast superiority of the Allied air arm. He was deeply impressed by the fact that in North Africa a numerically inferior air force had kept him, with 80,000 men, "nailed to the ground," as he expressed it . . . [Rommel] was of the decided opinion that the operations planned by Rundstedt and Geyr would either be nipped in the bud or at least so much delayed that they were bound to fail. To Rommel, the only hope of repelling the invasion seemed to lie [with] offering the strongest possible resistance to the actual landing.[14]

Arguments and Counterarguments

In one of Rommel's many letters extolling his strategy, he proclaimed, "The most decisive battle of the war, and the fate of the German people itself, is at stake. . . . Failing the early engagement of all our mobile forces in the battle for the coast, victory will be in grave doubt."[15]

The Desert Fox ordered his own subordinates to adopt the coastal defense posture and move all forces close to the beaches—infantry, artillery, even bread-baking units. His unorthodox strategy generated widespread disbelief and opposition. "As no man in his senses would put his head on an anvil over which the smith's hammer is swung," commented one astounded German officer, "so no general should mass his troops at the point where the enemy is certain to bring the first powerful blow of his superior material."[16] But Rommel had no authority over the ten panzer divisions, the only German force that possessed the striking power to defeat an invasion. To put the panzers at the beaches, Rommel needed to convince Rundstedt and Geyr that German victory demanded his heretical approach.

Geyr ardently rebuffed Rommel's efforts every step of the way. For every point Rommel put forth as a reason to adopt the coastal defense strategy, Geyr offered a counter claim or offsetting advantage associated with the mobile reserve strategy. Rommel's primary argument stipulated that the panzers must be near the coast to immediately attack the invasion site when it was most vulnerable. Geyr countered it was impossible to predict the invasion date or site, and any panzers near the coast would be battered by Allied warships, as had occurred in previous Allied amphibious operations. Therefore, the panzers must wait inland and launch their counterattack after the Allies progressed beyond the beaches.

Rommel warned that Geyr's counterattack would never occur, as the panzers would be pinned down by Allied airpower. Geyr wryly noted that the panzers' movement would be concealed by trees, commonly not found in the African desert where Rommel had earned his moniker. Geyr explained that the panzer forces could move at night, under the cover of darkness. Rommel pointed out that in the spring and summer, when the Allies were expected to invade due to favorable weather, European nights were at their shortest, barely seven hours long. Rommel worried fuel shortages would hold up panzers stationed too far inland. Geyr pointed out that the extensive French railway network would aid in rapidly bringing forward the reserve tanks.

Both leaders expected the Allies to drop paratroopers behind a beachhead as part of their invasion plan, and both believed that the threat of an airborne attack buttressed the correctness of their strategy. Rommel advocated that Allied airborne troops dropped during the invasion would disrupt and delay the mobile reserve's counterattack. Geyr claimed the mobile reserve strategy preserved freedom of movement, a critical factor to deal with an airborne attack.

Geyr's mobile reserve and Rommel's coastal defense strategy both offered compelling advantages. Yet the two respected, accomplished commanders advocated doctrinally and operationally incompatible strategies. Meanwhile, the question of where to put the panzers had to be answered because no coherent defense of western Europe could be adopted without a resolution.

Geyr, as the head of panzer training, needed to know if he should administer a curriculum emphasizing mobile attack or coastal defense. German logisticians had to know where to establish panzer supply and service depots for fuel, ammunition, and spare parts. Other combat arms such as infantry, artillery, and anti-aircraft units needed to position themselves relative to the panzers' locations. Without determining where to put the panzers, the Germans could not deploy a cohesive plan for the defense against the invasion. As one German general remarked, prior to D-Day the panzer controversy was "the main topic of conversation on the western front."[17]

The debate devolved into sharp, intense quarrels between Rommel and Geyr, unsurprising, given that both were headstrong individuals accustomed to getting their way. Witnesses described their interactions as explosive, violent, and "full of hard words." Class conflict fueled the fire. "Part of the problem was arrogance and aristocratic snobbery, especially from Geyr, an old-school aristocrat and General Staff officer who had spent most of his career in the cavalry," according to one historian. "He had spent two years on the Eastern Front and believed he knew everything there was to know about armored warfare. He looked down his nose at Rommel, who was a commoner."[18] Rommel, who had risen in the ranks without being welcomed into the elite General Staff, despised the Prussian aristocratic elitism that Geyr embodied.[19]

Rundstedt stayed above the fracas; his professional sensibilities were offended by the unseemly squabbling. He agreed with Geyr on the benefits of concentrating the panzers into a mobile reserve, yet shared Rommel's conviction that the panzers must be sufficiently forward to permit a rapid response. The unresolved question was paralyzing German strategy, yet Rundstedt, supreme commander in western Europe, equivocated.

Spring months approached, bringing weather favorable to the Allies. In February, Rundstedt convened a conference with Rommel, Geyr, and his other local commanders, at which time Rundstedt announced they would stick with his middle-of-the-road approach—the panzers would be deployed at multiple sites, close (but not too close!) to potential invasion beaches. Rundstedt seemed as intent on squelching the bickering as selecting the superior anti-invasion panzer strategy. "Neither Geyr nor Rommel was completely satisfied with Rundstedt's solution, even though his decision was clearly an attempt not to upset unduly either of his subordinate commanders," according to one account. "Rundstedt undoubtedly hoped his decision would signal an end to the dispute."[20]

It did not. Rommel would not desist. The Desert Fox held an ace up his sleeve, in the form of direct access to Hitler. Rommel had commanded Hitler's bodyguard unit earlier in the war, and the two kept in regular contact. Rommel's rank of field marshal included the privilege of requesting a meeting with the Nazi dictator at any time. Rommel played this card and went over Rundstedt's head, directly petitioning Hitler to endorse the coastal defense strategy. But Rommel did not stop there. He brazenly also asked Hitler to grant him command over all the panzer forces in western Europe, in effect stripping that authority from Rundstedt.

Rommel's audacity forced Hitler's hand. In March, with the invasion possible any day, Hitler hosted a planning conference with his senior commanders and staff at his Bavarian mountaintop chateau called the Eagle's

Nest. During the discussions Hitler requested a sidebar with Rundstedt and Rommel on the panzer issue. Rundstedt, aware of Rommel's earlier impudence, initially refused to participate but eventually was ordered to attend. The huddle did not last long. Rundstedt stormed out after a few minutes, grumbling about submitting his resignation if the usurping Rommel got his way.

For You History Buffs: Hitler's Headquarters and the Eagle's Nest

Contrary to common belief, Hitler spent little time in the German capital of Berlin during the war. Instead, he mostly lived and worked in one of his various Fuehrer Headquarters (FHQs). The Germans constructed fourteen FHQs across Europe at great expense and suffering—the projects consumed more than one million cubic meters of concrete and twelve million days of forced labor. One of Hitler's more heavily used FHQs was the Berghof, a large home and compound located in the Bavarian Alps near Berchtesgaden.

For a birthday present, Hitler's henchmen ordered the design and construction of the Eagle's Nest, a mountaintop chateau positioned on a six-thousand-foot (eighteen-hundred-meter) rocky peak above the Berghof, at a cost of more than $250 million in today's dollars. The Berghof was heavily bombed during the war and, like most of Hitler's FHQs, was demolished after Germany's surrender. However, the Eagle's Nest still stands, converted into a tourist restaurant and beer garden.

Rundstedt's sulky departure left Rommel alone with Hitler, an opportunity the Desert Fox pounced on. Over an uninterrupted thirty minutes, Rommel laid out his case, arguing for a full commitment to the coastal defense strategy, and restating his request to be granted control over all the panzers. Hitler seemed to concede, and Rommel left the conference confident his persistence and plan had prevailed. In his daily journal Rommel recorded, "Satisfied with result. The Fuehrer has completely accepted the commander's [Rommel's] opinion regarding the defense of the coast and agreed to a change in command organization."[21] Upon returning to France, Rommel instructed his staff to follow up with the German high command to secure the written orders confirming Rommel's new authority.

Outmaneuvered

Those orders never came. Unbeknownst to Rommel, after huffing out of the conference Rundstedt circled back with his contacts at the German high command, a group unsupportive of Rommel's unorthodox views and brash behavior. Within a few days, they undid all of Rommel's efforts and convinced Hitler to stick with Rundstedt's leadership. Rommel, after several weeks of vague and noncommittal responses from the high command about the new orders giving him control over the tank divisions, realized he had been outmaneuvered. A frustrated Rommel told his staff that when it came to working with Hitler, "The last out of his door is always right."[22]

The inexhaustible Rommel would not accept defeat. He continued proclaiming the need to adopt his coastal defense strategy, believing his nation's survival was at stake. Seeing that the conflict still festered, on April 27 Hitler publicly ruled on the long-running dispute. Hitler was sympathetic to his generals' competing viewpoints. The vision of decisively defeating the Allies at the shoreline tantalized the Fuehrer, but the dictator also recognized the conventional wisdom of concentrating the panzers into a mobile reserve primed for a massed counterattack.

Hitler lacked enough panzers to say yes to everything and was unwilling to say no to anything, so he doled out the tanks hither and yon. Of the ten armored divisions deployed in western Europe, Hitler assigned three to cover southern France should the Allies invade from that direction. In a partial nod to Rommel's pleas, the dictator placed three divisions close to potential invasion sites in northern France and Belgium. The remaining four panzer divisions would constitute Geyr's strategic mobile reserves. However, these four divisions were neither sited inland near Paris as Geyr had advocated nor proximate to potential invasion beaches as Rundstedt preferred. Rather, Hitler scattered these four panzer units across western Europe from Antwerp to Orleans, each division located as much as several hundred kilometers from the closest beach.

Hitler did not just parse out the panzers. He also took for himself direct authority over the tank divisions. Going forward, Rundstedt and Rommel could not move or order into combat any panzers without Hitler's explicit permission. The dictator inserted himself into the chain of command for the defense of western Europe, violating the traditional German military ethos of delegating decision-making to local commanders, and undoubtedly complicating German military decision-making at the start of the battle.

Hitler's April 27 ruling neutered any coherent anti-invasion strategy and doomed Germany's ability to rapidly counterattack the invasion, before the first Allied troops had even waded ashore. When the Allies finally invaded on D-Day, the panzers were too far from the beaches to participate in Rommel's coastline defense and too dispersed to launch any massed counterattacks as Geyr had advocated. "Hitler's decision made a fragile defense yet feebler," as one historian wrote. "The Allies could not have disposed German forces more favorably if they had done it themselves."[23]

Leadership Insights

The impending Allied invasion presented German leaders with an existential threat, which demanded only one military objective—defeat it. With their air force and navy in tatters, their only hopes of throwing the Allies back into the sea relied on their army and its powerful panzers. Consequently, the Germans' sole open question was: Which panzer strategy would maximize their chances of winning the impending battle?

This case study presents a compelling example of how business leaders should *not* research, select, and implement a strategy to achieve their desired objectives. Rather than relying entirely on personal experiences and long-standing tradition as the Germans did, business leaders should define and pursue strategic choices by clearly defining objectives, engaging all stakeholders, validating assumptions, and making fact-based decisions.

Commanders Rundstedt, Rommel, Geyr, and Hitler stumbled in their attempts to define and implement a battle-winning tank strategy. Today, historians and armchair generals still debate who was correct. Rommel and Geyr assessing their nation's military predicament differently is not an error in leadership. The leadership mistakes commenced as these two and the rest of the German senior command reacted to the conflicting threat assessments.

First, Rommel and Geyr made no serious effort to objectively analyze the situation, identify a range of panzer deployment options, and test conclusions. The two officers relied almost exclusively on idiosyncratic experiences and doctrinal traditions to justify their position and refute the other's. No fact-based process was applied, only a contest of personalities. The question of where to put the panzers—an issue expected to decide if Germany could win the battle and thus the war—disintegrated into a competition of who could pen the most memos, shout the loudest, or out-politic the opponent.

Rommel and Geyr did not corner the German market on lapses of leadership. Rundstedt, Germany's senior military officer in western Europe, permitted the row to drag on. He made no serious effort to adjudicate the issue; he barely understood tank forces beyond a superficial level. "Of all the German generals, Field Marshal von Rundstedt knew the least of panzer tactics," recalled one fellow German general after the war. "He and his staff were armchair strategists, who didn't like dirt, noise, and tanks in general—as far as I know, Field Marshal von Rundstedt was never in a tank."[24]

Micromanagement vs. Empowerment

Rundstedt's disdain for dirt was matched by his dislike of dealing with feuding subordinates. The field marshal lacked the energy to intervene, likely due to advancing age and a weary apathy about the war. Rundstedt was unwilling to install any coordinated anti-invasion strategy, abdicating that matter to his local subordinates even if Rundstedt opposed their methods. For example, Rundstedt watched in disagreement but took no action while Rommel pushed his troops forward to the shoreline. "While I did not like them being so near the coast, it would not have been right for me to interfere with the commander on the spot in such matters of detail," Rundstedt rationalized in a postwar interview. "It was only Hitler who interfered in that way."[25] German military doctrine emphasized empowering local leadership, but Rundstedt carried this to the extreme, surrendering strategy to subordinates who filled the vacuum with plans that were at best uncoordinated and at worst destructive to German objectives.

Rundstedt's inattentiveness opened the door for Hitler's interference. With his senior leaders in western Europe snarling at each other, the Nazi dictator inserted himself into the issue, taking ownership over a problem that his subordinate commanders should have resolved on their own. Hitler worsened the German defensive situation in two ways. First, he decided upon a panzer strategy that was no strategy at all, scattering them across the continent in violation of Prussian monarch Frederick the Great's dictum that "He who defends everything defends nothing." Selecting strategy involves choosing what to pursue at the expense of what to forgo, and Hitler was too indecisive (and egotistical) to admit that he and his empire could not accomplish everything.

Hitler's second fatal mistake was to take for himself direct command over the panzer divisions. At this point in the war his penchant for battlefield micromanagement was well established. Distrusting his field marshals and generals, Hitler concluded the panzers were too important to leave in anybody's hands but his own. Unfortunately for the Germans, when the invasion launched at Normandy on the early morning hours of Tuesday, June 6, Hitler was asleep.[26] Not until later that day did Hitler give the order to mobilize some of the panzers into counterattack, but by then D-Day was almost over and the Allies were firmly established onshore.

Strategic Planning

Today, corporate leaders possess a variety of methods to pursue their organization's strategic goals and plans. Most strategic planning approaches recognize and follow a similar methodology, usually including some variation of the following steps:

1. Clearly define and prioritize objectives and deadlines.
2. Engage all stakeholders.
3. Analyze the organization's current internal and external situation and environment, including its strengths, weaknesses, opportunities, and threats (SWOT analysis).
4. Identify and validate assumptions.
5. Make fact-based decisions.
6. Communicate the selected strategy and tactics across the organization.
7. Monitor performance and update goals and plans as needed.

While struggling to select their panzer strategy, the German military leaders either strayed from or skipped most of these steps. Rundstedt, Rommel, and Geyr disagreed on threats and priorities yet made little effort to pursue any consensus using data, objective analysis, or trials and testing. They heavily relied on unchallenged assumptions to form conclusions and propose policy. They elevated personal experience and assertiveness over facts and process. Rundstedt avoided dealing with details and difficult people. Hitler permitted subordinates to dump their problems on his plate. Unfortunately for the Germans, Hitler was incapable of choosing what to do and unwilling to trust his team.

Most business teams manage to avoid open shouting matches and desperate power plays like the Germans displayed. However, teams can omit or gloss over important steps when approaching and pursuing strategic objectives. Some business teams operate without clearly identifying the organization's top priorities across all stakeholders, objectively evaluating their strategic options, reviewing resources, and widely communicating a clear plan. In the short term, the team or organization may not experience any difficulties, but over time an incomplete or undefined business strategy will undermine profitable growth and value creation. Modern leaders will achieve greater success in pursuing their organization's strategic needs by observing these historical events and adopting superior leadership methods and practices.

Leadership Exercises

The following exercises revisit and expand on the historical events associated with "Where to Put the Panzers," and present leadership learning opportunities for individuals and teams to explore.

Exercise #1

German military commanders failed to identify and implement a coherent strategy for defending against the expected Allied invasion, especially with regard to adopting an effective plan for deploying their panzer forces.

- What was most interesting or surprising within this case study?
- What potential lessons does the case study offer to our team or organization?
- How effectively do we identify and select strategic goals and plans, including—
  - » Identifying priorities
  - » Engaging all the stakeholders
  - » Researching options
  - » Validating assumptions
  - » Making fact-based decisions
  - » Communicating objectives across the organization

Exercise #2

Prior to D-Day, Hitler and his German General Staff constantly shuffled army units, particularly the precious panzers, back and forth across the European continent in increasingly frantic efforts to defend their crumbling empire, such that prior to D-Day Germany occasionally possessed as few as one or two panzer divisions in western Europe. Recognizing the invasion was imminent, the Nazis managed to shift ten panzer divisions to western Europe before D-Day.

- What are our team's or organization's most important resources (or assets or capabilities)? How do these create a competitive advantage for us? Are we fully leveraging and deploying these advantages?
- Where within our organization do we wish we had "more of" something, such as staff, sales power, service capacity, operational knowledge, inventory, technology, or capital?
- What could we do to secure these additional resources or capabilities?

Exercise #3

Hitler's April 27 ruling on the panzer dispute would have been the last word for most people, but not for Rommel. The Desert Fox refused to accept the decision, believing his plan represented the only path for German victory. The first week of June, Rommel left his headquarters near Paris, confident the Allies would not invade, given the inhospitable weather forecasts.[27] His first scheduled stop was to visit his wife on her birthday. His second intended stop was to call on the malleable Hitler and again press for the coastal defense strategy. However, Rommel never made the appointment with Hitler. At home with his family for his wife's birthday on June 6, Rommel received word that the invasion had begun while he was away from his post.

- How important is creating alignment within a team around a major strategy, project, or policy? What are the consequences if all team members do not agree with or support the matter?
- What steps can leaders and managers take to build and maintain team alignment around an important objective or issue?
- When leaders and managers encounter a strategic initiative or policy they disagree with, in what circumstances should they fall in line and support it despite their disagreement? When can they or should they actively work to change it?

Exercise #4

Hitler tried to hold on to every piece of his Nazi empire as he prepared to meet the Allied invasion, unwilling to let go of or stop defending any conquest. Perhaps the most striking example occurred at the Channel Islands of Jersey and Guernsey, the only territory of the British Empire occupied by the Germans during World War II. While the German army struggled to find troops and materials to adequately defend continental Europe, more than 25,000 well-equipped German soldiers idled on the Channel Islands. Additionally, Hitler had ordered that ten percent of the steel and concrete allocated to construct the Atlantic Wall defenses must be used to fortify the islands. The islands had no practical military value beyond propaganda, yet Hitler refused Rundstedt's and Rommel's requests to evacuate them and redeploy the forces on the continent against the Allies.

- Part of strategic planning and execution is identifying what not to do, such as projects to leave idle, opportunities not to pursue, or markets not to serve. Leaders and teams often find this difficult. How can leaders and managers maintain disciplined focus on strategic priorities and resist pressure to pursue too much?
- Business leaders frequently face the need to accomplish more with the same resources, and even sometimes with less. Do we face any situations today or in the near future where we may need to achieve more with fewer resources?
- Are there activities, functions, markets, products/services, customers, etc. that we might discontinue or divest from so we can focus on more impactful needs or opportunities?

Exercise #5

In the middle of the panzer debate, German commanders in western Europe attended a war-gaming simulation exercise hosted by Geyr. The war game predicted that Geyr's panzer reserves would not be seriously impeded by Allied airpower and would defeat the invasion in a massed counterattack. Rommel left the exercise unconvinced, believing Geyr's game applied flawed assumptions.

- How can leaders create an environment in which assumptions are challenged, questions are encouraged, and new ways to solve problems are explored?

- What are the most important assumptions we have made in planning for our organization's future growth and objectives? Are the assumptions clearly summarized? How can we test and update our assumptions over time?

- Do we hold any long-standing beliefs, assumptions, or paradigms that might be less true or relevant today or in the near future? Consider factors or variables such as market conditions, competition, technology, customer needs and preferences, labor resources, supply chain health, capital resources, etc.

Exercise #6

By stepping into the panzer strategy debate and claiming authority over the panzer forces, Hitler took on for himself a responsibility that properly belonged to his experienced military commanders.

- Business leaders often encounter situations where a team member presents a problem or question and expects the leader to resolve it. When should business leaders directly solve the problem or answer the question, and when should leaders require their team members to keep responsibility and solve the issue?

- Which is the greater leadership challenge: resisting the impulse to let go of decisions or responsibilities, or getting subordinates ready and willing to take on greater decision-making and responsibilities?

- Do any leaders or managers in our organization currently hold responsibilities or authority that ideally should belong to somebody else? If yes, what would be the benefit of assigning that responsibility or authority to the ideal person or team?

Epilogue

The Allied invasion on D-Day suspended debate over where to put the panzers, but after the war, the dispute resumed among surviving commanders, military historians, and armchair strategists. Who was right—Rommel, Geyr, or Rundstedt? Read enough D-Day histories and you will encounter all possible answers. Like any counterfactual exercise, the question is impossible to determine. However, the battle's actual events suggest Rommel's coastal defense strategy may have offered the Germans the greater chance of defeating the invasion, however slim that chance may have been.

Once the combat began on June 6 on the beaches of Normandy, Rommel's pre-invasion fears of Allied air domination proved correct, and it quickly became apparent that Geyr had grossly underestimated the air threat. Practically every German general and foot soldier who served in Normandy pointed to Allied airpower as the primary factor for Germany's defeat. Geyr too found himself on the receiving end of Allied airpower. On June 7, with the battle only in its second day, Geyr set up his headquarters under the leafy canopy of an apple orchard near Caen. However, Allied signals intelligence intercepted the German unit's radio transmissions, and within hours British bombers and rocket-firing fighters swooped in over the treetops and attacked. Geyr was wounded and nearly two dozen of his staff were killed.

Shortly thereafter, a shaken Geyr was forced to acknowledge in a battlefield report: "The Allied air force is the decisive factor in success during the initial period of the invasion. . . . It is no longer possible to employ a panzer formation above company strength on the invasion front during daylight hours without heavy losses."[28]

An additional development on D-Day supports Rommel's coastal defense strategy. Rommel's implacable pursuit of putting the panzers at the coastline had produced one partial success. Of the ten panzer divisions that Hitler sprinkled across western Europe, the 21st Panzer Division was positioned near Caen, within striking distance of the D-Day beaches. That unit became the only significant German armored force to attack the beachhead on the invasion's first day. Its counterattack narrowly failed, largely due to Germany's lethargic response and convoluted command structure. But the incident suggests that if Rommel's aggressive petitions to deploy additional panzer forces near Normandy had been granted, Allied victory on D-Day could have been in greater jeopardy.

Rommel did not survive the war. Five weeks after D-Day, the Desert Fox was severely injured in an Allied air attack on his staff car while driving through the Norman countryside near Sainte-Foy-de-Montgomery. While Rommel recuperated, a group of German officers attempted to kill Hitler. The coup failed and Hitler's subsequent witch hunt ensnared Rommel, who had little actual involvement in the scheme. Rommel chose suicide to avoid a public trial, certain execution, and persecution of his family.

Geyr survived the war and was extensively interviewed by his American captors. Despite personally experiencing the suffocating Allied airpower during the attack on his headquarters, Geyr remained convinced that his concentrated panzer counterattack strategy would have been the superior approach to contest the invasion. "We should have waited unperturbed until all the reserve divisions involved had assembled and should then have launched them in a counter-blow against the enemy," Geyr lamented after the war. "However, this method was not possible. Neither Hitler nor Supreme Command West understood—nor had the courage—to let 'panzer situations' ripen."[29]

Geyr also praised Rommel's dedication, while throwing one last barb at his late foe's coastal defense strategy: "Rommel courageously supported his views in higher quarters as no other did in the West before or after him. This does the man honor." But, Geyr continued, "History will not absolve him from responsibility for having been the strongest motive force behind an inept use of the entirely battle-fit German Panzer Command."[30]

The Battle for the Bombers

SELECTING STRATEGY—PART 2

"To be strategic is to concentrate on what is important, on those few objectives that can give us a comparative advantage, on what is important to us rather than others, and to plan and execute the resulting plan with determination and steadfastness."

—Richard Koch, consultant, venture capitalist, and author of *The 80/20 Principle*

"This f----- invasion can't succeed, and I don't want any part of the blame. After it fails, we can show them how we win by bombing."

—General Carl A. Spaatz, commander—US Strategic Air Forces

For months prior to D-Day, both the Allies and the Germans fought internal battles to determine how to best prepare for and win the impending clash. These confrontations may seem less gripping compared to actual combat events, but the strategies adopted by the Allies and Germans significantly influenced the outcome of the military contest. To the modern business leader, these pre-invasion disputes reveal fascinating insights into how leaders and teams should identify and organize a shared strategy for success.

For the Allies, the most contentious pre-D-Day question was how to incorporate their thousands of large bombers already striking German industrial and urban targets from their English air bases. Some Allied commanders insisted that these missions against Germany should continue unimpeded, for destroying German industry and cities from the air would soon bring an end to the war. Others believed the massive fleets of bombers should be redirected to attack targets closer to Normandy's beaches to directly aid the D-Day invasion, the one battle that would determine Allied victory or defeat in Europe. This question turned into a rancorous debate that raged for months between British and American leaders across both sides of the Atlantic Ocean. As one prominent historian wrote, "Disagreements, even full-blooded quarrels, between the services were not uncommon either in Britain or America in World War II. But none generated more heat and passion or diverted so much attention from the struggle to defeat the Germans than that surrounding the proper use of the Allies' vast airpower in 1944."[1]

The Battle for the Bombers reveals how teams can devolve into parochialism and lose sight of primary objectives, and how great leaders can navigate disagreement and conflict to establish consensus around a shared vision and plan.

As you read the case study, consider the following questions, each of which will be explored in the exercises following the story:

- How important is having everyone on a team aligned around common priorities and objectives?
- What steps can leaders take to create and maintain team alignment?
- What are the signs that a team (or division or department) may be thinking and acting as a silo?

The Case Study: The Battle for the Bombers

In January of 1944, as he settled into his appointment as supreme Allied commander for Operation Overlord, US General Dwight D. Eisenhower reviewed the resources available to pull off—in just a few months' time— the most complex military operation in history. Examining the Allied situation, Eisenhower, commonly called Ike, identified multiple serious internal issues jeopardizing the D-Day attack: insufficient quantity of ships, inexperienced troops, and constant political and cultural tension across the multinational coalition.[2] In addition to the Allies' internal issues, Ike saw another serious obstacle blocking the path to victory—the powerful German armies waiting in Europe to meet them on D-Day.

The Overlord plan called for more than 150,000 American, British, and Canadian troops drawn from eight divisions and supporting units to land at Normandy on the invasion's first day. After D-Day, the Allies would expand the attack by more than two million additional soldiers waiting in England, plus more on their way from the United States. However, shipping these troops ashore would take time. Thus, at the battle's beginning the Allied invasion force would be comparatively small and vulnerable.

In opposition, the Germans could marshal approximately fifty-eight army divisions and supporting units totaling about 880,000 troops to defend their conquests in western Europe. Additional naval, air force, and miscellaneous units pushed up German combat personnel to about one and a half million. German forces varied in quality and were scattered from southern France to Norway. However, the Germans enjoyed the advantage of operating on land, able to rapidly move their forces to the invasion site via rail and road. At the invasion's start, Allied forces would be outnumbered, lightly equipped, and confined to a small beachhead with little room to maneuver. If the Germans could quickly redeploy their numerically superior units to counterattack the invasion before the Allies could muster their full strength, especially their panzer (tank) forces, Germany could win the battle and perhaps the war.[3]

Ike understood this. Allowing the Germans to move their combat units to the invasion site faster than he could build up his beachhead forces could lead to catastrophic defeat. The Germans had already come perilously close to defeating several previous Allied amphibious landing invasions in Italy. To win the buildup race, Ike needed what military strategists call an interdiction plan to delay, degrade, and destroy German forces before reaching the invasion site. A successful interdiction effort would limit the number of German units that the Allies would confront at the invasion's fragile beginning and give the Allies time to assemble their strength.

For You History Buffs: Allies' Near-Defeats Prior to D-Day

Prior to the D-Day landings in Normandy, the Allies had conducted a series of amphibious invasions in North Africa and Italy, several of which narrowly avoided defeat. During Operation Avalanche, an Allied amphibious landing at Salerno in September of 1943, German counterattacks successfully pushed back Allied forces such that Americans considered retreating and evacuating from the beachhead. Only a rush of reinforcements supported by naval gunfire and air support prevented an Allied disaster.

At Operation Shingle, an Allied amphibious landing at Anzio in January of 1944, the Germans organized a massive counterattack, rushing units from as far as Yugoslavia and southern France to encircle the beachhead. For weeks the battle's outcome was in doubt before the Allies finally broke through in some of the most intense combat of the war.

As part of their interdiction plan, the Allies developed a vast and ingenious disinformation campaign called Operation Fortitude to convince the Germans that the D-Day invasion in Normandy was a feint, and so they should withhold counterattacking Normandy to wait for the real landings. However, Ike could not be fully certain the Germans would fall for the trickery or stay fooled, for just one information leak could burst the entire effort. And deception could delay but not destroy or degrade German combat power. To win the Allies' most important battle of World

War II, Ike needed real combat power to interdict the German armies in western Europe. The Allies possessed this combat power in their air forces.[4]

For You History Buffs: Operation Fortitude

Operation Fortitude included two elements: Fortitude North aimed to convince the Germans that the Allies planned to invade Norway, and Fortitude South sought to mislead the Germans into believing that the Allies' main invasion would fall at Pas-de-Calais in northeastern France. The two misinformation campaigns were components of a larger Allied deception plan called Operation Bodyguard, named by Churchill because "in wartime truth is so precious that she should always be attended by a bodyguard of lies." Fortitude proved spectacularly successful and convinced the Germans to freeze in place many of their divisions for weeks after the Allies attacked at Normandy on D-Day.

Allied Airpower

To carry the war to Germany, the United States and Great Britain assembled air forces of size and scale unequaled in history, and likely never to be seen again. By the spring of 1944, the US Army Air Corps, the precursor to the US Air Force, possessed almost 7,000 combat aircraft in Europe. Britain's Royal Air Force (RAF) added over 4,000 more. The two nations' air forces contained scores of nimble single-engine fighter planes designed to shoot down enemy aircraft, and twin-engine "light" and "medium" bombers to strike tactical targets such as airfields, troop concentrations, fortifications, or naval bases. The battleships of the sky, however, were the large four-engine "heavy" bombers with familiar names such as the American B-17 Flying Fortress and B-24 Liberator, alongside the British Lancaster, Halifax, and Stirling. The two Allies combined fielded more than 3,500 of these machines, each carrying from seven to ten airmen plus thousands of pounds of bombs to attack targets hundreds of miles deep into occupied Europe and Germany.

Given the striking power these four-engine bombers possessed, some Allied military commanders believed that Germany could be defeated predominantly by bombing strategic targets such as manufacturing plants, energy facilities, and large urban areas. They professed Germany could be severely weakened or even defeated by strategic airpower alone, minimizing or avoiding the titanic land battles that caused millions of casualties during the First World War.

This vision of strategic airpower was in its infancy.[5] Prior to World War II, aircraft had been too feeble to pursue the vision; only a few years earlier bombers had been predominantly biplanes made of wood, canvas, and glue. Yet the rapid advancement of aviation technology in the 1930s and the Allies' ability to produce massive quantities of powerful new aircraft tantalized some Allied leaders with a dream of winning the war from the sky.[6]

American General Carl A. Spaatz (pronounced "spots")[7] and British Air Marshal Sir Arthur Harris were two of these visionaries, part of an unofficial faction nicknamed the Bomber Barons. In early 1944, Spaatz commanded the US Strategic Air Forces (USSAF) in Europe. Formerly a World War I fighter pilot, Spaatz was widely considered competent, intelligent, and professional. Spaatz had impressed Eisenhower when they served together in 1943 in the Mediterranean theater, and thus in early 1944 Eisenhower requested Spaatz be assigned to England to support Overlord. Spaatz was close to Eisenhower and a loyal officer, but he believed Overlord was misguided if not unnecessary, calling it a "highly dubious operation in a hurry."[8] Provided his air forces were given enough bombers and unimpeded time, Spaatz believed victory could largely be achieved from the air by destroying Germany's industrial capacity to wage war.

Air Chief Marshal Sir Arthur Harris, commander of Britain's Bomber Command, also believed the Allied path to victory lay through the air, but he disagreed with Spaatz's approach targeting German industrial facilities.

Instead, Harris directed Bomber Command to carpet-bomb German cities to kill, wound, or render homeless ("de-house") the civilian workers manning those industrial facilities. Harris once explained his area-bombing strategy to an American air officer—"You destroy a factory, they rebuild it. In six weeks they are in operation again. I kill all their workmen and it takes twenty-one years to provide the new ones."[9] Countless Allied leaders knowingly made decisions and pursued policies during the war that led to civilian suffering and deaths. Yet few unabashedly embraced the systematic and indiscriminate targeting of civilians as Harris did.

For You History Buffs: Allied Strategic Bombing Campaigns

Harris championed the strategy of area-bombing German cities, but he was not its author. Churchill and the British Chiefs of Staff embraced area bombing after a secret report in mid-1941 revealed that most British bombers were woefully inaccurate, often unable to drop a bomb within five miles of an intended target.

The Americans generally held fast to a principle that civilian casualties must be incidental in strategic bombing, although they never slowed their bombing efforts as those casualties grew to astronomical levels. Later in the war, the US fire-bombed Japanese cities under the premise that attacking urban centers was necessary to destroy the highly decentralized Japanese industrial base. A single raid by B-29 bombers on Tokyo during the night of March 9–10, 1945, likely killed more than 100,000 people—probably a greater number of casualties than occurred during either of the atomic bombings of Hiroshima and Nagasaki.

The military effectiveness and moral justification for Allied strategic bombing campaigns in World War II remains an intensely examined and debated topic.

Could Strategic Bombing Win the War?

The Bomber Barons believed that with American heavy bombers targeting German industrial targets by day and British heavy bombers striking German cities by night, the "round-the-clock" effort would eventually break Germany's military capacity and collective will to fight.[10] Consequently, a risky and grim D-Day invasion would become either a mop-up exercise or altogether unnecessary.

Spaatz and Harris believed their bombers just needed sufficient uninterrupted time and latitude to implement their war-winning strategies. Early in the war, the fledgling RAF Bomber Command and US Army Air Corps could barely muster several dozen to perhaps a few hundred aircraft on each mission. These initial raids featured inexperienced crews flying early-model planes, using primitive technology and unproven tactics. Two years later, much had changed. Both nations were launching 1,000-bomber missions using state-of-the-art aircraft flown by highly trained crews aided by technological innovations such as targeting radar and radio navigation. Finally possessing the means to pursue strategic bombing, Spaatz and Harris wished to ignore diversions such as D-Day. An aide to Eisenhower bitterly remarked that the Bomber Barons hoped "that Overlord will meet with every success but sorry they can't give direct assistance because of course they are more fully occupied on the really important war against Germany."[11]

Other Allied military leaders were unconvinced by strategic bombing's potential to win the war. Strategic bombing on this scale was new to warfare. Its ability to force German capitulation was only theory, and recent evidence undermined that theory. In the summer and fall of 1940, Germany had tried to bring the British to their knees by aerial bombing in what became known as the Battle of Britain. The indiscriminate area-bombing of London and other British cities had caused tens of thousands of civilian casualties, yet British political and civilian resolve did not weaken under attack, but rather hardened.

Other than Bomber Barons like Spaatz and Harris, most Allied military leaders held to the conventional belief that victory could not be achieved through bombing alone, leaving Overlord as the essential undertaking to defeat Germany. Eisenhower was among these, labeling the theory that the war could be won solely from the air as "dangerous nonsense."[12] Ike insisted that all Allied combat resources, including the four-engine strategic bombers, be utilized in the manner that would best contribute to the invasion's success. Unconvinced that bombing German factories and cities would win the war before D-Day, Ike sought a plan for redeploying the strategic bombers to interdict German forces prior to and after D-Day.

Zuckerman: The Man with the Air Plan

The person who provided the nucleus for a plan was Dr. Solomon "Solly" Zuckerman. Born in British colonial South Africa, Zuckerman possessed one of the more curious resumes of any figure in World War II. Prior to the war, Zuckerman was a zoologist studying the social behavior of apes. Once war broke out, as an anatomist he studied British casualties from German bombing attacks and designed a helmet for civilian defense personnel, called the Zuckerman helmet. Later he studied the effectiveness of Allied bombing attacks in Italy, and from there he became the scientific director of the British Bombing Survey Unit (BBSU), a group tasked with recommending how to use airpower to support the D-Day invasion.

Zuckerman was a pioneer of operational research—the disciplined use of data, statistical research, and modeling to enhance decision-making. Applying scientific process to experience gained studying bombing results in Italy, in January 1944 Zuckerman published a paper entitled *Delay and Disorganization of Enemy Movement by Rail*. Zuckerman's thesis formed the foundation of what would come to be known as the Transportation Plan.

Zuckerman's basic premise was simple. The most effective way to interdict German forces was to destroy over a two-to-three-month bombing campaign the seventy-six French, Belgian, and German railroad marshaling yards (a facility where railroad cars are stored and organized into trains) and service depots located within 150 miles (almost 250 kilometers) of the invasion beaches at Normandy. Bombing the yards and depots would create a "railway desert" limiting the Germans' ability to move their military forces by train, the most rapid and efficient means to transport armies. With rail service crippled, the Germans would have to increase reliance on trucks, consuming time and fuel—both in short supply for the Germans.[13] Finally, restricting Germans to the road networks would "canalize" their forces, increasing vulnerability to air attack.

Zuckerman recommended avoiding attacking railroad tracks and bridges, for he believed these targets were too difficult to hit and in the case of track lines comparatively easy to repair. However, marshaling yards and depots were large, sprawling targets more easily hit from the air with the bombing technology of that time. Zuckerman computed precise estimates for the bombing effort required. The typical yard was 500 acres in size, and four 500-pound bombs were needed per acre to seriously damage the facility, given known bombing accuracy ratios. The South African scientist concluded the Allies would need to drop 45,000 tons of bombs on the rail centers, which would consume almost half of the total Allied ordnance (total supply of bombs) in the months leading up to the invasion.

The Transportation Plan could not be implemented using only single-engine fighter planes and smaller twin-engine bombers, for those couldn't carry enough ordnance. Allied heavy bombers had to provide seventy-five percent of the bomb lift to implement the Transportation Plan, consequently interrupting the Bomber Barons' strategic bombing campaigns already underway against German industrial targets and cities.[14]

The Bomber Barons Push Back

Not surprisingly, Spaatz and Harris received Solly Zuckerman's Transportation Plan like a lead balloon, referring to it as Zuckerman's Folly.

The two men shared a vehement opposition to any dilution of their strategic bombing efforts, but they objected on different grounds. Spaatz warned the Transportation Plan would have a serious unintended consequence of benefitting the Luftwaffe, the German air force. Allied leaders unanimously recognized that a prerequisite for Overlord's success was defeating the Luftwaffe. Otherwise, German aircraft could strike the vulnerable invasion ships and beachhead.

Spaatz pointed out that American bombing missions against high-value strategic targets compelled German fighter aircraft to enter battle against the Allies, which was destroying hundreds of Luftwaffe aircraft and their irreplaceable pilots each month, thus clearing the skies of German planes in advance of D-Day.[15] Spaatz believed German fighters would not rise to contest bombing missions against French railroad facilities, but would stay safe on the ground. If he was correct, the Transportation Plan would give the weakened Luftwaffe a respite at a critical juncture shortly before D-Day.

Spaatz did not just attempt to shoot down the Transportation Plan. He also offered Eisenhower an alternative bombing target that he believed was superior to rail facilities—oil. Spaatz's Oil Plan aimed at bombing the fourteen synthetic oil plants and thirteen crude oil refineries that accounted for more than half of Germany's oil-production capacity. Oil was the military's lifeblood in World War II, much as it is today. Up to that point in the war, German oil production had received only cursory attention from American bomber squadrons.[16] Spaatz argued that "a concentrated attack against oil, which would represent the most far-reaching use of strategic airpower that has ever been attempted in this war, promises more than any other system a fighting chance of ending German resistance in a shorter period than we ever thought possible."[17]

Spaatz also believed the Luftwaffe would not ignore bombers striking their precious oil industry. "We believe," he summarized, "attacks on transportation will not force the German fighters into action. We believe they will defend oil to their last fighter plane."[18]

Britain's Harris also took aim against the Transportation Plan, dismissing Zuckerman as "a civilian professor whose peacetime forte is the study of the sexual aberrations of the higher apes."[19] Harris believed his strategic bombing campaign was too important to be interrupted. He also argued that RAF Bomber Command crews would be ineffective in precision bombing raids against rail facilities, for they were trained in nighttime area-bombing attacks against large urban centers. Harris, "an inflexible man, chronically resistant to negotiation and compromise, who treated those who disagreed with him as mortal enemies," believed retasking the bombers would be ruinous.[20]

General Eisenhower, supreme commander for Operation Overlord, the decisive military operation of the Allies' war in Europe, should have been able to overcome this resistance by simply ordering the Bomber Barons to comply. However, Eisenhower had no authority over the thousands of strategic bombers, arguably the Allies' mightiest military asset.

Eisenhower Enters the Fray as Relationships Strain

From the moment Ike assumed leadership of Operation Overlord, he anticipated this confrontation. First, he already recognized the importance of airpower in supporting an amphibious attack. Earlier in the war, Ike had led several beachhead invasions in the Mediterranean theater despite not possessing direct authority over Allied air forces, with nearly catastrophic results. Second, Ike already understood that the strategic bomber commanders enjoyed wide autonomy.

The British general who spent a year writing most of the Operation Overlord battle plan had warned Ike of the "problem persuading the Bomber Barons to play with us in spite of the overriding demands of their private war over the Reich."[21] Only days into his D-Day leadership position, Ike wrote to his boss General George C. Marshall, chair of the US Chiefs of Staff, sharing a worry that he would be "forever fighting with those air officers who regardless of the ground situation, want to send big bombers on missions that have nothing to do with the critical effort."[22]

For You History Buffs: The Man Who Wrote the D-Day Invasion Plan

General Frederick E. Morgan is an underappreciated figure in the D-Day story. In mid-1943, Morgan was charged with drafting the battle plan that eighteen months later would become Operation Overlord. Originally equipped with just a pair of aides and one borrowed staff car, Morgan later wrote that "never were so few asked to do so much in so short a time."[23]

Eventually he created a team of analysts, planners, logisticians, and economists; it was this team that sketched an Overlord invasion plan, which Eisenhower would later flesh out and implement. Ike subsequently made several significant changes to the plan, but the core remained Morgan's work.

The two strategic bomber forces were silos, accustomed to operating independently and opposed to any external jurisdiction. Neither the British nor American strategic bomber forces reported to Eisenhower. Harris reported to Air Marshal Charles Portal and the British Chiefs of Staff in London, and Spaatz's bosses were at the US Chiefs of Staff back in Washington. Ike's written orders from the two nations' Combined Chiefs of Staff instructed him "to enter the continent of Europe and, in conjunction with the other United Nations, undertake operations aimed at the heart of Germany and the destruction of her armed forces," but with regard to the bombers he could only "recommend any variation in these activities which may seem to you desirable."

Ike faced more than institutional intransigence. He also confronted fierce resistance from British leaders, including Portal and Prime Minister

Winston Churchill over the perceived loss of national prestige should the RAF's Bomber Command be subordinated to an American. Bomber Command was the one arm of Britain's military that had been relentlessly on the offense against Germany for the entire war, including during the war's darkest days when a desperate England stood alone against Nazi domination.[24] By early 1944, the US, due to its vastly greater economic might, had palpably surpassed Britain as the lead partner in the two nations' special bilateral relationship. Subjecting Bomber Command to an American's control was one pill too nationalistically difficult for the British to swallow.

Eisenhower was acutely sensitive to the dynamics of the Anglo-American relationship—US President Franklin D. Roosevelt had selected Eisenhower to lead Overlord in large part because he was the "best politician among the military men."[25] However, Ike was surprised by the dysfunction and discord he encountered within the leadership team.[26] Individuals were either confused or conflicted over roles and responsibilities. Air Chief Marshal Sir Trafford Leigh-Mallory, assigned to serve under Ike as Overlord's air commander-in-chief, expected that all air forces including the bombers would fall under his authority for the D-Day invasion. However, Harris and Spaatz objected because Leigh-Mallory had no experience with strategic bombers, having commanded exclusively fighter aircraft. Compounding the confusion, Ike had two air commanders on his senior team: Leigh-Mallory and RAF Air Marshal Arthur Tedder, whom Ike had made his deputy supreme commander. From day one the overlap between Leigh-Mallory and Tedder was obvious. One of Eisenhower's staff warned, "I don't think there is a place for both of them."[27]

Organizational disarray was exacerbated by interpersonal conflict. Many disliked Leigh-Mallory, whose confrontational demeanor regularly rubbed others the wrong way. One American general admitted after the war that "I just didn't know people at that level behaved like that. Nobody wanted to be under Leigh-Mallory, not even the British."[28] Spaatz did little to mask his disdain. In one instance, Spaatz attended a meeting chaired by Leigh-Mallory to preview the Transportation Plan. At this meeting Leigh-Mallory stated that he expected Spaatz to cede control of the strategic bombers as early as March 1. Spaatz stood up, gathered his papers, shouted, "Then I have nothing further to say," and stomped out of the room.[29] Meanwhile, Britain's Harris and his boss Portal were increasingly at odds. As the war dragged on, Portal grew less convinced that Harris's obsession with area-bombing German cities was producing results justifying the massive effort.

If this was not enough for Ike to deal with, American interservice rivalries created additional turbulence. During World War II, American air forces were not a separate military branch as today, but rather a part of the US Army. American air generals including Spaatz envisioned spinning off and forming an independent air force after the war. To support their cause, they must turn the billions of dollars America invested in tens of thousands of planes crewed and serviced by millions of men into demonstrable wartime results. Turning over the strategic bombers to a ground officer (Eisenhower) to support a ground operation (Overlord) undercut their pursuit of independence, especially if they suspected that ground operation might fail. At a meeting with some of his staff a few weeks before D-Day, Spaatz confessed, "This f------ invasion can't succeed, and I don't want any part of the blame. After it fails, we can show them how we can win by bombing."[30]

Ike Pursues an Aligned Team

Eisenhower's first step in the Battle for the Bombers was to secure consent from his superiors for command over the strategic bomber forces. While officially Ike reported to the Combined Chiefs of Staff of America and England, General Marshall was his primary boss, point of contact, and advocate. Shortly after Eisenhower's appointment to lead Overlord, Ike met with Marshall in Washington and petitioned for control over the bombers. Marshall did not deny Ike's request, but did not approve it either. Marshall had no authority over British Bomber Command. As for the American strategic bombers, Marshall would not back Ike's request until Eisenhower tried to unify his Overlord team in England.

After Eisenhower left for England, he maintained close communications with Marshall, continuously explaining his intentions and updating his superior on developments. "I feel that as long as you and I are in complete coordination as to purpose," Ike cabled, "that you in Washington and I here can do a great deal towards achieving the best overall results."[31]

With Marshall in Washington in his corner, Ike tasked his leadership team in England to create an air plan to support D-Day. Eisenhower ordered Leigh-Mallory to meet with the rest of Ike's air commanders—Portal, Tedder, Harris, and Spaatz—to form a Joint Bombing Committee and develop a bombing strategy in support of D-Day. Eisenhower was initially optimistic about the committee, telling an aide that while expecting some resistance, "This will probably work out all right."[32]

The committee met regularly over the next few months but accomplished nothing. Harris often skipped attendance, sending staffers in his stead who maintained the party line that British Bomber Command was only trained to attack cities and incapable of precision attacks against rail targets. Spaatz vigorously resisted any encroachment on his turf by Leigh-Mallory. The committee's members were too partisan, suspicious of each other's motives and protective of individual responsibilities and authority. Ike's Deputy Supreme Commander Tedder eventually reached "the unfortunate conclusion that the two strategic [bomber] forces are determined not to play."[33] Incompatible operational philosophies, competing agendas, and personality differences grounded Ike's hope for constructive, well-intentioned dialogue.

The committee's inability to gain traction revealed to Eisenhower the need to meet separately with the key players to build trust across the disarticulated team. Eisenhower applied reason and persuasion. (Eisenhower to Spaatz: "Proper credit has not been given to Leigh-Mallory's intelligence.")[34] Eisenhower even regularly included Churchill on his rounds, in part to keep the mercurial politician, famous for his impulsive ideas, out of Eisenhower's process. (Eisenhower to Tedder: Hurry up with getting an airpower plan, otherwise Churchill will be "in this thing with both feet.")[35]

Eisenhower Threatens to Quit

Ultimately, Ike could never secure authority over RAF Bomber Command as long as Churchill opposed the idea. On the evening of February 28, 1944, the issue came to a head. In discussions that Eisenhower later described as "quite violent," Churchill flatly denied Eisenhower's proposal for authority over the British bombers.[36] Churchill admitted he was also uncomfortable with Leigh-Mallory commanding strategic bombers, which frustrated Eisenhower, for it was the British who made Leigh-Mallory the Overlord air commander-in-chief. But while Churchill had concerns about Leigh-Mallory, he was adamantly against RAF Bomber Command falling under American control. Eisenhower was unwilling to back down; he told Churchill that if the prime minister and British Chiefs of Staff would not acquiesce, "he would simply have to go home."[37]

Eisenhower had dozens of disagreements with Churchill and both nations' Chiefs of Staff during the war, most minor but some quite fierce, but the bomber question was the only issue over which he threatened to quit.

Eisenhower routinely seconded his ego to maintain Allied team harmony, but by this point in the war he was aware of the tremendous individual clout he possessed. Stepping down would have triggered more geopolitical turmoil than perhaps any resignation letter in history. He was Roosevelt's handpicked leader for Overlord, and a hero in the eyes of the American public. "Going home" because the British were withholding resources from Overlord would have thrown the American and British relationship into chaos only a few months before the invasion.

Furthermore, Roosevelt and Churchill had promised Soviet dictator Joseph Stalin that the Allies would invade western Europe in the spring, and Ike would lead the invasion.[38] Soviet Russia was carrying the lion's share of the ground fighting against Germany—suffering millions of casualties in the process.[39] Dissention between America and Britain shortly before the invasion date could lead the distrustful Stalin to pursue a separate peace with Germany, a path he had previously threatened.

Caving to Ike's threat of resignation, Churchill suggested a path forward. If Eisenhower, as supreme commander of Overlord, could work with Portal, the British air chief of staff, to create a mutually acceptable airpower leadership arrangement, their ideas likely would be acceptable to the prime minister and the rest of the British Chiefs of Staff.

Ike agreed, but instructed his Deputy Supreme Commander Tedder to act as his emissary and meet with Portal. Tedder and Portal had a good relationship. Tedder also earned a reputation as an effective coordinator between air and ground forces during prior Allied operations in the Mediterranean.

Eisenhower's earlier optimistic attempts to engage a broad bombing committee had failed. His effort to secure from Churchill authority over the RAF bombers also had failed. Now Ike sought resolution through the smallest possible team of just two, but a team whose members understood the issue, appreciated its significance, and were committed to seeking a viable resolution.

With the invasion date fast approaching, the two Englishmen Portal and Tedder explored how the Royal Air Force Bomber Command could acceptably come under the control of an American Army general. In his postwar memoir Tedder explained, "During the first ten days of March I saw or spoke with Portal almost every day as we struggled to reconcile the differences between Eisenhower's wish for complete control of the heavy bombers and the Prime Minister's ruling that [Bomber Command] could not be handed over as a whole to Eisenhower."[40] They grappled with wording and phraseology such as "loose control," "supervision," and "detailed control," underscoring the tightrope they walked.

On March 9, less than three months before D-Day, Portal and Tedder produced a recommended framework for authority over air forces in support of D-Day. The Overlord leadership team would be reshuffled. Tedder, as Eisenhower's deputy supreme commander, would lead all air operations, in essence assuming Leigh-Mallory's role. Leigh-Mallory would retain the air commander-in-chief title but would be limited to commanding tactical air forces (i.e., fighters and small bombers), and would report to Tedder. Portal, representing the US and British Combined Chiefs of Staff, would review and approve the D-Day airpower plan, once submitted by Eisenhower. Once the airpower plan was set, Ike, with Tedder acting as his agent, would have "supervision of air operations out of England of all the forces engaged in [Overlord] including US Strategic and British Bomber Command."[41]

Portal and Tedder circulated a draft memo under their names summarizing the arrangement, but Eisenhower's fingerprints were all over it. Portal and Tedder would not have promoted this solution without his countenance.

A thankful Eisenhower wrote to Portal that the proposed leadership arrangement "was exactly what we want."[42] Churchill found the solution "very satisfactory." Spaatz agreed that the solution was a "logical, workable plan and, under the conditions which exist, cannot be improved upon."[43] The draft memo was submitted to both nations' Chiefs of Staff for approval. Eisenhower briefed his boss Marshall, cabling "This morning it appears to me the air problems are at last in good order . . .

All air forces here will be under Tedder's supervision as my agent, and this prospect is particularly pleasing to Spaatz."[44] With the Allied team in England finally in alignment, Eisenhower anticipated a speedy stamp of approval from Washington.

He was wrong. A week later, the US Chiefs of Staff in Washington denied the proposal, for it granted Eisenhower only "supervision" and not "command" of the strategic bomber forces. An astonished and discouraged Eisenhower confided to an aide that every time he believed he had the air command issue resolved, "Somebody else's feelings are hurt and I have another problem to settle."[45]

The rejection surprised Eisenhower. It should not have. For months he had insisted to Marshall and the rest of the US Chiefs of Staff that he must have unilateral command over the strategic bombers, because otherwise the various Allied leaders in Europe would continue to pursue their separate agendas, putting the D-Day operation in serious jeopardy. To Ike's bosses in Washington, the term "supervision" suggested he had accepted lesser authority. However, Eisenhower perceived no weakening of his position in the word "supervision." He had worked directly with Tedder and Portal; he knew they were of like mind with him and would implement his decisions. Ike scrambled to telegram Marshall that "the question of exact terms and phraseology did not arise at that time, but it was clearly understood that authority for operational control of forces definitely allocated to Overlord . . . should reside with me."[46]

Deeply frustrated, on March 22 Ike wrote in his diary that "unless the matter is settled at once I will request relief from this command."[47] Ike's renewed consideration of resignation was mercifully short lived. After a rapid flurry of telegraphs between the two nations' Chiefs of Staff (Eisenhower occasionally referred to these exchanges as "trans-Atlantic essay contests"), the word "direction" was proposed and quickly accepted. Eisenhower edited his diary entry and wrote "Amen!"

Eisenhower had finally secured authority over the combined Allied strategic bomber forces in support of the D-Day invasion. It had taken almost four months of cajoling, negotiating, bickering, and threatening. But, while Ike had won control over the bombers, there was still no resolution on how the bombers would be used in Operation Overlord. Whatever airpower strategy the Allies would finally select would take time to implement, and the invasion target date was nine weeks away. With "direction" over the strategic air forces in hand, Eisenhower set about resolving this second and final phase of the Battle for the Bombers.

The Final Showdown

Three days later, on Saturday, March 25, Eisenhower orchestrated the final showdown. He called a meeting at his headquarters west of London in Bushy Park, code-named Wildwing. All the players attended: Portal, Tedder, Spaatz, Leigh-Mallory, and Harris, supported by various aides and staff experts in intelligence, logistics, and economics. Tedder and Spaatz circulated memorandums prior to the meeting detailing their positions. For Eisenhower, the paramount question he must answer was: Which bombing strategy would provide the greatest aid to the invasion?

The Allied team remained sharply divided. Over the last few months, while the debate had raged over who would command the bombers, simultaneously the Transportation Plan (bombing French rail yards) and Oil Plan advocates (in favor of bombing Germany's oil industry) had been vehemently promoting their preferred choice and vigorously attacking the opposite. Tedder and Leigh-Mallory stood behind Zuckerman's Transportation Plan. Portal was coming around too. Spaatz was "jubilant and overjoyed" that he would not have to report to Leigh-Mallory, but remained solidly in favor of the Oil Plan.[48]

Harris found himself opposing both the Transportation and Oil plans. Steadfast in his conviction that RAF Bomber Command should not deviate from area-bombing German cities, he maintained that the "best and indeed only efficient support which Bomber Command can give to Overlord is the intensification of attacks on suitable industrial centers in Germany."[49] But Harris's stick-with-what-we-are-doing approach lacked weight. The Bomber Command leader had been predicting for too long that German collapse was just a few demolished cities away, even though the Nazi regime showed no signs of a weakened will to fight.

Furthermore, losses among RAF Bomber Command crews remained appalling. Harris's credibility had further eroded when his claim that Bomber Command crews could not accurately hit precision targets was debunked. Ordered by a dubious Portal to put the question to the test, on the night of March 6–7 Harris's strategic bombers hit six French rail yard targets with excellent results and lower-than-expected civilian casualties. As one historian wrote, the surprised Harris was "confounded by the virtuosity of his own men."[50] Ultimately, Harris could not offer Eisenhower a rationale for how carpet-bombing German cities would support an invasion on the beaches of Normandy, because it did not exist. At the March 25 showdown, Ike's only strategic options would come down to the Transportation Plan or the Oil Plan.

For You History Buffs: British and American Bomber Crew Casualties

Flying in a strategic bomber was proportionately one of the deadliest branches of combat service during the war. In the US Eighth Air Force, the primary European strategic bomber command, more than 26,000 crew lost their lives and tens of thousands more were injured or captured. Within RAF Bomber Command, 55,000 of the 125,000 total aircrew died during the war—more than two out of five. Almost 20,000 more British airmen were injured or captured.

Several months before D-Day, on the night of March 30–31, 1944, RAF Bomber Command suffered its worst night of the war. In a raid on the German city of Nuremberg, 96 of more than 700 bombers were shot down and a further dozen crash landed upon return. The RAF suffered 545 airmen killed and 163 captured. The mission is remembered by the Royal Air Force as Black Friday.

As the meeting opened, Tedder was given the floor and formally nominated the Transportation Plan to cripple France's rail yards and thus interdict German forces once the Allies invaded. However, he conceded Spaatz's point that pressure must be kept on the Luftwaffe—the implication being that if German fighters did not attack bombers conducting rail yard missions, the Allies would have to rethink things. Tedder acknowledged that bombing rail facilities would not prevent all rail traffic from getting through. But he believed that sufficient rail traffic would be interrupted, and "D-Day would have no chance of success" without the Transportation Plan.[51] According to the official meeting minutes, "considerable discussion" ensued thereafter.

Eisenhower listened as the attendees argued the Transportation Plan's particulars, merits, and weaknesses. Their deliberations strayed far and wide, addressing what portion of French rail traffic could sustain German military needs, how quickly damaged trains could be repaired, how much food from last year's harvest was on hand to feed the French civilian population without further rail deliveries, and to what extent Germany could alternatively source coal and bauxite if rail traffic was compromised.

After listening to these diversions, Ike narrowed the group's focus. He reminded them of the paramount need to take every possible step to ensure that the invasion got ashore and stayed ashore. Given this objective, Ike declared "the greatest contribution that he could imagine the air forces making to this aim was that they should hinder enemy movement."[52] His conclusion was if the Transportation Plan provided any "reduction in military traffic, however small," it should be adopted unless this team could identify an "alternative plan which would produce greater results."[53]

That was Spaatz's cue to propose the Oil Plan as an alternative strategy to both starve German vehicular traffic in Normandy and sever the lifeblood of Germany's war-making capacity. The American Bomber Baron believed the issue came down to a tradeoff between the Transportation Plan's short-term limited effects—which Spaatz doubted—versus the Oil Plan's titanic long-term effects, of which Spaatz was confident. Spaatz claimed the Oil Plan "will lead directly to sure disaster for Germany. The Rail attack can lead to harassment only. In weighing these two, it appears that too great a price may be paid merely for a certainty of very little."[54]

Time was the key consideration for both bombing strategies. Eisenhower needed time for his invasion to withstand the inevitable German counterattacks and win the buildup race. Spaatz required time for his bombers to destroy Nazi industry. Someone in the meeting asked how much time was required for the Oil Plan to achieve a decisive potential. A British oil expert provided the answer—about six months. Germany possessed six months' worth of oil stockpiles and thus bombing oil production would not negatively impact German military power until those reserves were depleted. An aide to Spaatz conceded the point, admitting that there was no guarantee that "attacks on oil targets would have an appreciable effect during the initial stages of OVERLORD."[55]

The Transportation Plan Is Adopted

Eisenhower and Overlord did not have six months. D-Day was two months away, and once ashore the Allies would be outnumbered for weeks. Eisenhower acknowledged that the Oil Plan held great potential for contributing to the eventual defeat of Germany, but it could not contribute to his primary objective of getting and keeping the invasion troops ashore. The Supreme Commander instructed his team that the

"Oil Plan should be considered as soon as the first critical situation in OVERLORD had passed," but otherwise "there was no alternative to the Transportation Plan."[56] Thus, the Transportation Plan was selected as the Allied airpower strategy to support D-Day.

The March 25 meeting escaped the rancor that permeated the previous four months because the participants understood that Eisenhower was now firmly in charge and would choose the strategy that offered the greatest immediate support of D-Day. Eisenhower had turned a collection of individuals fractured by competitive silos, egoism, personal animosity, and international tension into a team organized around a singular mission and the strategy to pursue it. It was an imperfect arrangement, held together only through Ike's will and clout, aided by Tedder's unifying demeanor. However, Eisenhower secured authority over all Allied airpower, and the Transportation Plan was adopted as the airpower strategy to support the D-Day invasion.

Leadership Insights

This case study explores what can happen when a leader faces an unorganized set of subordinates and managers who possess unconnected or competing agendas. Eisenhower's mandate was "to enter the continent of Europe" and pursue the destruction of Nazi Germany's military forces. To accomplish his objective, Ike sought to gain authority over every major resource that could help his armies get ashore and stay there. This included the strategic bomber forces, because Eisenhower knew that if left on their own, these silos would continue pursuits that offered no synergistic support to D-Day.

Business leaders can observe the methods and tactics Eisenhower doggedly applied in his attempts to create a functional team and unified strategy. Initially, he optimistically asked the stakeholders to meet in committee, explore the issues, and collaboratively define an invasion airpower strategy. The bombing committee never jelled, its members divided by partisanship and distrust. But their struggles revealed to Ike which people were his early supporters, which were in active resistance, and where the relationship fault lines lay. With D-Day only a few months away and the committee languishing, Ike met individually with opponents and doubters, tearing down barriers and building up consensus. He demonstrated a willingness to listen and compromise, but a refusal to enter arrangements that undermined his mandate, to the point of putting his career and reputation on the line. Throughout the affair he kept Marshall, his superior officer but also advocate and confidant, appraised of developments and primed to support him.

Modern business leaders may use similar methods and tactics when leading teams and mobilizing support around objectives, especially in the face of open or sometimes concealed opposition. Eisenhower's most effective weapon in the Battle for the Bombers was Tedder, his deputy supreme commander. Eisenhower deployed Tedder as his emissary and implementer, delegating the legwork of participating in the bombing committee, evaluating the Transportation Plan, and conferring with Portal to reach the breakthrough arrangement. (Business leaders may recognize the Tedder-Portal effort was a mid-twentieth-century Tiger Team—an ad hoc group of subject-matter experts often from diverse backgrounds formed to address and resolve a single high-stakes or time-sensitive problem or challenge.) At the end, the contest for the bombers was resolved when Eisenhower did something he had emphatically insisted he would not do—he put somebody other than himself directly over the strategic bombers, specifically Tedder.

After the leadership reshuffle, which promoted Tedder above Leigh-Mallory, Tedder's aviation role was carefully described by the official documents as Eisenhower's "agent," avoiding the title of air commander-in-chief, which had been assigned to Leigh-Mallory. (Churchill described Tedder's role to be the "aviation lobe of Eisenhower's brain.")[57] This was window dressing. Tedder immediately became Eisenhower's de facto chief air commander. The months of squabbling had revealed to Eisenhower that promoting Tedder in role but not title would limit damage to British sentiment, de-escalate personality conflicts, and gain American acquiescence. In elevating Tedder, Eisenhower quietly dropped his prior insistence that the bombers should be his alone to directly command, because Ike never confused the means with the end. Wrestling away control over the bombers for himself was not Ike's true objective. His goal was to ensure the bombers were used against targets that best aided the D-Day invasion.

A lesser leader than Eisenhower might not have agreed to his apparent dilution of authority. However, Eisenhower recognized that Tedder possessed two qualities that he did not—Tedder was English, and he held a background in military aviation including coordinating air and ground forces. Tedder's nationality diffused one objection from Churchill, Portal, and the rest of the British Chiefs of Staff. Tedder's aviation experience diffused a second objection from Spaatz. Furthermore, Tedder had more going for him than just nationality and resume. He was competent, respected, and empathetic. According to one wartime observer, Tedder "could always see the other fellow's point of view and tolerate it, even if he did not welcome it. It was because of his tolerance and understanding that he gained the tolerance and understanding of others."[58]

Once Tedder was elevated to Eisenhower's aviation "agent" (or "brain lobe"), then selecting the Transportation Plan as the Allied airpower strategy quickly became feasible and less contentious. After that point, Eisenhower and Tedder co-managed the air campaign during Operation Overlord. Eisenhower focused on strategy and critical relationships while Tedder directed implementation of the airpower plan, including tasking the strategic bombers according to Ike's vision.

Eisenhower won the Battle of the Bombers by maintaining focus on his top objectives, thinking flexibly, and adapting his team to leverage each person's strengths, experience, and relationships. The Eisenhower-Tedder relationship was the linchpin for resolving the leadership disarray and selecting a coherent airpower strategy. In today's business organizations, their relationship might be described as "chief executive officer—chief operations officer," "visionary—implementer," "outside leader—inside leader," or simply "number one—number two."

There are innumerable ways executives and managers can formally or informally arrange teams and work together to pursue important objectives. Leadership teamwork leverages individual talents and increases the likelihood of achieving shared objectives. Few individuals are equally skilled and effective in all leadership functions. Defining vision, setting strategy, planning for growth, building teams, molding culture, creating processes and systems, fostering accountability, and coaching development—these are common examples from the extensive and diverse demands put on today's leaders. Eisenhower recognized his needs, skills, and constraints, and employed and elevated Tedder into a leadership partnership that together accomplished what neither could do on his own.

Leadership Exercises

The following exercises revisit and expand on the historical events associated with "The Battle for the Bombers," and present leadership learning opportunities for individuals and teams to explore.

Exercise #1

Eisenhower was given an absolute objective but a team fractured by personality conflict, silos, and competing agendas. Through his creative diplomacy, Eisenhower aligned his team around an overall airpower strategy to support the D-Day invasion. After reviewing the case study, consider the following questions:

• What was most interesting or surprising within this case study?

- What potential lessons does the case study offer our team or organization?
- What specific steps did Eisenhower take to build consensus and alignment around the Transportation Plan bombing strategy? Are any of his methods applicable within our team or company?

Exercise #2

Eisenhower encountered two powerfully entrenched silos in the British and American strategic bomber arms. The leaders of the two air forces envisioned winning the war through strategic bombing and resisted pausing their efforts to support Overlord. The two bomber forces also made little effort to collaborate operations with each other and pursued different targeting philosophies.

- What are the signs that a team (or unit, department, division, etc.) may be thinking or behaving like a silo?
- How can leaders and managers achieve and maintain effective communication and collaboration across multiple teams? Within our company, do I or we see any opportunities for improved information sharing or collaboration across multiple teams?
- Are there any situations within our organization where multiple teams are pursuing common objectives but employing different and non-synergistic methods or tactics? Could these efforts be coordinated and complementary?

Exercise #3

During the debate over the best use of airpower, Allied commanders lacked proven methods to measure progress in their new and unproven strategic bombing campaigns. Without shared key performance indicators

(KPIs) or similar tools, the Bomber Barons could manipulate data and produce arcane metrics to validate their efforts.

For example, a British report in early 1944 offered that Germany "has irretrievably lost 1,000,000 man-years" due to area-bombing its cities. The report continued that "this represents no less than 36 percent of the industrial effort that would have been put out by these towns if they had remained unmolested . . . Expressing these losses in another way, 2,400,000,000 man-hours have been lost for an average expenditure of 116,500 tons of bombs claimed dropped, and this amounts to an average return for every ton of bombs dropped of 20,500 man-hours."[59] One historian observed that "seldom in the history of warfare have attempts been made to measure victory or defeat by such remarkable mathematical yardsticks."[60]

- What key performance indicators (KPIs) should we focus on to measure our success?
- Are there any areas within our company where we would like to have more visibility and performance information?
- Do all employees within our team or company understand our top objectives and KPIs?

Exercise #4

A secondary question during the Transportation Plan vs. Oil Plan debate involved the efficacy of bombing bridges. Leigh-Mallory refused to send his tactical air forces against bridges, in compliance with Zuckerman's prescription. Spaatz and others disagreed and pushed for a test. On May 7, twelve US P-47 Thunderbolt single-engine fighter planes struck a railway bridge over the Seine River at Vernon, northwest of Paris. The bridge was destroyed using only seven tons of bombs, and only five French civilians were lightly wounded.

The next morning Leigh-Mallory and every senior Allied air commander found pictures of the destroyed bridge on his desk. A converted Leigh-Mallory ordered Allied fighters and two-engine bombers to prioritize "bridge-busting" missions. By D-Day every major road and rail bridge crossing the Seine River was down or heavily damaged, greatly inhibiting the movement of German forces into Normandy.

- Where do we have underappreciated or underutilized potential or capabilities? What gains could be achieved by better accessing and deploying these abilities?

- Do we have new opportunities that we could explore and prove with quick and low-cost testing and experimentation?

- Are we effective at circulating within our organization important news such as major breakthroughs, victories, lessons, or changes in our plans or tactics?

Exercise #5

After the March 25 meeting, Eisenhower observed Spaatz and Harris lagging in implementing the Transportation Plan. As of April 19, Spaatz's strategic bombers had not yet attacked a single target on their Transportation Plan mission list. Harris, who each morning unliterally selected Bomber Command's nightly urban target in a meeting called Morning Prayers, consistently claimed unfavorable weather prevented his squadrons from hitting Transportation Plan assignments. Eisenhower and Tedder had to closely monitor the two strategic bomber forces for compliance throughout the Overlord campaign.

- What steps can leaders take to ensure that all team members actively support a strategy, initiative, or policy once it has been adopted?

- Have we ever experienced individuals or teams deviating—intentionally or accidentally—from an agreed-upon plan or strategy? If yes, what steps were taken and what lessons learned?

Exercise #6

Spaatz's prediction that German fighter planes would avoid combat against bombers attacking French rail targets proved accurate. The Allies could not afford to give the Luftwaffe a respite shortly before D-Day, so Tedder and Eisenhower allowed Spaatz to mix some oil targets into his Transportation Plan assignment list. German fighters resumed their vigorous defense against these oil missions, and consequently suffered losses from which they could not recover. Spaatz's supplemental oil missions never exceeded twenty percent of the US bombing effort, but even the small number of oil raids proved catastrophic for Germany. Aviation fuel monthly supplies fell from 180,000 tons in April to 50,000 tons in June and barely 10,000 tons in August. After seeing the ruin being inflicted on Germany, Tedder admitted, "I suppose we'll have to give the customer what he wants," and quietly permitted Spaatz to continue his attacks on oil targets.[61]

- How can leaders and managers balance the need to focus and remain committed to a particular strategy or process, but maintain flexibility to adapt and modify methods if necessary?
- How can leaders remain open to recognizing mistakes or discovering incorrect assumptions and promptly taking corrective action?
- Do we maintain the desired balance between disciplined execution of a plan while remaining open to adaptation when assumptions or data change?

Exercise #7

After the war, many Allied leaders described their Transportation Plan infighting as the most divisive and partisan during the war. It was the only issue over which Eisenhower threatened to resign, and both Tedder and Spaatz also considered quitting during the episode. The deliberations were often combative rather than collaborative, the leaders more focused on discrediting the plan they opposed rather than objectively evaluating the merits of either.

- Which can be more difficult—getting all team members to freely and fully express their opinions and beliefs when discussing an important issue, or team members debating different ideas and points of view without descending into destructive arguments? What steps can individuals and teams take to be effective at both?

- Does our team or organizational culture permit an environment of frank dialogue and discussion?

Epilogue

World War II barely ended before wartime military leaders and politicians, joined by postwar historians and armchair generals, picked up the Transportation Plan arguments anew. The debate continues, for as one historian observed, "Much ink and emotion have flowed over the benefits from the Transportation Plan."[62] Many credit Zuckerman's plan as playing an instrumental role in winning at D-Day and thus the war. Churchill concluded that "sealing-off of the Normandy battlefield from reinforcement by rail may well have been the greatest contribution that the bomber forces could make to OVERLORD."[63] In one of the last interviews Eisenhower gave before his death, he stated that selecting the Transportation Plan airpower strategy was his greatest contribution to Overlord, a remarkable perspective given the incredible range of decisions he made during the campaign.

German commanders on the other side of the battle generally agreed. In a postwar interview, Field Marshal Karl von Rundstedt, Germany's top military commander in western Europe, concluded that one of the primary reasons his nation lost in Normandy was the "systematic destruction of all railway communications so that it was impossible to bring one single railroad train across the Rhine. This made impossible the reshuffling of troops and robbed us of all mobility."[64]

Other historians and military strategists disagree, judging the Transportation Plan overrated, flawed, or misdirected. The most common criticism is the Transportation Plan's high opportunity cost. "The pre-D-Day attacks against French rail centers were not necessary," according to one analysis, "and the seventy thousand tons [of bombs] could have been devoted to alternate targets," particularly oil related.[65] Other charges against the Transportation Plan include: it errored in its prescription against bridges, Allied disinformation and German indecision played the greater interdictory role, French Resistance attacks against rail targets proved more destructive, and the civilian casualties did not justify the outcomes.

Regardless, once the invasion commenced, the Germans could not quickly amass sufficient forces to challenge the beachhead. The large strategic four-engine bombers continued their attacks on transportation targets while smaller bombers and fighter planes hunted trains, trucks, cars, barges—anything that moved. German forces were "nailed to ground."[66] In one of many examples, on June 7 a German tank division stationed in southern France near Toulouse was ordered to move to the Normandy invasion site. The four-hundred-mile transit normally would have taken seventy-two hours by rail, but the division did not reach the combat area for seventeen days.[67]

Eisenhower won the Battle for the Bombers, and consequently the Allies won the Battle of the Buildup. One week into the invasion, the Germans possessed only about 120,000 troops in the immediate combat area, often short of ammunition, fuel, and supplies. More than one million German military personnel remained far from Normandy, frozen in place by disinformation and delayed by Allied airpower. In contrast, by one week into the campaign the Allies had disembarked more than 300,000 troops and thousands of tanks, vehicles, and artillery pieces. One month into the invasion, Allied forces in France exceeded one million. The risk the invasion would be unable to stay ashore had long passed, and Allied armies marched toward Nazi Germany's borders and eventual defeat.

Ike's Call

MAKING EFFECTIVE DECISIONS

"Deficiency in decision-making ranks much higher than lack of specific knowledge or technical know-how as an indicator of leadership failure."

—John C. Maxwell, leadership expert and best-selling author

"Probably no one who does not have to bear the specific and direct responsibility of making the final decision as to what to do can understand the intensity of these burdens."

—General Dwight D. Eisenhower, supreme Allied commander—Operation Overlord

It is illustrative that historian Carlo D'Este opens his 864-page biography *Eisenhower: A Soldier's Life* with General Dwight D. Eisenhower's decision to launch the D-Day invasion. Eisenhower—"Ike"—spent the majority of his seventy-eight-year life serving his country: as an Army officer, where he eventually ascended to the rare rank of a five-star general; after the war as the first supreme Allied commander of NATO; and finally as the thirty-fourth president of the United States. During those decades of service, Ike made countless decisions of immense importance and impact. Yet, Eisenhower's momentous call setting D-Day in motion was the apex decision of his career, and a turning point in history. It also offers a fascinating study in effective decision-making for today's business leaders.

Successful leadership and management requires effective decision-making. Effectiveness does not mean accuracy; no leader gets every decision right. Instead, an effective decision-maker applies a reliable and repeatable process that isolates what is important, balances patience while gathering relevant information against the urgency of time, considers potential options, and then cleanly chooses the best course of action. Effective decision-making is not idiosyncratic. Decision-making can incorporate deep, difficult-to-verbalize feelings, but it is not solely rooted in one's gut.

This case study explores the events leading up to Ike's decision to commence Operation Overlord. As the supreme commander, his was the sole authority to launch history's largest and most complex combined amphibious and airborne military operation. Before giving the order to launch, Ike had more to worry about than just the German army; his second nemesis was Mother Nature.

The invasion's success demanded favorable weather. Unfortunately for Ike and the Allies, in the final days immediately before the invasion the weather turned worse, threatening to disrupt carefully laid plans or perhaps even cause a catastrophic defeat.

The modern business leader may gain a valuable insight into effective decision-making methods by reviewing Ike's approach to this momentous decision, and the steps he took to improve his odds for making a successful call and thereby achieving victory.

As you read the case study, consider the following questions, each of which will be explored in the exercises following the story:

- How would you describe your (and your team's) decision-making process or culture?

- Do you and your team regularly evaluate your accuracy on important decisions, predictions, assumptions, or forecasts?

- Does your culture consistently embrace and promote individual and team accountability for important decisions?

The Case Study: Ike's Call

D-Day could never occur, and the Allies could never win in Normandy, without cooperative weather.

On D-Day, the Operation Overlord plan called for 156,000 American, British, and Canadian soldiers and their equipment to land on French soil, transported by vast fleets of planes and ships. Poor weather would keep those planes sitting on their tarmacs and those ships tied up at their berths, stopping the Allied attack before it ever started. But favorable weather on D-Day was not enough. Once the Allies landed, they would be outnumbered and surrounded by the Germans for weeks. The Allies would need at least several days of continued acceptable weather immediately after D-Day to protect, supply, and expand their fragile beachhead. Ike and his team understood that hostile weather presented at least as great a potential threat to their cause as the Germans.[1]

Therefore, victory in Normandy demanded predicting the weather accurately, ideally at least four to five days in advance. However, northern France's coastal weather patterns during summer months are notoriously volatile. Under 1940s technology and methods, weather forecasts in the area could be questionable beyond twenty-four hours and unreliable beyond forty-eight. Shipping timetables presented additional complexity. The 7,000 ships and seacraft participating in the assault were collected in over 150 ports and harbors throughout the United Kingdom, many of which were three or four days' sailing time from their assigned beach. For this massive fleet to comply with an invasion timetable scheduled down to five-minute intervals, hundreds of ships needed to depart for the attack several days before the Allies could reasonably predict weather conditions at their destination.

Further complicating matters, amphibious landings and airborne paratrooper missions have extremely particular tolerances beyond just weather-related wind, sea, and rain conditions; they must also factor in ocean tides and moon cycles. Allied planners faced a daunting task in aligning all desired variables. One historian calculated that

> Amphibious forces needed offshore surface winds not greater than Force 4—thirteen to eighteen miles per hour—for three consecutive days, as well as apposite tides. Pilots wanted a cloud ceiling of at least 2,500 feet for transport planes, with visibility of no less than three miles, and, for heavy bombers, no overcast thicker than the partly cloudy condition designated 5/10. Paratroopers required surface winds below twenty miles an hour, without gusts, and illumination of not less than a half a moon at a thirty-degree altitude. The odds against such conditions aligning on the Norman coast for seventy-two hours in June were placed at thirteen to one.[2]

By early 1944, Allied planners identified a three-day window from Monday, June 5, through Wednesday, June 7, as offering the desired combination of moonlight and tidal conditions.[3] D-Day thus was set for June 5, with the following two days as alternates. If weather conditions were favorable during that window, Ike would launch the invasion. If weather conditions were inhospitable, then Ike and more than two million Allied soldiers, sailors, and aircrew must wait two weeks for the next acceptable tidal conditions. (Even then, the desired moonlight would be lost.) If the weather conditions between June 5 and 7 were borderline, Ike would have to make a decision that could determine Allied victory or defeat.

For You History Buffs: The Importance of Tides on D-Day

Tidal considerations dictated the potential dates for D-Day. The invasion plan called for the first assault waves on D-Day to land at low tide so that beach obstacles could be seen and destroyed. The low tide had to occur in the early morning about an hour after sunlight to give Allied warships time to bombard beach defenses before the first landing craft hit the beaches. Then, the rising tide during the day would minimize landing craft getting stranded on the beach. Finally, a second low tide had to occur before the end of daylight to allow for a second wave of landings on D-Day.

Weather Report Threatens Launch

On the morning of Friday, June 2, Ike was getting bad news.

The bearer was Royal Air Force (RAF) Group Captain James M. Stagg. Scottish by birth, Stagg was tall with a thin face and sour demeanor. (One British admiral described him as "six feet two of Stagg and six feet one of gloom.")[4] Stagg was a surprising choice for the unenviable job of leading the multinational scientific team that forecast the weather for Eisenhower. Although he wore a military uniform, Stagg was a civilian who had been given rank and livery to minimize any confusion about his service. His formal education had not been in meteorology, but rather geology. Understandably, some Allied leaders doubted Stagg's qualifications for this immense assignment. However, Stagg had spent the previous two years with the British Meteorological Office, which provided weather services for the British armed forces. While there, he had been responsible for collating disparate teams and scientific processes into coherent weather analyses. This had brought Stagg to Ike's attention, less for Stagg's weather knowledge and more for his skills managing a diverse team and synthesizing their technical deliberations into coherent recommendations.

In the final days leading up to the scheduled invasion date of Monday, June 5, Stagg and his key staff met with Eisenhower and his senior commanders twice per day to give the latest weather reports, first at 4:15 a.m. and then at 9:30 p.m. Stagg's reports were delivered in the library at Southwick House, an estate home dating to 1800 that served as Ike's advance headquarters in southern England near Portsmouth. Southwick's spacious library featured floor-to-ceiling French doors, dark oak wall paneling, and a wide, deep blue rug. Emptied of its intended books, the room had been functionally refurnished with a large table, several sofas, and a supply of armchairs arranged concentrically so Ike and his team could sit in rows by rank during the weather briefings.

At 4:15 a.m. on Friday, June 2, Ike and a dozen commanders and aides filled those sofas and armchairs to receive Stagg's unwelcome news. Stagg dryly announced that inclement weather could be coming. However, he admitted that his team of American and British scientists disagreed about how bad the weather could become or for how long inclement conditions could last—the very information Ike needed. Eisenhower told Group Captain Stagg to keep at it and bring an updated forecast at that evening's briefing. Stagg would later write, "Had it not been fraught with such potential tragedy, the whole business was ridiculous . . . I was expected to present to General Eisenhower an 'agreed' forecast for the next five days which covered the time of launching of the greatest military operation ever mounted, when no two of the expert participants in the discussion could agree on the likely weather for the next twenty-four hours."[5]

Stagg spent that day poring over data and moderating his team's debates which "went on furiously if inconclusively."[6] By the evening briefing at 9:30 p.m., Stagg's forecast had clarified and worsened. The weather over the next three or four days—through the invasion target date of Monday, June 5—"would be potentially full of menace" with strong winds, low clouds, and rough seas.[7] However, Stagg admitted his scientific team remained divided. Ike, knowing he soon must make a go or no-go decision, and understanding how quickly weather in the English Channel and Norman coastal area could change, ordered the invasion to continue as planned.

As the Friday evening meeting wrapped up, one of Ike's aides pulled Stagg aside and urged him, "For Heavens' sake, Stagg, get it sorted out by tomorrow morning before you come to the commander's conference. General Eisenhower is a very worried man."[8] Anticipating the choice that he might soon face, that night Ike wrote in his diary, "Probably no one who does not have to bear the specific and direct responsibility of making the final decision as to what to do can understand the intensity of these burdens."[9]

Unfortunately, Stagg's early morning briefing on Saturday, June 3, brought no better news. Eisenhower was running out of time. He must give the order to launch the invasion by that same time tomorrow for the thousands of ships and planes to be in proper position for Monday's (June 5) assault.

For You History Buffs: Gathering Weather Data for D-Day

Knowing the invasion's success depended on identifying favorable weather, the British and Americans had established an unprecedented array of weather information-gathering resources. "More than five hundred weather stations were scattered across the United Kingdom, most reporting hourly," according to one historian. "Eight US Navy ships also took meteorological readings in the western Atlantic, and reconnaissance planes packed with instruments flew every day from Scotland, Cornwall, and Gibraltar. British beach watchers at fifty-eight wave observation stations thrice daily noted the height of every breaker during a three-minute interval, then sent their reports to a Swell Forecast Section."[10]

The Allies also had secured a secret agreement to collect weather information from Ireland, a neutral country during World War II. Stagg

continued

and his team even incorporated stolen enemy weather data into their forecasts, intercepting and decoding weather reports from German U-boats
patrolling at sea. This wealth of data helped Stagg and his team refine
their methods and forecasts.

Pressures Mount and Security Is Strained

That Saturday was undoubtedly an anxious one for Ike, Stagg, and their
respective teams. (In his diary, Stagg described the day as one of "extreme
strain.")[11] Despite having slept precious little for days, Stagg spent the
entire day with his scientists studying the latest information, debating
their interpretations, and arguing the implications.

Eisenhower spent Saturday in anguish. Smoking four packets of
cigarettes a day and dealing with high blood pressure, he paced and
pondered, half-heartedly playing checkers or bridge in a struggle to
occupy his mind. There was little else for him to do. Early that evening,
his stress boiled over and his temper exploded, chewing out an aide
for privately screening a movie for him before the film had been made
available to regular troops.

At 9:30 p.m. Ike's team reconvened as per their schedule. "The fears
my colleagues and I had yesterday about the weather for the next three
or four days have been confirmed," Stagg glumly reported.[12] To a room
of stunned general and admirals, Stagg predicted nothing but unaccept-
ably strong winds, rough seas, and thick clouds for Monday, June 5, and
potentially beyond. Before dismissing the meteorologist, Eisenhower
asked if Stagg's scientists were in consensus with this forecast. They were,
Stagg replied. The conference concluded shortly thereafter, every leader
dejected and worried. Eisenhower alone, however, carried the responsibility and burden to determine the course of action the following morning.

At 4:15 a.m. on Sunday, June 4, the dark skies were clear and winds
deceptively calm as Eisenhower, his top commanders, and Stagg met yet

again in the Southwick House library. Stagg could offer no encouragement. Over the next few days, weather conditions in the invasion area would be more like mid-winter rather than early summer. One of the outlying weather stations feeding information into Stagg's team had detected ominous pressure readings lower than any previous recordings that century. Stagg predicted Monday's winds could reach forty-five miles per hour (over seventy kilometers per hour) with seas impossibly rough. Beyond Monday, the weather was too uncertain for Stagg to predict.

Eisenhower listened quietly. Time was almost up. The one-half million soldiers, sailors, and aircrew involved in the first day's attack were positioned to launch. Of them, tens of thousands of troops had already been at sea for several days, cramped, bored, wet, cold, and often seasick. If the assault was going to proceed on schedule, within a few hours the rest of the fleet must depart for the shores of France. At dozens of airfields across England, nearly a thousand transport planes and gliders carrying more than twenty thousand paratroopers waited for takeoff orders. Everybody was anxious to end the wait and get on with it.

Ike knew the Allies could not keep the operation hidden indefinitely. Secrecy was paramount. If the Germans somehow discovered the invasion location even a day or two in advance, the entire operation would be in peril. In southern England, hundreds of thousands of British, American, and Canadian troops were quarantined behind concertina wire fences guarded by armed military police in seventeen temporary staging areas called "sausages" because of their elongated shape on a map. English civilian traffic near the sausages had been banned. A ten-day delay was imposed on military mail to grant the censors more time to review, redact, and reject where necessary. Since February, all civilian travel between Britain and neutral Ireland was suspended to stem the flow of information to German spies operating from Dublin. Since mid-April, diplomats and their couriers had been blocked from entering or leaving England, causing severe international protests. Even the handful of English civilian carpenters who had built a massive plywood invasion map hanging on the wall at Southwick House were being held in detention, unable to return to their families until the invasion commenced.

Despite such herculean efforts to maintain secrecy, the dam had sprouted leaks. In mid-April, an American general got drunk at a hotel bar and blabbed that the invasion would occur before June 15.[13] A British naval officer accidently left a top-secret copy of Overlord's naval plans in the backseat of a London taxi. (The driver found it and turned it in to Scotland Yard.) In yet another near catastrophe, a chance gust of wind blew twelve copies of the Overlord order—one of the most secret documents of the war—out an open window at the British War Office. A frantic scramble only located eleven copies. Two nerve-racking hours later, a stranger walked up to the British sentry on duty and turned in the missing copy. The stranger was never identified.

The press presented another concern. Shortly before D-Day the Associated Press put out a story trumpeting "Eisenhower's forces are landing in Paris!"—a false report sent by a typist practicing her skills on the telewire. The bulletin was recalled twenty-three minutes after issue, but not before it had been picked up by CBS and Radio Moscow.

Despite this immense pressure to get on with it, the invasion could not commence if planes could not fly and ships could not sail. Gripping Stagg's weather report in one hand, Eisenhower turned to his senior commanders and polled them for their recommendations. Admiral Bertram Ramsay, the naval commander-in-chief for Overlord, advised that the invasion be postponed. Eisenhower's senior airman, Air Chief Marshal Trafford Leigh-Mallory, agreed. Overlord's overall ground commander, General Bernard "Monty" Montgomery, recommended proceeding with the landings. Other officers weighed in, some in favor of keeping the schedule and some opposed. Ike's team was divided.

Weighing all that was at stake, Eisenhower decided to postpone the invasion by twenty-four hours, from Monday, June 5, until Tuesday,

June 6. A few years after the war Ike called the postponement the "most agonizing decision of my life . . . The consequences of that decision at that moment could not have been foreseen by anyone . . . that decision at that moment could possibly have cost us additional thousands in lives."[14]

As their meeting adjourned, Admiral Ramsay reminded Eisenhower that troopships that had already been at sea for several days would soon run low on food and fuel. After this twenty-four-hour delay, those ships must either go forward with the invasion or return to port. Ike had played his only postponement card. If the invasion could not launch on Tuesday, June 6, it must be called off until the next tidal window opened two weeks later.

Ike's order for a one-day pause initiated a ripple of commands, and at least one close call. A coded radio message—"Hornpipe Bowsprit"—was sent to all ships at sea alerting them to hold positions. However, not all vessels received the broadcast. Nearly 150 ships in Convoy U-2A obliviously continued toward France. Two destroyers were dispatched at top speed to intercept and relay the news using bullhorns and signal flags, given the need for radio silence so close to occupied France. Minesweepers at the head of Convoy U-2A were barely thirty miles (about fifty kilometers) from their target at Utah Beach before finally getting the word to turn back, narrowly avoiding catastrophe.

For the rest of Sunday morning and afternoon, Ike could again do little but wait. He spent much of the day alone, chain-smoking, walking aimlessly. Military news and intelligence continued to flow into his headquarters, much of it not good. Reports indicated the Germans probably had moved yet another army division into the invasion area. There was no way to know if this was just bad luck, or if the Germans had somehow gotten wind of the invasion site. At one point, Ike invited a news reporter assigned to cover his headquarters to take a walk. The reporter later described the supreme commander as "bowed down with worry . . . as though each of the four stars on either shoulder weighed a ton."[15]

That afternoon, Stagg's predicted storm arrived, exactly on schedule.

At 9:30 p.m. Sunday evening, Ike and his generals and admirals met for the fourth night in a row for Stagg's latest forecast. With coffee mugs in hand to combat the universal lack of sleep, they somberly took seats around the library. Outside, hard rain and surging winds bashed Southwick House, rattling the room's tall windows. Ike motioned for Stagg to begin.

Possible Break in the Weather

"Since I presented the forecast last evening," Stagg opened, "some rapid and unexpected developments have occurred over the North Atlantic."[16] He explained that the approaching depression had slowed down, creating a possible window of at least one day's tolerable weather on Tuesday, June 6. "I am quite confident that a fair interval will follow tonight's front," Stagg offered.[17] After then, the weather remained uncertain. One attending general later wrote, "A cheer went up. You never heard middle-aged men cheer like that!"[18]

The commanders grilled Stagg for more information, and for a longer look into the future. One day of favorable weather was good news but far from the four- or five-day stretch of hospitable conditions the Allies needed to be safe. If Ike launched the invasion but immediately after D-Day the weather subsequently worsened, the first waves of troops could be stranded ashore with no reinforcements or air and naval support, and no hope of evacuation. Stagg stiffly replied that offering any more information "would make me a guesser, not a meteorologist."[19]

Admiral Ramsay brought the group into focus, alerting Eisenhower that if the invasion was to resume, he had to issue orders to the fleet within thirty minutes. With that cue, Ike dismissed Stagg so the senior military leaders could discuss the situation.

Once again, Eisenhower went around the room, polling each of the subordinates to state aloud his recommendation. Air Marshal Leigh-Mallory again counseled against proceeding. Air Marshal Arthur Tedder, Ike's deputy commander, waffled and described going forward as "chancy." General Walter Bedell "Bettle" Smith, Ike's trusted chief of staff, called going forward "a helluva gamble, but one to take."[20] Monty, consistent with his earlier stance, said he believed the invasion should go forward. For the second time, Ike's team presented conflicting recommendations.

According to accounts later given by several of those in attendance, Ike silently paced around the room. After some time, addressing nobody in particular, he asked aloud, "The question is, just how long can you hang this operation on the end of a limb?"[21] The most important Allied attack in the war was primed to launch. The chance of an uncontained security leak would only increase. Stagg could only offer the narrowest window of barely compliant weather. If Stagg was wrong and the weather on D-Day proved worse than forecasted, the invasion might fail before even getting started. If the weather did cooperate on D-Day but inclement conditions returned a day or two later, the Allied troops ashore would still be in terrible jeopardy. The weight on the end of the limb was heavy and the bow bending.

Ike finally announced his decision. "I am quite positive we must give the order," he said. "I don't like it but there it is. I don't see how we can do anything else."[22]

With that, Ike made his call.

Ike had just set Overlord in motion, but he would have one final chance to call off the invasion the following morning, if Stagg's forecast worsened during the next few hours. Eisenhower, his commanders, and Stagg would meet again one last time at 4:15 a.m. on Monday, June 5. As the meeting broke for that night, Ike sought out his chief meteorologist and gave him the news. "Well Stagg, we're putting it on again. For heaven's sake hold the weather to what you've told us and don't bring any more bad news."[23]

Ike Makes the Call: "Let's Go"

The next morning's conference came quickly. Ike and his commanders quietly filed into the library, each having slept a few restless hours. Eisenhower took a seat by himself on one of the room's sofas, an empty bookshelf behind him. The continued pounding rains and high winds must have led some to question Stagg's prediction of an imminent break in the storm. However, when Stagg entered the room, several participants noted that the Scottish weatherman was not his usual dour self. With a hint of a smile, Stagg and his team affirmed their earlier forecast of a favorable weather window on June 6. If anything, he said he was more confident than he had been the previous evening. He cautioned, however, that the weather was volatile. The most they could predict was twenty-four to perhaps thirty-six hours of acceptable conditions. Beyond then was impossible to know.

With the update, Ike polled his subordinates a third and final time. He did not speak, but merely pointed his chin at each commander in turn around the room. They knew what he wanted. Each offered his recommendation. While the ever-cautious Leigh-Mallory remained in opposition to launching the attack, the remaining generals and admirals recommended proceeding. Ike listened without comment.

As for what happened next, a half-dozen eyewitness accounts give conflicting testimony. Some say Eisenhower paced, while others say he remained sitting. Some say he was quiet for only a moment, but others claim Ike said nothing for five full minutes. (Eisenhower himself later said his silence could only have been about thirty to forty-five seconds in duration, for "five minutes under such conditions sounds like a year.")[24] Time had run out. His experts could offer nothing more than marginal weather predictions for a day or perhaps a day and a half, even though the battle plan demanded four or five days at minimum. His senior leaders were divided. Ships were running out of fuel. There was no backup plan. The cost of failure was incalculable.

When the supreme commander finally spoke, some remember that he said, "OK, let's go." Others recall that Eisenhower said, "Well, we will go." In an article published a few months after D-Day, *Reader's Digest* magazine reported the portentous words were "OK, let 'er rip." However he phrased it, Eisenhower ordered irrevocably forward Operation Overlord.

Ike's team only had time for an enthusiastic but quick cheer before rushing from the room. His commanders had work to do. Aides waited outside the library with two sets of prepared orders—one if the invasion was on, and one if the ships were to come back. The proper set of orders was issued. Tuesday, June 6, would be forever known as D-Day.

Ike was left alone in an empty room. Two decades later, in a television interview with Walter Cronkite on the twentieth anniversary of D-Day, President Eisenhower sat in that same room and reflected on that moment he'd stood by himself in the Southwick House library. "That's the most terrible time for a senior commander," Eisenhower said. "He has done all that he can do, all the planning and so on. There's nothing more that he can do."[25]

For You History Buffs: Ike's Call in *The Longest Day*

The scene of Eisenhower deciding to launch the invasion is dramatized in the Academy Award–winning film *The Longest Day* (1962), considered a classic World War II movie. Eisenhower reportedly turned down an offer to play himself in the film. Instead, a Hollywood set director named Henry Grace was cast in the role due to his remarkable resemblance to Ike.

Leadership Insights

The story of Eisenhower's D-Day decision is frequently told by historians and has been dramatized on screen. The sheer magnitude of Eisenhower's decision is staggering and validates Ike's credentials as a leader in any realm. For business leaders and managers, this story stands as a powerful demonstration of effective decision-making. Eisenhower—

- Diligently gathered information from subject matter experts
- Engaged all his advisors and subordinates, requiring them to openly participate and offer their unambiguous recommendations
- Listened
- Remained functionally calm despite enormous pressure
- Weighed options carefully and thoroughly
- Never lost sight of the strategic priorities
- Watched the clock

Applying these steps, Ike's decision-making exemplified strong leadership applicable to today's business issues.

However, a less well-known aspect of Ike's decision-making process may be even more valuable and relevant to contemporary business leaders. As momentous (and thankfully correct) as Ike's call was, the way the general prepared himself to make his decision reveals his finest skills as an effective decision-maker.

Before launching D-Day, Eisenhower first needed to assess how much he could rely on analysis presented by expert members of his team. Ike had to determine how much he could trust Stagg's judgment and recommendations. To understand how Ike gained confidence in Stagg, we must explore further the working relationship between these two men and examine what most history books leave out of this incredible story.

Ike's faith in Stagg's analysis was not blind, accidental, or unearned. From the moment he assumed command of Operation Overlord, Ike appreciated the critical role weather would play in the invasion's outcome—it was the operation's largest variable for which Ike had no control nor influence. Therefore, long before D-Day Eisenhower prioritized working with Stagg, testing and evaluating the accuracy, reliability, and consistency of Stagg and his team of meteorologists.

Starting two months before the invasion, Eisenhower held almost daily meetings with Stagg and the weather scientific team, following a weekly schedule set by Eisenhower. Each Monday, Ike would challenge Stagg to present an invasion recommendation for a fictitious D-Day to launch on that Thursday, which Stagg took to calling "Dummy D-Days."[26]

Ike's and Stagg's Monday weather forecasting discussions could last hours, delving far deeper into the issues and processes than later would be possible during Stagg's fifteen-minute morning and evening updates presented during the final days before the invasion. Ike used this extended time to extensively question Stagg and the meteorological team, evaluating how they made their recommendations and the processes they applied. Eisenhower did not seek to learn meteorology; he sought to understand Stagg's capacity for rational analysis, ability to synthesize data from his own scientific team, confront uncertainty, and formulate conclusions. At the conclusion of each Monday's in-depth discussion, Ike would then decide based on Stagg's forecast to launch that week's Dummy D-Day on the coming Thursday, or postpone the imaginary attack.

After each Monday's decision, Ike, Stagg, and their respective teams would meet once and sometimes twice per day during the balance of the week to review the accuracy of Stagg's forecasts. These reviews gave Eisenhower additional opportunities to watch Stagg and his process in action. Finally, at the end of each week the team reconvened and scored the outcome of Ike's mock go or no-go decision made that Monday, undoubtedly gaining wisdom from each successful or incorrect decision.

Ike even incorporated these weekly weather dress rehearsals into the Allies' invasion training schedule. In early May, the US Army's 1st Infantry Division and other units were scheduled to conduct a practice landing at Slapton Sands in England, chosen for its resemblance to Omaha Beach. After one of Stagg's in-depth weather briefings predicted questionable weather for the exercise, Ike postponed the training operation by twenty-four hours, foreshadowing his decision thirty days later to postpone the actual D-Day invasion.

Eisenhower came to understand Stagg's methods and resources and grew confident in Stagg's capabilities. "In these trial forecasts," one biographer wrote, "Eisenhower had learned that the man whose opinion and nerve he could trust in the hour of decision was Stagg."[27] Additionally, whether Ike intended this or not, these repeated exercises must have acted as mental and emotional rehearsals for Eisenhower himself, preparing him for the possibility that he might have to make an impossibly difficult decision, as he ultimately did. Ike's decision to launch the greatest military operation in history despite uncertain and unfavorable weather was made on hard-earned research, tests, risk assessments, and performance measurements.

Ike's preparations during those months before the D-Day launch may be the more insightful and relevant business lesson. While Eisenhower's historic decision to launch D-Day is inspiring, most business leaders will never face any choice as world-impacting and risk-filled as what Eisenhower faced. However, all business executives must make difficult decisions, some of which might lead to ultimate success or failure in an important project, or in extreme cases perhaps determine the fate of the entire organization. All leaders must decide when and how far to trust in their team's analysis and recommendations. Today's business leaders and managers can borrow a page from history and emulate Eisenhower's dedication to preparing himself and utilizing his team before making the decisions that count.

Effective decision-making may be one of the least studied leadership skills. For some leaders and teams, decision-making is something that just happens—questions arise, some analysis and discussion may occur, options are considered, and then decisions are made. Many leaders and teams do not measure or track their decision-making effectiveness, even though high-performing organizations know the value of measuring critical processes and results. Remarkably few leaders pursue formal training or development in decision-making skills. Many leaders and teams do not follow a consistent framework or set of best practices for making decisions. Rather, decision-making tends to be idiosyncratic—individual experiences, perspectives, and intuition strongly influence the process and outcome.

Developing decision-making skills and applying sound processes translates into superior business performance. For example, a study summarized in *Harvard Business Review* found that managers who made decisions using consistently applied best practices achieved expected results ninety percent of the time, and forty percent of them exceeded expectations.[28]

In today's competitive business environment, making effective decisions has never been more important. The wrong decision on the wrong issue at the wrong time can derail or destroy a team or a company. Compounding this, leaders and their teams increasingly must make decisions with greater speed than ever before, thereby exacerbating the potential for error.

Of course, it is impossible to eliminate all risk of making an incorrect call. Behavioral and psychological factors such as groupthink, overconfidence, and cognitive biases can muddy the water. Reducing decision-making risks produces superior business performance.

Leadership Exercises

The following exercises revisit and expand on the historical events associated with "Ike's Call," and present leadership learning opportunities for individuals and teams to explore.

Exercise #1

Faced with potential hostile weather that could devastate the Allies' chances for victory in Operation Overlord and cost thousands of lives,

Eisenhower made the call to launch the attack after applying a well-practiced and sound decision-making process. After reviewing the case study, consider the following questions:

- What was most interesting or surprising within this case study?
- What potential lessons does the case study offer our team or organization?
- How would I describe our team's decision-making methods, processes, or culture?

Exercise #2

When Ike and his team faced a critical decision, Ike followed a consistent decision-making process, which included asking every team member to weigh in. Non-participation or silence was not permitted. "I have no sympathy with anyone, whatever his station," Ike said, "who will not brook criticism."

- How can leaders and managers encourage dissenting points of view during team discussions? Is this an opportunity for improvement within our company?
- What are the pros and cons of applying a consistent decision-making process versus making decisions largely based on individual experiences and intuition? Are there situations when leaders should follow a process? When should they just make a call?

Exercise #3

The Eisenhower Matrix is a decision-making and prioritization tool developed from a quote often attributed to Ike: "What is important is seldom urgent, and what is urgent is seldom important." The model, depicted next, organizes issues and decisions according to impact (importance) and time sensitivity (urgency), and then offers a prescriptive course of action for each issue or decision.

Eisenhower Matrix
Urgent-Important Matrix

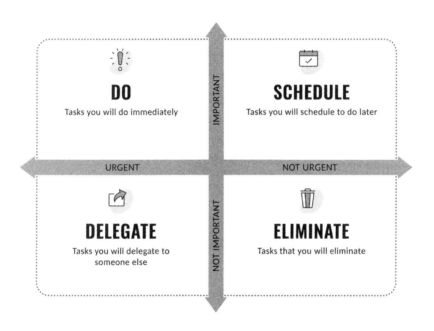

DO
Tasks you will do immediately

SCHEDULE
Tasks you will schedule to do later

IMPORTANT

URGENT   NOT URGENT

DELEGATE
Tasks you will delegate to someone else

ELIMINATE
Tasks that you will eliminate

NOT IMPORTANT

The model's purpose is to focus prompt decision-making on higher-impact matters and eliminate distractions. Review the model, and then discuss:

- How well do I or we focus on issues and tasks that occupy the top two quadrants of the model—those that are important? Do issues or matters that are urgent but not important (the lower left quadrant) regularly interrupt or distract me or our team?

- Do I or we occasionally fall into the trap of focusing on tasks with deadlines (urgency) over tasks without deadlines, even if they are more urgent? (Psychologists refer to this as the "mere-urgency effect.") What changes could we make to our individual and/or team prioritization and decision-making methods to overcome this tendency?

- Should we apply the Eisenhower Matrix to our organization?

Exercise #4

Starting several months before D-Day, Eisenhower and Stagg regularly practiced their weather forecasting and decision-making, tracked their results, and discussed their successes and failures. When Ike found himself facing the real test, he had the benefit of knowing Stagg's capabilities and performance record. Eisenhower also had prepared himself for the possibility of facing a difficult weather-related decision, which ultimately he had to make.

- What are the benefits of conducting postmortems to review major decisions, efforts, projects, or initiatives once concluded?
- What are the advantages of keeping score on the accuracy of forecasts such as sales projections, financial budgets, or market trend predictions? Are there opportunities for our team or company to improve its scorekeeping?
- Do I or we face any potentially important decisions in the near future? How are we preparing for those decisions?

Exercise #5

In preparing for D-Day, the Allies created an unprecedented network of weather data-collecting resources and deployed a multinational team of scientists to analyze and interpret that data. In contrast, the Germans were largely blinded to weather data. Their data-gathering ships had been sunk, remote weather stations destroyed, and long-range air patrols curtailed due to heavy Allied defenses. As a result, the Germans did not detect the break in the storm that Stagg's team identified.

- Does our team or organization have sufficient sources of reliable external data, such as market trends, economic indices, customer preferences, and competitor actions?
- How is this information incorporated into decision-making?

Exercise #6

After making his historic call, Ike ate breakfast alone and then made his way to nearby Portsmouth harbor to watch invasion ships depart. Within a few hours, the wind and rain eased as per Stagg's prediction. Later that afternoon, back in his trailer, Ike found a piece of scratch paper and on it composed a statement he intended to issue if the invasion failed. His now famous "In Case of Failure" memo read:

> Our landings in the Cherbourg-Havre area have failed to gain a satisfactory foothold and I have withdrawn the troops. My decision to attack at this time and place was based upon the best information available. The troops, the air and the navy did all that bravery and devotion to duty could do. If any blame or fault attaches to the attempt it is mine alone.

After the successful landings, Ike threw the memo away, but an aide retrieved it. The handwritten note is preserved at the Eisenhower Library.

- Does our culture consistently embrace and promote individual and team accountability for important decisions?

- What steps can leaders and managers take to turn failures and mistakes into learning lessons?
- Do I or we properly acknowledge and celebrate successes?

Epilogue

The D-Day invasion proceeded on Tuesday, June 6, as per Ike's decision. Weather conditions were permissible but not favorable—strong winds, choppy seas, and thick clouds still challenged many elements of the operation. Perhaps most tragically, twenty-seven out of thirty-two amphibious tanks, a top-secret new weapon, sank in the heavy swells off Omaha Beach, drowning many of their crews and denying the desperate soldiers ashore their fire support.[29]

The weather was worse than the Allies had hoped for, but better than the Germans had predicted. Consequently, weather ironically proved to be the Allies' ally on D-Day. The Germans, lacking forecasting resources, did not anticipate the improved weather conditions that Stagg's team had predicted. Lulled into believing the Allies were confined to England for the next few days, the Germans kept reconnaissance planes on the ground and canceled naval patrols. Additionally, several top German military commanders in Normandy were away from their posts when the Allies invaded, including Field Marshal Erwin Rommel, the famed Desert Fox, who had departed to be with his wife on her birthday on June 6. Their absence contributed to the German leadership's slow and confused response to the invasion.[30]

The last postscript to "Ike's Call" is what could have happened if Eisenhower had not made the decision to launch the invasion on June 6. The Overlord plan called for the invasion to commence when the Norman low tide arrived near sunrise, preferably under full moonlight. If Ike had not launched during the June 5 to 7 tidal window, the next date when low tide occurred near dawn would be June 19. As it turned out, the worst Norman summer storm in decades rolled into the invasion area on June 19 with little advance notice. The tempest battered the invasion beaches for four days, sinking or grounding nearly eight hundred ships and crafts, destroying one of the Allies' two massive artificial prefabricated harbors called Mulberries, and setting back by a week the critical flow of troops and supplies. If Ike had waited and launched D-Day on June 19, the invasion likely would have been the disaster he most feared. Reflecting on these events several months after D-Day, Ike wrote Stagg a commendation letter and scrawled in the margin, "I thank the gods of war we went when we did."[31]

Eisenhower would later serve two terms as president of the United States, succeeded by another World War II veteran, John F. Kennedy. On the day of Kennedy's inauguration, as the two men rode in a motorcade, President-Elect Kennedy asked Ike why the D-Day operation had been so successful. "Because we had better meteorologists than the Germans," Ike replied.[32]

US General Terry de la Mesa Allen, shown while leading the US 1st Infantry Division, the famous Big Red One. Before D-Day, he was controversially dismissed from command.

Source: University of Texas at El Paso Library Special Collections Department, MS307 Terry de la Mesa Allen papers.

**US General Omar N. Bradley, pictured shortly after the end of the war.
Bradley led all American ground forces on D-Day.**

US General Dwight D. Eisenhower, shown during the middle of the Battle of Normandy. Ike, as he was commonly called, was the top Allied military leader for the invasion.

Source: NARA

US Admiral John Hall led American naval forces supporting the Omaha Beach assault. His decisions contributed to the Americans' confusion at Omaha regarding their new secret weapon, the amphibious tank.

Source: NARA

British Air Marshal Arthur Harris commanded the Royal Air Force (RAF) Bomber Command during much of the war. He resisted Eisenhower's efforts to task British strategic bombers to attack French railroad targets in support of the invasion.

US General Clarence Huebner commanded the 1st Infantry Division on D-Day at Omaha Beach. Despite his effective leadership, Huebner is largely overlooked in most D-Day histories.

British Air Chief Marshal Trafford Leigh-Mallory was initially put in command over Allied air forces for the D-Day invasion. But most of the American air commanders and even some British leaders objected to Leigh-Mallory having authority over the Allies' strategic bombers.

Source: Wikicommons

US General George C. Marshall served as the chief of staff for the US Army during the war. Marshall wanted to command the D-Day invasion, but US President Franklin Roosevelt believed Marshall was too indispensable in Washington, DC. Thus the D-Day command went to Marshall's protege, Eisenhower.

Source: Wikicommons

British General Bernard L. Montgomery, during his first press conference in Normandy several days after D-Day. Monty, the most famous British military leader of the war, commanded all British ground forces during the invasion.

Source: Wikicommons

US General George S. Patton, pictured shortly after the end of the war and before his death in a traffic accident. Patton might have been given command of all US ground forces on D-Day, but he had been benched by Eisenhower for slapping two hospitalized American soldiers and accusing them of cowardice.

British Air Marshal Charles Portal presided over the Royal Air Force for most of the war. Portal did not agree with Eisenhower on all issues, but he saw the need to maintain alignment across the senior American and British military leadership team.

Source: Wikicommons

Field Marshal Erwin Rommel led German army forces in Normandy. Known as the Desert Fox due to his battlefield exploits in North Africa earlier in the war, he was unable to mount a successful defense against the invasion.

Field Marshal Gerd von Rundstedt commanded all German forces in western Europe. However, his advancing age, and Nazi dictator Adolf Hitler's micromanagement, undermined Rundstedt's effectiveness in organizing a coherent anti-invasion defense strategy.

Source: German Federal Archive

German General Leo Geyr von Schweppenburg commanded German panzer (tank) forces in western Europe. Geyr vigorously argued with Rommel about the proper strategy for deploying tank forces to best defeat the Allied invasion.

US General Carl Spaatz commanded American strategic bomber forces during Operation Overlord. Spaatz disagreed with the need for the risky D-Day invasion, believing his bomber forces could defeat Germany by destroying military and industry targets from the air.

Source: NARA

Group Captain James M. Stagg led the Allies' meteorological team, providing
Eisenhower with weather forecasts leading up to D-Day. Ike came to trust in Stagg's
leadership and recommendations.

British Air Marshal Arthur Tedder served as Eisenhower's deputy supreme commander for Operation Overlord. Tedder helped Ike address and overcome the personality conflicts and organizational silos that threatened to fracture the senior Allied leadership team.

||||||||||||||||||||||||||||||||||||||||||||||||||||||||||||||||||||||||||

The Tanks That Sank off Omaha

APPLYING BUSINESS PROCESSES

*"If you can't describe what you are doing as a process, then you
don't know what you're doing."*

    —W. Edwards Deming, business strategist, author, and consultant

*"I am not proud of the fact nor will I ever cease regretting that
I did not take the tanks all the way to the beach."*

    —US Navy Ensign R. L. Harkey, officer-in-charge of LCT 602 on D-Day

Prior to Operation Overlord, amphibious assaults against an enemy beach had required the first groups of soldiers to wade ashore without protection from tanks, which could only be delivered once the beach was safe for ships to unload them. Allied military commanders and planners wished to change this and rewrite the invasion playbook on

D-Day by putting hundreds of tanks on the beaches *prior* to the foot soldiers landing, which could give the Allies a decisive advantage at the crucial start of the attack.

To achieve this change, the Allies invented and manufactured a secret weapon, so important that the US assigned it the same priority as the development of atomic weapons known as the Manhattan Project. The Allies created a tank that could float and swim to the beaches under its own power, surprising the Germans and revolutionizing amphibious warfare.

Unfortunately, things did not go as planned for the top-secret swimming tanks. Choppy seas on D-Day morning seriously challenged the tanks' fragile technology. At Omaha Beach, senior US leaders failed to create and communicate a sound process for their subordinates to determine if the swimming tanks should deploy in the difficult seas. Consequently, one of the more senseless D-Day tragedies occurred, causing lost lives in the waters off Omaha and contributing to the Americans' desperate struggle on the beach.

This case study examines the importance of creating and applying sound processes to help organizations maximize their likelihood of sustained success and minimize risk and the potential for failure.

As you read the case study, keep in mind the following leadership questions:

- What are the characteristics of an effectively designed and applied business process?

- Within our team or organization, are different individuals or teams pursuing similar objectives but applying different decisions, methods, or processes?

- What are some reasons why people do not follow a given process or procedure?

The Case Study: The Tanks That Sank off Omaha

In the predawn hours of Tuesday, June 6, 1944, a flotilla of sixteen US Navy ships called "landing craft, tank" (LCT) approached the Normandy coast of northern France. The gray LCTs, each less than 120 feet (about 36 meters) long and 33 feet (about 10 meters) wide, were too small to merit either a name or a formal captain, so instead each seacraft was known only by a three-digit hull number and was commanded by a junior naval officer merely called the "officer-in-charge." Specially designed for amphibious warfare, the LCTs' flat-bottomed hulls and bow ramps enabled them to offload vehicles, troops, and cargo directly onto a beach. However, lacking a traditional V-shaped hull also meant that in anything other than a calm sea the steel craft swayed and slapped down on the waves, often inducing seasickness for all but the most experienced sailors.

These sixteen LCTs and their crews of about a dozen sailors each plowed through the moonlit waters of the English Channel toward a beach code-named Omaha. Many miles on either side to their east and west, more than forty additional LCTs in similar-sized flotillas proceeded toward the four other D-Day beaches, code-named Gold, Juno, Sword, and Utah. Together, these LCTs constituted only a fraction of the seven thousand ships in the invasion fleet, but they carried a secret new weapon that Allied leaders expected would provide a decisive advantage. Loaded into the open belly of each LCT making its way toward Omaha sat four specially modified tanks capable of swimming under their own power from the sea onto the enemy shore. For the first time in history, on D-Day Allied leaders would launch an amphibious attack led by armored tanks rather than vulnerable infantry.

Duplex Drive Tanks: Part Boat, Part Submarine, Eventually All Tank

The secret weapons were called "duplex drive" tanks, commonly abbreviated to "DD" tanks. "Duplex drive" indicated the tanks had two means of propulsion—traditional tracks to move across terrain, plus a pair of bronze eighteen-inch propellers installed in the rear to propel the tank through the water at speeds up to five knots (about six miles per hour). The term duplex drive was inspired by their dual means of propulsion but chosen to mask these weapons' revolutionary amphibious capability.

To achieve flotation, the tanks would erect a nine-foot watertight rubber-and-canvas screen. Once on the water, the DD tank became part dinghy and part submarine. Once ashore, the crew quickly collapsed the canvas shroud and shifted the transmission from powering the propellers to driving the tracks. With the DD now all tank, it could bring heavy firepower and armored protection to the invasion beach, a capability desperately needed for the exposed first waves of an amphibious attack. A British general involved in planning D-Day witnessed the DD tank and said, "At last was found that for which every army in the world had been searching for years."[1]

For You History Buffs: The Development of the DD Tank

Armored warfare theorists and tacticians had long dreamed of tanks that could freely move through seas or deep rivers. The obvious challenge was devising a practical way to float a vehicle that weighed tens of tons.

In 1940, Nicholas Straussler, a Hungarian inventor and émigré to England, devised the solution by applying simple principles of flotation. Generally, any vehicle will float once its mass is equal to the mass of the water it displaces. Straussler wrapped a tall watertight collapsible shroud made from rubber and canvas around a tank, secured at the base to the tank's hull. Pumping compressed air into thirty-six telescoping pillars raised the shroud, held in place by foldable metal struts. With the screen thus erected, the tank would float in the water. Two propellers installed in the tank's rear, linked to the drive mechanism turning the tracks, gave forward propulsion.

After the DD tank entered the water, the tank commander sat on a small platform erected behind the turret, peering over the canvas shroud and steering using an installed hand tiller. The tank driver, sitting deep inside the tank nearly ten feet below the water's surface, also could drive and navigate by way of an attached periscope. Safety equipment included a bilge pump to remove seawater that leaked or splashed into the vehicle, and water rescue gear for the crew.

The British were the first to conduct operational experiments with DDs. In late 1943, as planning for Operation Overlord accelerated, the British shared the DD tank technology with their American partners. The Americans enthusiastically offered to expand the program and convert US Sherman tanks into DD tanks for all the Allied forces to use on D-Day. To manufacture[2] hundreds of DD Shermans and ship them to England in time for D-Day, the top-secret program was designated the highest "AAA" status in Washington, DC, the same priority level assigned to the Manhattan Project.

Today, many people are familiar with images taken on D-Day morning, showing the first waves of soldiers wading ashore while German machine guns and cannons fire into their defenseless ranks. Modern D-Day depictions, such as the epic film *Saving Private Ryan*, perpetuate this view. The widespread belief that the first infantry and engineers waded ashore without tank support is not entirely accurate and was definitely not the Allied plan. Having developed their DD tank secret weapon, Overlord planners devised an amphibious assault plan that opened the beach attack with about 280 DD tanks[3] swimming onto the five invasion beaches ten minutes before the first infantry and engineers arrived. The DD tanks would emerge from the water to surprise unsuspecting Germans, eliminate enemy fortifications and troops, and shield the first waves of soldiers. This was the plan for the five Allied target beaches on D-Day morning, yet unfortunately things did not go according to plan.

For You History Buffs: The Magnificent Eleven Photographs

Photographer Robert Capa took perhaps the most famous set of pictures from a beach during the D-Day morning assault. Capa went ashore with the first waves at Omaha Beach, photographing the attack while he was under heavy fire and struggling to avoid drowning in the rough surf.

Unfortunately, a darkroom processing accident destroyed all but eleven of the pictures, which are now referred to as the "Magnificent Eleven" series. Their grainy, frightening images are among the most well-known photographs not just from D-Day but from the entire war.

Rough Seas Threaten the New DD Tanks

Before the American, British, and Canadian forces commenced battle against the German defenders on the shore, first they had to confront the weather at sea. D-Day had originally been scheduled for June 5, but a severe summer storm had forced Eisenhower to postpone the attack by twenty-four hours with hopes the weather would improve.[4] It did, if only barely, and on June 6 the seas in the English Channel off the Norman coast were mostly described as Force 4: "moderate" conditions with wind speeds from twelve to sixteen knots (about thirteen to eighteen miles per hour) and waves from three to six feet.[5] For the Allied battleships, cruisers, destroyers, transports, and other large ships in the invasion fleet, Force 4 conditions presented no significant challenge. However, for the thousands of small invasion seacraft, even these moderate seas made crossing the English Channel uncomfortable, and dangerous if not skillfully piloted. For the swimming tanks, these conditions presented a serious threat.

The DD tanks' design limitations were well known to Allied leaders. For months prior to D-Day, American, British, and Canadian tankers and LCT crews had tested and trained on the swimming tanks and their operation from the LCTs, exercising in secure areas guarded against German spies. The crews, themselves sworn to secrecy at the risk of court-martial, trained on all aspects of this new technology: raising and lowering the canvas shroud, steering and navigating the tanks in the water, operating the bilge pump, emergency escape procedures, loading the duplex drives onto the low-hulled landing craft, and launching the DD tanks into water from an LCT's bow ramp.

At the conclusion of this extensive program, thirty-two-year-old US Navy Lieutenant Dean Rockwell, the primary naval officer in charge of the American LCT-DD training, submitted a written report to his senior commanders. Rockwell, a thickly built, dark-haired former champion wrestler in high school and college before the war, strongly recommended using the DDs on D-Day, noting that in over a thousand practice launches only two tanks had sunk and no personnel were lost. However, he warned, "No launchings have been attempted in anything over a Force 3 sea as the difficulties of launching and navigation preclude operation."[6] Once afloat, the DD tank's canvas hull was almost fully submerged, barely providing one foot of freeboard—the distance between the water and the top of the screen. Even small waves could swamp the tank.

Across the five invasion beaches, the assault plan called for LCTs to transport the DD tanks to a defined point between 7,000 and 5,000 yards (6,400 to 4,600 meters) from shore—safely out of range of German artillery—and then launch the DDs to swim to the beaches and arrive before the first waves of infantry and combat engineers. On D-Day morning, however, high-ranking Allied leaders at four of the five invasion beaches determined that the seas and winds were too hostile for the DD tanks to launch from their intended point of departure. Thus, the British at Gold and Sword Beaches, the Canadians at Juno Beach, and the Americans at Utah Beach ordered their LCT fleets to carry the DD tanks closer to shore before launching, or in some cases deposit the tanks directly on the sand.

At Omaha Beach, the decision to launch or not launch the DD tanks into the sea would not be made by high-ranking officers, but rather by two US Army captains. One made a prudent decision, but the other made a tragic error in judgment.

For You History Buffs: Most Leaders Decide Seas Are Too Rough

On D-Day morning, Allied commanders at four of the five invasion beaches decided to launch their DD tanks closer to shore or all the way onto the beach due to rough seas and winds. At British Gold Beach, seventy-six DD tanks, half from the 4th/7th Royal Dragoon Guards and half from the Nottinghamshire Yeomanry (Sherwood Rangers), were scheduled to launch 7,000 yards from shore to support the British 50th Infantry Division.

Instead, British commanders ordered their LCT crews to take the tanks nearly all the way to the shore, launching them several hundred yards from Gold. Even after taking this precaution, eight British DD tanks sank before reaching the beach. The remaining DD tanks arrived and entered the battle, although many were delayed or arrived out of position due to the difficult sea conditions.

In the waters off Britain's other target beach, code-named Sword, weather conditions were calmer, but British commanders still elected to bring the DDs about 2,000 yards closer to shore before authorizing the launch with the code word Floater. Several DDs still sank, including a pair swamped by passing ships from the invasion fleet, but most of the thirty-eight British DD tanks from the 13th/18th Royal Hussars (Queen Mary's Own) made it to Sword Beach that morning, providing valuable support for the British 3rd Infantry Division.

Off Juno Beach, Canada's target on D-Day, forty DD tanks from the 10th Canadian Armored Regiment (Fort Garry Horse) had intended to launch from 7,000 yards and swim to the beach ahead of the Canadian 3rd Infantry Division. However, like their British counterparts, Canadian leaders ordered the LCTs to bring the DD tanks and their crews closer in, launching only a few hundred yards from the beach. Still, five of these forty tanks foundered before they could reach the battle.

Off Utah Beach, eight US Navy LCTs carried thirty-two DD tanks from the US Army's 70th Tank Battalion toward the shore. Utah Beach is located at the base of Normandy's Cotentin Peninsula, a landmass that shelters the local seas from higher winds and currents. However, American commanders at Utah, like their British and Canadian peers, still chose to launch the DD tanks from only 3,000 yards offshore rather than the planned 5,000. One DD tank succumbed to the waves and four more were lost when their host LCT exploded on a German mine, but the remaining twenty-seven DD tanks arrived at Utah to support the US 4th Infantry Division.

Troubles on Omaha Beach

Of the five D-Day beaches, Omaha was the most heavily defended. American leaders knew taking it would be difficult and cost many lives. Unfortunately, at Omaha on D-Day everything initially went wrong for the attackers. To start, under the attack plan American warships and heavy bombers would blast the beaches to "soften up" the German defenses before the DD tanks and infantry arrived. From the sea, two battleships, three cruisers, and twelve destroyers hurled naval shells at Omaha, but only for thirty-five minutes, failing to inflict significant damage on the well-camouflaged German concrete fortifications. Additionally, eight landing craft modified to each carry more than a thousand rockets approached the shore and fired their ordnance, creating an impressive pyrotechnic display; but their crude aiming technology sent most rockets into the water.

For You History Buffs: Pre-Invasion Bombardment Controversy

The duration of the pre-invasion shore bombardment was hotly debated by Allied leaders planning the D-Day invasion. Many commanders wanted a longer bombardment prior to their assault to maximize destruction of German defenses before the troops came ashore. However, at D-Day the pre-assault naval bombardment was limited to thirty-five minutes to minimize the Germans' time to rush reinforcements to the invasion beaches.

continued

> For comparison, in the Pacific theater of the war, American warships often bombarded Japanese-held islands for several days prior to an amphibious landing, because the islands were cut off from reinforcement. In hindsight, at Omaha both the pre-landing naval bombardment and pre-paratory air attacks were poorly designed and executed, contributing to the high loss of life among American soldiers that morning.

From the air, 450 US heavy bombers completely missed Omaha Beach because the aircrews intentionally waited an extra thirty seconds before dropping to minimize the risk of hitting friendly forces. Consequently, their thirteen thousand bombs fell onto Norman farms and cows rather than Nazi pillboxes and soldiers. One American soldier later suggested that his country's airmen "might have done better if they had landed their planes on the beach and chased the enemy out with bayonets."[7]

Finally, in one of the biggest intelligence breakdowns of the invasion, Allied leaders failed to detect and warn that elements of the German 352nd Division had relocated to the area, increasing by almost threefold the number of German troops defending Omaha Beach.

The Americans aboard the sixteen LCTs ferrying sixty-four DD tanks and their tank crews toward Omaha had no way of knowing about these problems. Regardless, they would soon have serious difficulties of their own. The ships, led by Lieutenant Rockwell, had departed England at about 0300 (3 a.m.). Proceeding through a narrow channel swept of German mines, the flotilla eventually split into two eight-ship squadrons, and each turned toward the separate halves of Omaha Beach. Rockwell kept command of eight LCTs, carrying thirty-two DD tanks from the US Army 743rd Tank Battalion toward the western end of Omaha. The other eight LCTs fell under the command of US Navy Lieutenant John Barry and ferried thirty-two DD tanks from the US 741st Tank Battalion toward the eastern half of Omaha.

Around 0400, the officers-in-charge on each LCT, mostly ensigns not yet out of their twenties, called general quarters. Normandy's northern latitude[8] creates short summer nights, and the skies already had begun to lighten. The LCTs, each loaded with four thrity-two-ton tanks plus ammunition, fuel, crews, and supplies, ran low in the choppy seas, their decks often awash with up to a foot of water. The sailors woke any sleeping tankers, who were curled up on spare life rafts because the spartan LCTs had too few bunks. The five-man tank crews forced down hot coffee and ate K rations, their rising adrenaline helping push down any seasickness. Tankers removed chains lashing their vehicles to the LCTs' decks, warmed up their engines, and spun open compressed air valves that inflated the DDs' canvas shrouds. LCT crews passed navigational headings to tank commanders so they could orient their gyro compasses for the swim to the beach.

As the two separate eight-ship columns advanced toward the Norman coast, Ensign R. L. Harkey, officer-in-charge of LCT 602, reported, "Sporadic flashes, apparently bombs, and many flares, could be seen on the shore which stood out darkly but not clearly."[9] The LCTs soon arrived at their line of departure, an imaginary boundary in the sea where the LCTs turned to launch their secret weapons (the DDs) into the waters and toward battle.

Here, the confusion and troubles began.

Barry, leading the LCTs ferrying DD tanks from the 741st Tank Battalion toward the eastern half of Omaha, was missing two of his eight ships. Unknown to Barry, the two absent LCTs had mistakenly followed the other column heading for the west half of Omaha Beach. Unfortunately, one of the two missing LCTs carried US Army Captain James Thornton, the ranking DD tank officer in the flotilla for the 741st Tank Battalion. Thorton had been given authority to decide if the 741st Tank Battalion's thirty-two DD tanks would launch in the seas or be carried by the LCTs to the shore. His counterpart riding in the second column of eight LCTs, US Army Captain Ned Elder, would make the same decision for the thirty-two DD tanks of the 743rd Tank Battalion.

A little after 0500, the time had come for Thornton and Elder to decide. Rockwell, guiding the eight LCTs carrying Captain Elder's 743rd tankers, was certain from his experience running the DD tank training program that the tanks could not survive the sea's rolling swells. Wasting no time, at 0505 Rockwell took the initiative and "contacted Capt. Elder via tank radio, and we were in perfect accord that the LCTs carrying tanks of the 743rd Battalion would not launch but put the tanks directly on the designated beaches."[10]

Heeding Rockwell's advice, Elder decided that his 743rd DD tanks would proceed directly to Omaha Beach.

To Launch or Not to Launch the 741st DDs

Meanwhile, US Army Captain Thornton had his decision to make for the 741st Tank Battalion, whose DD tanks and their crews were riding in the LCTs commanded by Lieutenant Barry. But Thornton was in one of the two wayward LCTs, and thus out of sight from Barry and unable to communicate by signal flag. Thornton had access to his tank's radio, and so he contacted somebody to discuss the situation. But Thornton did not radio Barry, the senior naval officer in charge of the eight LCTs carrying his tanks, as one might expect. Instead, for reasons lost to history, Thornton contacted US Army Captain Charles Young, the second-ranking tank officer from his 741st Tank Battalion. According to the official after-action report of the 741st battalion,

> The two commanders discussed the advisability of launching the DD tanks, the sea being very rough, much rougher than the tanks had ever operated in during their preparatory training. Both commanders agreed that the advantage to be gained by

the launching of the tanks justified launching the tanks in the heavy sea. Accordingly, orders were issued for the launching of the tanks.[11]

Thornton's order to launch was radioed to the rest of the LCTs carrying 741st DD tanks. Barry, the naval officer Thorton logically should have consulted, was caught by surprise, reporting after the battle that

> No signal was received by me from the army concerning their intentions or anything else. When I endeavored to contact the next senior army officer by visual signal, he had already started to launch. It was obvious even before launching that the sea at that distance was too choppy for the tanks.[12]

Many of the LCT sailors, and even some of the tankers, were incredulous about the decision to launch into the ocean swells. One naval officer on the scene later wrote, "The sea, I will say at this point was pretty rough, but the signal was given to drop the ramp. At 0535 all the tanks were launched and were floating in the water, apparently underway on their own power."[13]

Another LCT commander later wrote that the Army officer on his craft "reported to me that word had been received over his tank radio that the tanks were to be launched as previously planned . . . We both felt it was a little too rough to launch."[14]

Yet others seemed comfortable with the decision. On a different landing craft, the naval officer-in-charge later reported that "the ramp was lowered. Sea appeared to be at least no. 4 with a strong breeze. The tank corps men however appeared confident of their being able to make the beach."[15]

Within minutes, the well-practiced Army and Navy crews launched all four DD tanks from each host LCT, plunging the 741st DDs and each's five-man crew into the rolling seas. Almost none of the secret weapons and their crews made it to shore. Several tanks sank immediately after swimming off their LCT's ramp. On board Ensign Harkey's LCT 602, he reported that the first tank initially swam cleanly away. However, "the second tank went off . . . it bobbed for a moment then suddenly sank. The soldiers in it inflated a rubber life raft. The third tank hesitated, whether this was because of engine trouble or because of the fate of the second tank is not known. The third and fourth tanks were launched and when both were in the water, one sank."[16]

Other DD tanks made it closer to the shore, but eventually nearly all succumbed to the seas. In many cases the three- to five-foot waves crested over the canvas shroud's one-foot freeboard, rapidly filling the vehicles with water. In other tanks, strong waves simply crushed the canvas screens, despite some tank crews futilely using their bodies to brace the screens against the battering seas.

Of the thirty-two tanks in the 741st, twenty-nine tanks with 145 crewmen launched into the water.[17] Of those twenty-nine vehicles, twenty-seven disappeared under the waves, plunging to the bottom of the English Channel as much as one hundred feet below. Tank crews scrambled to escape thirty-two-ton Shermans that sank faster than any stone. As one tanker later recalled scrambling to abandon his flooding tank, "I was the last one to step off the tank into the raft. The tank disappeared from under my foot in a swirl of water, gone."[18] Those men who initially escaped found themselves adrift in the frigid gray water, praying life vests and rafts would keep them alive before drowning from exhaustion or dying from hypothermia.

Some sailors aboard the LCTs were unaware of the catastrophe developing in the water, having immediately turned back after disgorging their load of DDs. In LCT 602, Ensign Harkey launched his four DD tanks and began to turn away, but his sailors heard cries for help from the water. They spotted several survivors struggling to stay afloat, and one man wearing a life vest yet floating face down in the water. Harkey's men threw life preservers and tried to extract the tankers, but in the rolling waves the risk was too great; their swaying three-hundred-ton LCT would crush the swimmers. Harkey abandoned the rescue attempt, hoping a smaller craft could retrieve the men. After D-Day, Harkey sorrowfully concluded a four-page handwritten report: "Needless to say, I am not proud of the fact nor will I ever cease regretting that I did not take the tanks all the way to the beach."[19]

Many of the tank crew members ultimately were pulled from the water, but not all. The exact number of 741st Tank Battalion men who perished in the waters off Omaha Beach is unknown, but the most common estimate is thirty-three—about one in four from the twenty-seven DD tanks that sank. On D-Day, thousands of other Allied soldiers, sailors, and airmen lost their lives. Yet, among the day's tragedies, few seem as senseless as the loss of the crew members from the 741st DD tanks. They left their families and homes to serve their country in a foreign land and spent months training for the most important seaborne invasion in the biggest war in history, only to forfeit their lives a few minutes before and a few hundred yards away from the battle's beginning. It is difficult to conclude that their sacrifice was not in vain.

The sinking of Captain Thorton's 741st tanks and their crews contributed to America's near defeat on Omaha Beach. And even though Captain Elder opted that his 743rd Tank Battalion DDs should be carried directly to the beach, his tanks were delayed by the rough waters, reaching shore too late to clear the German defenses before the American infantry arrived as planned.

Leadership Insights

All businesses are a collection of systems and processes and the people who establish and interact with them. In some situations, the systems and processes may be informal: unwritten, unmeasured, and not widely communicated or understood beyond one or a few people. However, to scale and sustain growth, at some point companies and their leaders must design and follow processes that are formalized: documented, communicated, measured, re-evaluated, and continuously improved over time.

Formal processes are the internal skeleton upon which companies are built. They enable organizations to gain capacity, reduce inefficiencies and waste, minimize risk, promote desired values and norms, win a larger share of opportunities, and consistently deliver products and/or services of a target quantity and quality. Practically every business result that leaders and teams strive to achieve requires robust systems and processes: long-term financial growth, premium profit margins, operational efficiency, engaged employees, satisfied customers, positive brand and organizational reputation, and superior market value.

The loss of the 741st DD tanks off Omaha Beach is a familiar story to those who have read about D-Day or watched popular films and documentaries.[20] While tragic, the event reveals how an organization can fail to achieve desired results if a team lacks well-crafted and clearly communicated processes. What most historical accounts do not reveal is how US Army and Navy leaders at Omaha Beach failed to clearly determine who would decide whether or not to launch the DD tanks into the sea, and what process must be followed.

General Bradley: Top Army and Navy Officers Jointly Decide

On May 17, 1944—three weeks before D-Day—General Omar Bradley, the overall commander of US Army ground forces in Operation Overlord, issued a top-secret half-page memo regarding the "Launching of DD Tanks." The body of Bradley's memo contained only one brief paragraph:

Although the control of DD tanks in the final analysis remains
a responsibility of the [Army] Corps Commander concerned,
it is appreciated that the decision to beach the LCT's is a
responsibility of the Naval Task Force Commander and must
be the result of close collaboration with the [Army] Corps
Commander. It is believed that to delegate the authority for
either of the above decisions to Commanders of craft would
result in an uncoordinated and piecemeal attack."[21]

In his memo, Bradley made two key points. First, because the US
Army held responsibility for its DD tanks, and because the US Navy
held responsibility for its LCT ships, the two services must closely collaborate on the DD tank launch process. Second, Bradley instructed that
the highest-ranking Army and Navy officers at each US beach (Omaha
and Utah) should decide if the DD tanks assigned to that beach would
launch into the sea or not. Bradley did not want the lower-ranking officers—specially the ensigns, lieutenants, and captains in the LCTs and
DD tanks—making the launch decision. Bradley feared that different
leaders would make different decisions and thus produce "an uncoordinated and piecemeal attack." As we have already seen, neither of Bradley's
guidelines were followed in the waters off Omaha.

Bradley sent his memo to the relevant top American commanders
on D-Day, including the four highest-ranking officers at Omaha Beach:
US Army General Leonard T. Gerow, General Clarence Huebner,
Colonel Severne McLaughlin, and top US Navy leader Admiral John
L. Hall. Bradley's memo did not define the process these leaders should
follow on the DD tank launch issue, but handwritten records from
two weeks before the invasion indicated that on D-Day morning US
Army leaders Gerow, Huebner, and McLaughlin would sail together
on a command ship so they could closely collaborate regarding the
DD tank launch decision.

Admiral Hall: The Officers at Sea off Omaha Will Decide

While US Army General Bradley's memo stated how he envisioned the DD tank launch process should be handled, the US Navy leaders at Omaha had different ideas. On May 29, 1944, two weeks after Bradley's memo and about one week before D-Day, Admiral John Hall issued the Navy's final Omaha operational plans. On the question of the DD tanks, Hall's plan stated on the first page of Annex F: "If the sea state is such to *prevent* the DD tanks from being launched and proceeding to the beach under their own power, LCT (DD's) will land them with the first wave."[22]

Then, in a double-asterisk notation inserted at the bottom of the same page, Hall's plan added: "This matter will be decided by the Senior Naval Officer in charge of LCT (DD)s and the Senior Army Officer in charge of DDs."[23]

In other words, Hall delegated the DD launch decision jointly to the Navy and Army leaders in the LCTs and DD tanks, contradicting Bradley's recommended process of keeping the DD launch decision at the highest leadership levels.

In a written report issued several weeks after D-Day to address the DD tanks disaster, Hall explained the reasoning behind delegating the launch decision down to the Navy and Army officers in the waters off Omaha:

> (a) They had more experience than any other officers in the Assault Force in swimming DD tanks from LCTs.
>
> (b) The decision should be made by someone actually on the spot where launch was to take place and embarked on an LCT rather than a large naval vessel. A decision under such conditions should be sounder than one made on a large vessel miles away where the sea conditions might have been much different.
>
> (c) If a decision were to be made elsewhere and action had to await an order, confusion and delay might result in the absence of such an order, and it was anticipated that communications

might be interrupted by enemy action so that it would be impossible to transmit orders by radio.[24]

Hall's logic is sound, but his process directly conflicted with Bradley's—even though Hall received Bradley's memo too.

Further Confusion between Bradley's Generals

Curiously, Hall's post-D-Day report also stated that he worked with US Army Generals Gerow and Huebner to determine that the Navy and Army officers on the water off Omaha would decide if the DD tanks launched. Hall wrote that he, Gerow, and Huebner discussed the DD tank matter "at length" and "it was agreed that the senior decision should be left to the Senior Army Officer and Senior Naval Officer of each of the two LCT units carrying DD tanks."[25]

Why were Gerow and Huebner—Bradley's two highest Army generals at Omaha Beach—collaborating with Admiral Hall to create a DD tank launch process that contradicted Bradley's instructions?

The only thing that is clear is that the senior American commanders responsible for the Omaha Beach assault were remarkably unclear about who would decide to launch the DD tanks and how the decision would be made.

A Completely Different Process at Sea off Omaha

As it turned out, the mid-level and junior officers on the water off Omaha Beach followed an altogether different process that conflicted with both Bradley's and Hall's directives. As we have already seen, on D-Day morning the DD tank launch decision was made solely by the Army DD tank battalion officers—Captains Thornton and Elder—not a joint Navy–Army decision.

Navy Lieutenant Rockwell made this clear in his post-battle report, where he wrote, "The question of launching was finally left to the senior army officer of each battalion." Navy Lieutenant Barry, in his after-action report, also recorded that "the senior army officer was the person to decide on launching or not. This was established at the briefing."[26] The official Army reports from both the 741st and 743rd Tank Battalions also agreed. The latter's stated that "the Army directed that the senior captains of each battalion involved in the actual DD landing would make the decision on the spot as to whether to launch or not."[27]

Pulling all this together, Bradley told his top generals to collaborate with the Navy and keep the DD launch decision at a high level, without defining who or how. But two of those generals (Gerow and Huebner) worked with the top naval leader (Hall) to delegate the decision down to the lower-ranking commanders that Bradley specifically did not want involved. Then, the top naval leader (Hall) issued orders stating the DD tank launch must be a joint Navy–Army decision, but his naval subordinates (Rockwell and Barry) deferred the decision exclusively to the Army officers on board their ships (Thornton and Elder), who were under orders to make the launch decision by themselves.

The confused and jumbled leadership regarding the DD tank launch decision process is jarring. I reviewed hundreds of original D-Day reports and records regarding these events, most of them unpublished, and the paper trail is unsurprisingly fragmented. It is tempting to assume that the American commanders involved in this affair must have been better organized than this, but the historical records that would connect these dots have been lost. Unfortunately, the records we have confirm serious leadership breakdowns leading up to the moment when the DD tanks from the 741st drove into the water.

Rockwell stated in his post-battle report that before departing Portland-Weymouth harbor in England at 0300 on D-Day morning, he raised the question "as to the course to pursue in the event of a sea too rough for launching."[28] By all accounts, Rockwell was a competent and dedicated naval officer. Rockwell—the overall naval commander for the sixteen-LCT flotilla—would only have asked about the DD launch process on D-Day morning for one likely reason—he did not know it.

Other historical records confirm the communication lapse. Despite the enormous effort and investment in the DD tank program, none of the pre-invasion operational plans issued by the various US Army units at Omaha provided guidance regarding the DD tank launch decision process. The ill-fated 741st Tank Battalion's pre-invasion orders issued two weeks before D-Day are silent regarding the DD tank launch decision. The US Navy's operational plans for Omaha ran into hundreds of pages, with many sections and annexes getting updated and reissued several times in the countdown to June 6. Within that mass of documents, the only guidance for the DD launch decision question is the previously mentioned footnote squeezed on to the bottom of a page within Annex F, sent by Hall only a few days before the invasion.

Hall's footnote stated that the decision would be made jointly by "the Senior Naval Officer in charge of LCT (DD)s and the Senior Army Officer in charge of DDs." Reading this process creates more questions than clarity, and perhaps it did for Rockwell too. What if the Navy and Army officers did not agree with each other? What if the Navy and Army officers could not contact each other—a serious possibility in wartime conditions and difficult weather. Finally, under Hall's joint-decision process, was the Army officer supposed to decide if the DD tanks launched or not, and the Navy officer would *subsequently* decide if the LCTs went to the beach or not, or were both officers supposed to have an equal say on both steps in the process? Bradley's memo suggests he advocated the former approach, whereas Hall's pre- and post-D-Day comments show that he expected the latter.

If before D-Day Rockwell received and read the final version of the naval plan and saw the singular footnote in Annex F, he may have been wrestling with these uncertainties as his LCT flotilla departed for the invasion. Or, Rockwell might have lacked any instructions on the matter. Either way, it illustrates a serious leadership breakdown. Conflicting priorities went unresolved. Communication lapses were rampant. The only sparse guidance that was issued was vague, inconsistent, and buried at the bottom of the pile.

As a result, on D-Day morning mid-level Army leaders Thornton and Elder were tasked with deciding a critical issue for which they had insufficient training and inadequate skills.

Thornton and Elder had never trained in the Force 4 seas prevalent on D-Day morning. Thornton and Elder were told to make the DD launch decision on their own, not procedurally required to seek consent or even input from people with more maritime expertise, namely Rockwell and Barry. Elder chose not to launch the 743rd Tank Battalion into the water, but only after Rockwell contacted him and lobbied for that prudent path; we do not know if Elder would have asked for Rockwell's advice had the naval officer not reached out first.

Thornton did not contact Barry for consent or input, and the process given to him did not require him to do so. The only input Thornton sought was from fellow Army officer Captain Young, for reasons probably never known. Thornton ultimately made a poor decision, likely due in part to the adrenaline-filled overconfidence and the determination to fulfill one's mission that often comes in combat. But, Thornton and Elder were handed a flawed process. Consequently, they exercised an independent authority that their senior leaders emphatically did not wish for them to have, and which they were not trained to handle.

Leadership Exercises

The following exercises revisit and expand on the historical events associated with "The Tanks That Sank off Omaha," and present leadership learning opportunities for individuals and teams to explore.

Exercise #1

American top commanders at Omaha Beach failed to define and communicate a sound process describing who would make the DD tank launch decisions in the event of difficult sea conditions, and what steps they should follow. Consequently, the Army officers ultimately tasked with the authority were unprepared and followed an ill-advised process that maximized risk.

- What was most interesting or surprising within this case study?
- What potential lessons does the case study offer our team or organization?
- What are the characteristics of an effectively designed and applied business process?
- What processes do we heavily rely on to pursue our business growth and objectives? Do any processes need to be reviewed or improved upon?

Exercise #2

In the waters off Omaha Beach, two teams with identical missions, training, equipment, and operating environment made two completely different decisions.

- Why did this happen? What were the contributing factors?
- What is the desired balance between requiring team members to adhere to defined processes and procedures versus permitting team members to exercise judgment and deviate from process and procedure? How well do we maintain this balance?
- Within our team or organization, are different individuals or teams pursuing similar objectives but applying different decisions, methods, or processes? If so, are the differences enhancing or detracting from the results?

Exercise #3

Only two of the twenty-seven tanks from the 741st that launched into the water reached Omaha Beach. Sergeant Turner Sheppard, commanding one of the pair, arrived and made "the smoothest landing the crew had ever managed."[29] The second DD was commanded by Sergeant George Geddes. Both commanders had experience in piloting small boats before the war, likely a key factor contributing to their successful journey to the shore.

- Do we have personnel or teams who could significantly benefit from more cross-training, such as learning a new skill or gaining new knowledge, to enable them to pursue their current responsibilities more effectively or potentially expand into new capacities or roles?

- Do we have any soldiers that we wished could sometimes be adequate sailors, or any sailors that we wished knew a little more about soldiering?

Exercise #4

After overseeing more than a thousand practice launches with the DD tanks, five weeks before D-Day US Navy Lieutenant Rockwell submitted a detailed report recommending the procedures for using the DD tanks in the amphibious assault, including several clearly stated restrictions. For example, DD tanks should not launch in seas stronger than Force 3, and must not launch farther than four thousand yards from shore. However, these warnings never made it into operational plans. American battle orders did not mention the Force 3 restriction, but only vaguely stated that the DD tanks should be launched "if weather permitted." Additionally, the final assault plans called for the DD tanks to launch from five thousand to six thousand yards from shore, to keep US ships farther back from German artillery.

- What steps could the US Navy and Army leaders have taken to better define and communicate the weather conditions required to launch the DDs into deep water? How could this have been incorporated into the DD launch decision process?
- What are some of the biggest causes of communication breakdowns, especially across different teams or departments?
- Do we have processes and procedures that are not as clearly stated or understood as they ideally should be?

Exercise #5

While the historical records contain gaps, it is likely that on D-Day morning at every Allied beach except for Omaha, senior Army and Navy officers actively participated in the DD tank launch decision for their nation. Only at Omaha Beach was the launch decision delegated to the mid-level tank officers riding in the LCTs. And, only at Omaha Beach did any DD tanks launch from their originally planned distance, without compensating for sea conditions by moving closer in or landing directly on the beach.

- What is our team or organizational culture regarding delegating authority and decision-making? Is the preference or tendency to keep authority at higher levels unless there is a compelling reason to delegate it lower, or do we consistently push decision-making down unless there is a compelling case to keep it at a higher level?
- Do we have functions or situations where an existing authority should either be delegated down or moved up to a higher leadership position?
- What are some reasons why people do not follow a given process or procedure? Do we have any situations where people or teams do not follow processes or procedures as closely as is desirable?

Epilogue

The twenty-seven DD tanks from the 741st Tank Battalion lost at sea were already on the bottom of the English Channel before the first assault waves had even crashed ashore at Omaha Beach. With D-Day just the opening act of the most important attack of the war, the Allies had little time to assess and mourn what had happened off Omaha, usually only giving the event a single sentence or two in the official after-action reports.

However, the Army and Navy understood that the DD tanks' technological limitations had been badly exposed on D-Day morning. Designers made some improvements to the DD tank's equipment, but the inherent vulnerability could not be overcome. DD tanks were used again in several Allied operations, but never on the same scale as on D-Day, and only in calm seas or river crossings. The DD tanks failed to revolutionize beach assaults as Allied planners had hoped, and the technology quickly faded into obsolescence.

US Army Captain Ned Elder and his thirty-two DD tanks from the 743rd Tank Battalion unloaded directly on Omaha Beach, where their presence significantly contributed to the razor-thin American victory. Immediately after landing on the beach, Elder led the 743rd tanks against German defensive fortifications. Several times, he dismounted from his tank in the middle of combat to better lead the operation, and he eventually was wounded but refused to evacuate. For his actions on D-Day, Elder received the Purple Heart and the Distinguished Service Cross (DSC), the US Army's highest award for bravery other than the Medal of Honor.

Elder died in combat about thirty days later, and thus his thoughts about the events off Omaha Beach early on D-Day morning were lost long before the Battle of Normandy had concluded. His wise decision not to launch the 743rd Tank Battalion DDs into the sea has largely been forgotten. Rockwell lived long after the war and gave multiple media interviews, and over time many D-Day books and articles came to credit solely Rockwell with ordering the DD tanks not to launch at sea and thus saving the day. Rockwell undoubtedly served his nation well during the war, and on D-Day he demonstrated courage and initiative. However, the historical documents, including Rockwell's own wartime words, state without ambiguity that the decision to launch or not was Elder's alone to make. I wish to correct the record and appropriately honor Elder for his leadership, valor, and sacrifice.

US Army Captain James Thornton, who made the unfortunate decision to launch the 741st DDs into the ocean swells, went missing in action about ninety days after D-Day, and was presumed to have been killed in battle. Captain Young, the fellow Army officer whom Thornton radioed on D-Day morning to discuss the launch question, was also killed during the war. Thus, their perspectives are also lost to history. Many D-Day histories criticize Thornton's launch decision in the strongest terms, though often omitting his name out of a sense of decency. Thornton's decision was undoubtedly incorrect and cost lives. However, more senior leaders put Thornton into a situation for which he had inadequate training and instructed him to follow a process that increased the risk of making a bad choice. More D-Day histories need to acknowledge the difficult hand that Thornton was dealt.

The fate of Lieutenant John Barry, the leader of the eight LCTs carrying Thornton's 741st DD tanks, is unknown. Immediately after the catastrophe, Rockwell instructed all sixteen of the LCT officers-in-charge to promptly submit individual reports of their events during the day. Rockwell's unusual step preserved the D-Day memories and thoughts of Barry and the other LCT commanders. Barry submitted his handwritten account, and as far as I know, subsequently disappeared from history.

As for sunken tanks from the 741st, several decades after the war French authorities recovered and moved many of the wrecks, leaving in place any tanks containing human remains. Several of the recovered DDs can be found at the D-Day Underwater Wrecks Museum in Normandy. Since 2000, underwater surveys by the US and British governments have confirmed that at least seven DD tanks remain sunken off the beaches of Normandy, respected and protected as war graves.

||||||||||||||||||||||||||||||||||||||||||||||||||||||||||||||||||||||||

Hitler Snoozes

PURSUING CRITICAL SUCCESS FACTORS

*"Critical success factors are the limited number of areas in which results,
if they are satisfactory, will ensure successful competitive performance for
the organization. They are the few key areas where 'things must go right'
for the business to flourish. If results in these areas are not adequate, the
organization's efforts for the period will be less than desired."*
　　　—John F. Rockart, director, MIT Center for Information Systems Research

"The first twenty-four hours will be decisive."
　　　　　—German Field Marshal Erwin Rommel, commander
　　　　　of Army Group B in France during the Normandy battle

Pick up a handful of books about D-Day, and many mention that
Adolf Hitler slept late on the morning of the Allied invasion.
Historians' reactions range from merely commenting on the absurdity
of the moment, to claiming that Hitler sleeping late cost the Germans

the decisive battle in western Europe. While the military consequences of Hitler snoozing may be debated by historians, for today's business leaders the events surrounding Hitler sleeping on D-Day morning present an opportunity to examine the importance of identifying and pursuing an organization's critical success factors (CSFs) that determine mission success or failure.

Prior to the invasion, Hitler and his commanders widely recognized that their critical success factor to defeat the Allies was to rapidly counterattack the landings, immediately throwing the invaders back into the sea before they could gain a firm footing on the ground. Without a timely counterattack, the Germans appreciated that they likely would lose the battle and with it perhaps the war.

This case study tells the story of how the Germans lost focus on their critical success factors—CSFs—and delivered an unnecessarily confused and disorganized response at the start of the invasion, most vividly portrayed by Hitler remaining asleep long after his senior commanders knew an attack was underway. For today's business executives, the Nazi lethargy on D-Day presents a powerful example of the need to identify and act on an organization's critical success factors.

As you read the case study, keep in mind the following leadership questions:

- What is the most important objective we are currently considering or pursuing? What is/are the critical success factor(s) for that objective?
- Do we have any challenges that are taking our focus away from our top objectives and CSFs?
- What steps can leaders and managers take to make sure all team members understand top organizational objectives and their associated CSFs?

The Case Study: Hitler Snoozes

In preparation against an Allied invasion, Germany deployed fifty-eight army divisions in western Europe containing about 880,000 soldiers. Combined with air and naval forces, Germany possessed about one and a half million personnel to defend against the expected attack.[1] Against these figures, the Western Allies would be vastly outnumbered on D-Day. However, those German divisions were scattered across much of western Europe defending almost 2,500 miles (4,000 kilometers) of coastline stretching from southern France to northern Norway.

Once the Allies struck, the bulk of the German forces needed to redeploy to the invasion site to play any role in the battle. Thus, Operation Overlord was in a real sense a race—a Battle of the Buildup—to see which combatant could get the most forces to the critical locations fastest. If the Germans could rapidly counterattack the invasion within the first hours or days, before the Allies could solidify into an unbreachable position, they could throw the Allies back into the sea and potentially turn the entire war to their advantage.

There was another reason Germany had to rush its counterattack against an Allied invasion to maximize its chance to prevail. Amphibious invasions (military attacks launched from ships at sea against land targets) are weakest at the start and strengthen with time. This is the opposite of conventional land-based attacks. In a land-based operation, the attacker is typically strongest at its beginning for it has yet to suffer any combat attrition. In contrast, in an amphibious invasion the effect is reversed. At the start of an amphibious attack, the attacker's few troops are vulnerable (and often seasick) while transitioning from ship to shore. Additionally, heavy equipment like vehicles, tanks, and artillery require time to disembark from ships. Only with time does an amphibious attack accelerate in strength as increasing numbers of troops and weapons deploy ashore and gain room to operate. Therefore, Germany's best opportunity to repel the invasion would come at its beginning. Every hour and day that the Allied invasion endured, the possibility of German victory would diminish.

Field Marshal Erwin Rommel understood this as well as any German leader. At D-Day, he commanded Army Group B, one of the most important units tasked with defending against the invasion. For months prior to D-Day, Rommel had worked eighteen- to twenty-hour days studying the terrain, assessing German defenses, and preparing his troops. According to the tireless and capable Rommel, "The first 24 hours would be decisive. Once the Allies established a large beachhead it would be impossible to drive them back into the sea."[2]

To swiftly counterattack an invasion, the first task for the Germans was to identify the time and location for the start of the Allied attack. It would seem like this would be a straightforward task: The Allies would attack, German troops in that area would report they were under attack, and then German senior commanders would know when and where the invasion had started. However, the Germans managed to make this apparently simple task unconscionably harder on themselves, because after the shooting started on D-Day, they could not decide what constituted an "invasion" and what did not.

Hitler and his commanders not only believed an invasion was coming, but they also believed that the Allies would launch one or more diversionary attacks before revealing their main effort. More than six months before D-Day, Hitler had warned, "Holding attacks and diversions on other fronts are to be expected."[3] The Germans had sound reasoning; common military sense dictated that the Allies would make every effort to mask their true invasion plans to confuse, misdirect, and slow a German counterattack. But, rather than believing that the Allies might use diversionary attacks, the Germans talked themselves into believing it was a certainty. "Everybody agreed on several landing attempts at different points simultaneously or at short intervals," recalled one German general interviewed after the war.[4]

Germans Incorrectly Guess the Invasion's Location

The Germans made a second assumption about Allied intentions, this dealing with the invasion's primary location. Prior to D-Day, German leaders engaged in a constant guessing game about where the Allies would strike, making predictions all over the map. Few Germans offered a steadier stream of speculations than Hitler. In late 1943, the Nazi dictator forecast that "not even the possibility of a large-scale offensive against Denmark may be excluded."[5] Only a few months later he said with agitation, "At no point along our long front is a landing impossible, except perhaps where the coast is broken by cliffs. The most suitable and hence the most threatened areas are the two peninsulas in the west, Cherbourg and Brest."[6] But, even though at some point the Germans fretted over practically every stretch of western European coastline, they consistently assumed that the most likely invasion target would be the French region of Pas-de-Calais.

For You History Buffs: Did Hitler Predict the D-Day Location?

Some histories give credit to Hitler for correctly predicting the Normandy invasion site. This is inaccurate. Hitler did issue several warnings to his commanders in France that Normandy was a potential target, including one alert shortly before D-Day, coincidentally. However, Hitler made many predictions about where an attack would fall. By guessing about everywhere, inevitably one of his hunches proved correct.

Looking at a map, the Germans deduced that Pas-de-Calais presented the Allies with multiple compelling advantages. The Pas-de-Calais coast juts out from northern France, near the Belgian border, and points directly at the extreme southeastern tip of England, thus creating the shortest distance between Britain and Nazi-occupied Europe. The English Channel, which had served for centuries as Britain's protective moat against continental invaders, is only about twenty miles (thirty-three kilometers) wide at this point. (On a clear day a person standing on one coast sometimes can see across to the opposite.) Launching an invasion across the Channel's narrowest stretch would increase the time Allied aircraft operating from British airfields could patrol over the combat area. Allied ships would minimize transit time, speeding up the delivery of troops, equipment, and supplies to the invasion site.

Pas-de-Calais is also close to the major Belgian port of Antwerp, and the Germans believed the Allies would need to quickly capture a large port to facilitate the rapid unloading of troops and matériel.[7] Finally, an invader striking at Pas-de-Calais would open the shortest path to Germany's border and industrial heartland in the Ruhr Valley. If the Allies invaded at Pas-de-Calais, they would carve a direct route to Germany proper. For this combination of geographic and military considerations, the Germans most consistently assumed that the main Allied attack would be aimed at Pas-de-Calais.

Consequently, the Germans installed substantially stronger coastal defenses at Pas-de-Calais, such that the region earned the nickname "The Iron Coast." The Atlantic Wall, a string of anti-invasion coastal forts and defenses, was significantly more formidable in Pas-de-Calais. The German Fifteenth Army was assigned to the region, its eighteen divisions totaling more than 300,000 troops tasked with defending about 430 miles (700 kilometers) of coastline. In contrast, the German Seventh Army defending the actual Allied invasion site in Normandy possessed only thirteen divisions with about 200,000 troops, despite having to cover more than 1,000 miles (1,700 kilometers) of coastline.

The Germans convinced themselves that the Allies would use diversionary raids followed by a main attack at Pas-de-Calais. Through code-breaking, the Allies learned of these German assumptions. In what one US general rightly called the "biggest hoax of the war," the British and Americans turned the Germans' own assumptions against them.[8] In a broad and multilayered counterintelligence campaign called

Operation Fortitude, the Allies created a masterful illusion. Fortitude and its subsidiary operations created fictional armies stationed in England directly across from Pas-de-Calais, fabricated dummy fleets of inflatable tanks and plywood airplanes, broadcast streams of radio messages from mythical units, and fed the Germans bogus information via an extensive network of double agents.

Fortitude's purpose was to play to the Germans' assumptions that Pas-de-Calais was the primary Allied invasion site, duping them into not counterattacking the Allied invasion at Normandy but rather withholding their strength for the expected main operation at Pas-de-Calais. Operation Fortitude worked, probably to a greater degree than even the most optimistic Allied leaders could have expected.

For You History Buffs: Patton Serves as a Decoy

US General George S. Patton played an important role in deceiving the Germans. Patton was benched prior to D-Day after slapping, for alleged cowardice, two American soldiers who were suffering from combat fatigue.

However, Patton was a high-profile figure well known to the Germans, so as part of the Allied deception Patton was put in command of the fictitious First United States Army Group (FUSAG), which contained eleven nonexistent divisions. Then, the boisterous Patton toured England with Willie, his white bull terrier, speaking to town meetings and women's clubs, dropping seemingly overconfident references about how soon he would be in Calais. (Patton's tour is partially recreated in the 1970 biographical film *Patton*, which won seven Academy Awards including Best Picture.) The ruse worked, and the Germans waited until long after D-Day for Patton to land at Pas-de-Calais.

Germans Intercept Reports of Allies' Imminent Attack

In the evening hours of Monday, June 5, German intelligence services intercepted an Allied radio broadcast that contained code words known to alert French Resistance forces that an invasion was at hand.[9] Some

Germans believed the broadcast was genuine, while others dismissed its significance—one German admiral doubted that the Allies would be stupid enough to "announce the invasion in advance over the radio."[10] Shortly after midnight on June 6, reports started arriving from multiple locations that Allied paratroopers had been sighted and engaged by German troops. As is common in combat, these initial messages were chaotic, fragmented, and often conflicting.[11] Yet, news of airborne attackers spread. Soon the Germans captured their first prisoners and discerned that multiple Allied airborne divisions had landed in Normandy.[12]

As German commanders received these initial reports, some began arguing whether the operation in Normandy was the "real" invasion or just a feint. For example, by early morning on D-Day, commanders at the three most important army headquarters units in France already disagreed. "The Chief of the General Staff from the Seventh Army emphasized that this was a large-scale attack, as the depth and width of enemy landings demonstrated. [But] the Chiefs of the General Staff of Army Group B and OB West were of the opinion that it was not a matter of a large-scale attack."[13] These debates broke out in Normandy and spread all the way to Berlin, wasting time the Germans did not have.

While some Germans suspected that the unfolding Allied attack was the actual invasion, others—including Hitler and most of his top commanders—concluded Normandy was the widely expected feint.[14] Believing this, Hitler scrapped the carefully crafted German pre-battle plans to immediately reinforce Normandy with seventeen divisions stripped away from adjacent districts.[15] Instead of rapidly mobilizing these seventeen divisions—a move that would have perilously threatened the Allied invasion—the Germans transferred only five divisions to Normandy over the first two weeks of the battle.[16]

In addition to making a pair of ill-advised assumptions, another factor that undermined the Germans' commitment to rapidly counterattack the Allied invasion was their cumbersome chain of command.

At about 2:00 a.m. on D-Day morning, German Field Marshal Gerd von Rundstedt was urgently awakened by his staff. Rundstedt was the commander-in-chief of German-occupied western Europe. The sleepy Rundstedt initially doubted the news of an Allied attack—he dismissed radar reports[17] of Allied ships at sea as likely to be seagulls.[18] Yet as multiple reports of Allied paratroopers dropping into Normandy arrived at his headquarters, Rundstedt acknowledged an attack was underway but believed it to be the expected diversion. Despite this belief, by 4:00 a.m. Rundstedt had heard enough. He ordered the two most powerful German panzer divisions located within striking distance of the Normandy coast to immediately counterattack an enemy amphibious invasion.[19]

German Commander Rundstedt Pushes Back

Rundstedt acted promptly and decisively. More than five decades of military experience convinced him of two things. First, he correctly anticipated that an Allied amphibious landing was on its way, even though no ships would appear off the beaches for several more hours. Rundstedt properly deduced the Allies would not drop massive numbers of paratroopers without an accompanying seaborne invasion to support and exploit their airborne attack.

Second, Rundstedt understood that the Atlantic Wall beach defenses would be insufficient to repulse an invasion.[20] He knew that coastal defenses at best could stall an assault from the sea, buying time until he could bring forward panzer divisions to strike. In a comprehensive memo prepared for Hitler eight months before D-Day, he wrote that the proper response to an invasion must be "to smash the enemy with fire when he is still on the water, that is to say in a weak moment, or to weaken him to such a degree, that he either turns back or can only land with disorganized elements. . . . Every hour is precious."[21] On D-Day Rundstedt attempted to urgently follow through on this exact course of action.

Rundstedt did not wait for visual confirmation of Allied ships on the horizon. He did not wait to see how the beachhead defenses fared. He did not wait to learn if the attack was a feint or the main invasion, despite his own belief it was diversionary. Rundstedt reasoned that whether the Normandy attack was a feint or not was irrelevant. Any Allied incursion could disrupt German operations and, if left unchecked, could fester into a full-scale threat. Furthermore, in Rundstedt's clear logic, even if the attack developing in Normandy was a feint, the quicker he deployed overwhelming forces to defeat it, then the sooner his forces could be redeployed to meet the main Allied attack once it manifested.

Rundstedt also did not wait for permission to order the panzer divisions forward. Even though he nominally led all German forces, he lacked authority to send into battle the panzer divisions stationed in his area. That command could only come from above. But, to save crucial time, Rundstedt simultaneously ordered the panzers forward and instructed his staff to notify the leaders in the high command of the German Armed Forces (known as OKW) of what he had done.[22]

Many D-Day histories have criticized Rundstedt's performance in the Normandy campaign, suggesting he was out of touch, lacked vigor due to his age (sixty-nine at the time), and was only a rubber-stamp leader under Hitler. Criticism of Rundstedt is justified at other points in the battle. Yet in the predawn hours of June 6 when time was precious, Rundstedt never lost sight of the critical need to rapidly counterattack the invasion, and he acted decisively in an attempt to achieve that mission.

German Response Halted until Hitler Wakes Up

However, Rundstedt's quick initiative would not stand. Back at OKW, Rundstedt's prompt actions were reviewed by General Alfred Jodl, chief of operations at OKW and the second most powerful officer in the German military. At about 7:30 a.m., Jodl countermanded Rundstedt and said the panzers must hold fast. Jodl did not disagree with the need for urgency—just the opposite. Several months before D-Day, Jodl had visited Rundstedt in France to review the anti-invasion plans. In his follow-up report, Jodl wrote that at the start of an attack "at first everything must be committed at one place and the situation fully cleaned up at that place. Should the enemy subsequently land elsewhere, operations must then be concentrated at that place."[23]

Jodl halted the counterattack because Rundstedt did not have the authority to send in the panzers. Neither could Jodl nor anybody else at OKW. The decision to send forward the panzers could only come from German supreme leader Adolf Hitler. And Hitler was asleep, with standing orders not to be woken.

Hitler had reserved for himself the authority to mobilize these tank divisions.[24] For Jodl and Rundstedt, obeying Hitler was not merely a professional obligation but a matter of life and death. German officers who disobeyed Hitler had been court-martialed and in extreme cases arrested and killed.

On D-Day morning Hitler slept late, as was his custom. The previous evening Hitler had entertained guests at the Berghof, his vacation home in the Bavarian Alps in southern Germany. The Fuehrer and his entourage had watched the latest newsreels, filled with images from the world at war around them. However, when entertaining guests Hitler usually steered the conversation away from military matters, so the talk that night had focused on art, film, and theater. Hitler finally retired around two or three in the morning. As Hitler was going to bed in Bavaria, about 650 miles (1,000 kilometers) to his west the first of more than 20,000 elite American and British paratroopers already had dropped onto French soil in the opening act of Operation Overlord.

While Hitler slept through the night and into the morning, the vanguard of more than seven thousand Allied ships arrived off the Normandy beaches and began disgorging the initial waves of American, British, and Canadian soldiers. Meanwhile, Rundstedt's aides continued unsuccessfully to lobby Jodl at OKW to rescind the hold on sending the tanks forward.

Finally, sometime between 11 a.m. and noon, Hitler woke.[25] Despite learning of the attack underway in Normandy, Hitler did not immediately consider Rundstedt's request to advance the two panzer divisions. Rather, the dictator, who earlier had demanded that "the enemy's entire landing operation must under no circumstances be allowed to last longer than a matter of hours or days," had breakfast and then drove an hour to attend a previously scheduled meeting with the leader of Hungary. Rundstedt's request idled until Hitler's regular afternoon military conference, at which time the dictator finally approved Rundstedt's request to send the tank divisions into battle.

By then approximately twelve hours had passed since the start of the invasion. The crucial first day had been forfeited. It was late afternoon when the panzers finally received a green light to proceed, but with almost forty miles (more than sixty kilometers) still separating them from the beaches, insufficient daylight hours remained to counterattack. A fog that earlier in the day could have provided protection for the German tanks against Allied air attack had burned away.

For You History Buffs: The German Counterattack: Too Little Too Late

At 3:55 p.m. on D-Day afternoon, the German army in Normandy finally received permission to order the tank units to counterattack the invasion— nearly twelve hours after Rundstedt's initial attempt and almost ten hours after the first Allied troops landed on the beaches. The orders said "to have the enemy in the bridgehead annihilated by the evening of June 6 since there exists the danger of additional sea- and airborne landings for support. The beachhead must be cleaned up by not later than tonight." Upon reviewing the order, a German general in Normandy replied, "That would be impossible."[26]

The powerful armored strike against a fragile Allied invasion would have to wait. When those two German panzer divisions finally entered the battle over the following days, they faced surging Allied forces too strong to overcome.

Over the coming days and weeks, additional German efforts to dislodge the Allies also would fail. As one German commander involved in the D-Day campaign later lamented, "As early as 6 June the original principle in the conduct of battle i.e. to employ all available forces against those enemy forces that landed first was broken. The Battle for Normandy had already been lost on the first day."[27]

Leadership Insights

By the spring of 1944, the Germans' preeminent objective in western Europe was to defeat the Allied invasion they correctly expected. Every German military and political leader from Berlin to the French coast recognized this was their best and final chance to salvage some form of victory in the war. This precarious military situation ironically provided German leaders with absolute clarity and alignment around this singular goal.

The Germans were also clear that the critical success factor to defeat the invasion was to rapidly counterattack the Allies. Of course, the Germans in World War II did not use the phrase "critical success factor" (CSF). But practically every senior German commander understood that the invasion must be defeated within hours or at most a few days, otherwise the Allied invasion forces would quickly grow too strong if permitted to take root. While the Germans enjoyed alignment around their mission (defeat the invasion) and the critical success factor (counterattack rapidly), they failed to consider their CSF and organize themselves in a manner that effectively pursued it. Their failures illustrate for business leaders the necessity of identifying the critical success factors for a specific objective and focusing and organizing their teams around those factors to reach a desired objective.

First, consider the Germans' assumption that the Allies would make at least one diversionary attack before the main invasion. That they didn't question this assumption and held on to it for weeks after D-Day demonstrates astonishingly rigid thinking. However, the leadership mistake relevant to business executives is not the military assumption around an Allied feint attack, but the German failure to examine how this assumption affected their ability to launch a rapid counterattack.

As long as the German commanders assumed that the first Allied attack would be a feint, they boxed themselves into waiting an unknown period of time for the "real" attack to appear, a monumental violation of their CSF. Before D-Day, senior German commanders acknowledged it would take time to discern if an attack was diversionary. In a letter to Rommel just a few weeks before the invasion, Jodl wrote that the panzer divisions would be released "the moment we can be certain about the enemy's intention and focus of attack."[28] Strangely, nobody questioned how long it would take to be certain or the disastrous implications of this limiting belief. Rundstedt, too, failed to see the dilemma. He wrote prior to the battle that "within the whole area of possible enemy landings, the real focal point cannot as yet be determined definitely. It will only come to light during the course of the landing engagements."[29] German leaders never reconciled that waiting for "certainty" and for it to "come to light" if an attack was diversionary or primary quashed any real possibility of promptly countering the invasion.

Further complicating their predicament, some Germans theorized that the Allies might employ multiple diversionary attacks. Contemplating this possibility would force the Germans to delay even longer until the real invasion somehow became manifest. How many diversionary attacks the Allies might employ, how much time might occur between diversionary attacks, and how long it would take the Germans to finally decipher which incursion was the main threat was a mystery. If Hitler or any of his field marshals, generals, and admirals fully appreciated their quandary, their thoughts are not found in the historical record. Rather, the German leaders marched toward D-Day holding tightly to two irreconcilable convictions: First, they must rapidly counterattack the Allied invasion to have any chance of success; and second, they must wait some unknowable period to determine using some unknown method when and where the real invasion was occurring.

If the Germans had critically examined their CSF and embraced its implications, they might have at least explored their predicament and perhaps considered tactics or procedures to preserve their ability to promptly counterattack despite what might be merely diversionary raids. One reasonable step would have been to predetermine what likely constituted a diversionary attack versus a full-scale invasion. For example, the Germans could have looked to an attack's size and mix of forces as evidence of the operation's true nature. Once an Allied attack began, the Germans could have studied the incursion, compared it to their expectations, and quickly assessed whether that attack was likely diversionary or not.

Some local units in Normandy did exactly this, barely a few hours into the invasion's start. In one example, by midday on D-Day the German 84th Corps headquarters notified their superiors that they believed Normandy was the main attack, reaching this logical conclusion after identifying from captured prisoners that the Allies' best divisions were active in Normandy.[30] "Three airborne divisions have been identified beyond doubt," they reported. "That makes three-quarters of all airborne units we know to be based in England. There are, moreover, the crack units of the 4th and 1st US Army divisions. It is out of the question that the enemy would sacrifice some of his best assault troops for the sake of a mere feint."[31]

Another German officer who engaged in combat against British and Canadian forces reported on D-Day, "The British 3rd and Canadian 3rd Divisions had been identified by about noon. We know that the 50th

London and 7th Armored Divisions are also there . . . If this isn't the invasion, what are they going to come with?"[32]

While these local German commanders rapidly deduced that the June 6 attack must be the main effort, top German leaders did not apply the same critical thinking. Rather, they continued to hold on to the belief that Normandy was a diversion, even to the point of making comically wild rationalizations to explain away the facts. At a conference in Berlin on July 3—almost one month after D-Day—Jodl acknowledged that the elite Allied divisions were in Normandy. However, he concluded that this meant the additional Allied forces in England poised to launch the real invasion must be of inferior quality, and therefore "we have every confidence of defeating them."[33]

We cannot say with certainty that if German senior commanders had created prior to D-Day a shared definition of what constituted a diversionary attack, then the German response on D-Day would have been rapid and effective. But we can say that making the effort to predefine the characteristics of a feint might have mitigated some of the German paralysis that set in on D-Day, and lingered long past. The Germans failed to critically think through the operational steps to uphold their CSF and never attempted meaningful steps to remedy their predicament.

Hitler's Ego and Paranoia Prevented Timely German Response

Another impediment to maximizing the speed of their invasion counterattack was the dysfunctional German chain of command. Rundstedt lacked permission to deploy the strategic panzer forces crucial for an invasion counterattack. Hitler reserved that authority for himself. Hitler's penchant for micromanagement was well understood by this point in the war. (In a postwar interview, Rundstedt quipped that despite his role as the top German commander in western Europe, during the Normandy battle his "only real authority was to change the guard in front of my gate.")[34]

After German Headquarters OKW countermanded Rundstedt's predawn orders to send forward the panzers, throughout that day his aides pleaded unsuccessfully to get the tanks moving without waiting for Hitler. Writing after the war, one of Rundstedt's staff officers remembered in frustration being told that "the main landing was going to come at an entirely different place. . . . OKW stuck to its guns—the Fuehrer had to decide first."[35] To maximize the speed of counterattack, Hitler would have needed to delegate proper latitude to his local commanders. That was not going to happen. Hitler's political paranoia, ego, and penchant to micromanage outweighed considerations of military speed and efficiency.

If the German critical success factor of counterattacking quickly was not already sufficiently undermined by uncritical thinking and a cumbersome chain of command, the dictator's sleeping habits further crippled the German response on D-Day. Hitler's sleep pattern was well established; his advisors knew their leader went to bed late and typically did not rise until close to midday. With standing orders to not be woken, simple math shows that during one-third of each twenty-four-hour period, a German counterattack might be delayed while waiting for Hitler to wake.

Furthermore, if the Germans fully examined their situation, they should have realized that Hitler's sleep schedule was practically certain to overlap with an Allied attack. Common military sense pointed to the Allies invading at night or early dawn, to maximize daylight hours on the amphibious operation's precarious first day—the exact time when Hitler was likely to be sound asleep. If any Germans connected those dots, they would have realized before the D-Day battle even began that they were practically certain to lose up to eight or more irreplaceable hours waiting for their Fuehrer to get out of bed. While military historians armed with hindsight debate how much those lost hours ultimately mattered, the German leadership at the time was absolutely convinced that those precious hours were the single critical success factor in their best and perhaps only chance to repel an invasion.

Despite their conviction, they did nothing to overcome this barrier to their critical success factor.

A simple and obvious procedural remedy would have been to secure Hitler's permission to wake him upon the first reports of an Allied invasion. (For example, British Prime Minister Winston Churchill issued standing orders during the war to not wake him unless Britain was being invaded.) This did not happen. And while the historical record is unclear, a reasonable deduction is this policy was not even considered. After the war many surviving German field marshals, generals, and admirals vigorously blamed Hitler for their country's mistakes and defeat, if only to mask their own culpability. If a Hitler subordinate had offered the logical and prudent suggestion to secure permission to wake the dictator once the Allied attack began, but Hitler had unwisely refused this suggestion, that incident almost certainly would show up in the postwar finger-pointing directed at the Nazi dictator.

Critical success factors are the very few things that a team or organization must get right to accomplish their goals—the wildly important activities that will make or break success. Hitler, Jodl, Rundstedt, Rommel, and practically the entire German leadership organization recognized what they needed to get right, but in practice they merely gave lip service to their CSF and did little to organize themselves around it. They unquestioningly accepted operational assumptions that ended up dulling their ability to read the situation. They blissfully countenanced their dictator's sleep cycle and forfeited precious hours. Consequently, their D-Day counterattack was fragmented, lethargic, and ultimately ineffective.

Thankfully, business teams and companies are unlikely to face a situation where rapidity of counterattack against an invading foe is their critical success factor. Yet all teams have goals or objectives, and thus all teams should identify those very few steps or activities that they must get right to be successful. CSFs will vary across companies, teams, industries, situations, and with time. Examples could include the following:

- Increase market share
- Maximize cross-selling of existing accounts
- Accelerate project completion rate
- Shorten launch time for new products or office locations
- Reduce costs of goods sold (COGS)
- Increase recurring revenue
- Minimize materials wastage
- Improve customer satisfaction or renewal rate

Avoid confusing CSFs with key performance indicators (KPIs). CSFs focus on the actions or steps that make the greatest contribution to success, while KPIs measure the pace and impact of those actions or steps.

Convene stakeholders to discuss and identify CSFs to create a team aligned around its highest-impact activities. Once you define the CSF, identify and implement the managerial, operational, cultural, financial, and other steps your team must take to best achieve it. Doing this exercise will reduce distractions and wasted resources, channel your efforts, accelerate desired change, and maximize likelihood of reaching the stated objective or goal.

Leadership Exercises

The following exercises revisit and expand on the historical events associated with "Hitler Snoozes," and present leadership learning opportunities for individuals and teams to explore.

Exercise #1

German leaders understood that their critical success factor on D-Day was to rapidly counterattack the landings, immediately throwing the invaders back into the sea before the Allies could establish a strong beachhead. However, the Germans never focused on the steps necessary to execute against their CSF, and on D-Day their leadership decisions and actions were slow and disorganized.

- What was most interesting or surprising within this case study?
- What potential lessons does the case study offer to our team or organization?
- Identify an important objective that we are currently considering or pursuing. What is/are the critical success factor(s) for that objective? Are we well focused and organized around the CSFs related to that objective?

Exercise #2

The Germans consistently overestimated how many divisions the Allies had available in England, which fueled their confirmation bias that the Allies would launch multiple attacks. In the months leading up to D-Day, Colonel Alexis von Roenne, head of the German army's intelligence department, noticed that his estimates of Allied troop strength (already overinflated due to British trickery) were being cut in half by his bosses the German high command (OKW) before being presented to Hitler, to avoid upsetting the dictator. Roenne responded by doubling the figures that he submitted, unknowingly restoring the exaggerated figures that the Allies hoped the Germans would continue believing.

- What are our important business reports, forecasts, or models? Are they accurate and effective? Are there opportunities to improve their value and relevance?
- How can leaders and managers create an environment where people are willing to bring them bad news in a timely and unfiltered manner?

- Where could our organization benefit from better data or visibility?
- Do any of our forecasts or projections suggest that we may currently face a difficult situation or challenge that we are not yet adequately prepared for?

Exercise #3

Some D-Day historical accounts claim that Jodl sharply rebuked Rundstedt on D-Day morning after learning of his initiative to order the panzer divisions forward to attack the Allied invasion beaches.

- How can leaders and managers build teams and cultures that encourage desirable personal initiative and decision-making?
- Currently, do our employees take too much personal initiative, not enough personal initiative, or just the right amount?

Exercise #4

After waking on D-Day, Hitler did not immediately consider Rundstedt's counterattack request. Instead, he left for a meeting with the Hungarian regent, Admiral Miklos Horthy. Hungary had been an ongoing problem for Hitler. The country had fought alongside Germany up to that point in the war but, sensing a German defeat, sought a separate peace with the Allies. The situation had escalated to the point that several months before D-Day, Hitler had diverted German army units to occupy Hungary and keep the country under his domination.

- Discuss this statement: "Being overburdened is the same as being underprioritized."
- Do we have any problems or challenges that are taking our focus or time away from more important objectives and CSFs?

Exercise #5

After the war, one of Jodl's direct subordinates wrote that on D-Day morning Jodl "was not yet fully convinced that here and now the real invasion had begun. He did not therefore consider that the moment had arrived to let go our last reserves and felt that the Commander-in-Chief West [Rundstedt] must first try to clear up the situation. This would give time, he considered, to get a clearer picture whether the operation in Normandy was not a diversionary attack prior to the main operation."[36] If this account is true (and other accounts differ), then on D-Day Jodl traded time for clarity—time that the Germans emphatically stated prior to the battle they would not have once an attack started.

- What steps can leaders and managers take to make sure all team members understand top organizational objectives and their associated CSFs?

- Do we currently face any situations where we would prefer to trade time for clarity? How should leaders decide when it is time to act?

Epilogue

As soon as German leaders received the first reports of Allied paratroopers landing in the early morning hours on June 6, they began guessing and second-guessing if the Normandy attack was the precursor for a bigger Allied amphibious operation, likely in Pas-de-Calais. On June 8, two days after D-Day, Hitler ordered infantry reserves in Pas-del-Calais to redeploy to Normandy, and at noon on June 9, he instructed two panzer divisions in Poland to redeploy to France. But later that same day, an uncertain Hitler changed his mind and instructed troops in Pas-de-Calais to stay in place, in effect scrapping "Case Three"—the Germans' carefully predetermined schedule to reinforce Normandy in the event of an invasion at that location.

Through code-breaking, the Allies eavesdropped on the German indecisiveness. Upon learning Hitler had reversed orders to send troops to Normandy, one Allied leader later recalled they "were all smiles . . . there it was. Hitler had cancelled Case Three. We'd won, and what an astonishing moment that was. We knew then that we'd won . . . there would be heavy battles, but we'd won."[37]

For You History Buffs: The Double Agent Named Garbo

Allied deception efforts including Fortitude continued past D-Day, aimed at keeping the Germans second-guessing for as long as possible what was the real invasion. One of the most effective elements of Fortitude was the British network of double agents known as the Double Cross Committee (also known as the XX Committee or Twenty Committee). Of the more than 120 double agents created—some real and some fictional—an agent code-named Garbo likely did the most damage to the Germans.

Garbo was a Spanish national named Juan Pujol Garcia. Even though Spain was a neutral country, early in the war Garcia walked into a British embassy and volunteered to become a double agent, motivated purely by his moral objections to Nazism. Garbo's wartime service is a fascinating and courageous story, and his masterpiece occurred three days after D-Day. Garbo sent the Germans a 122-minute radio message containing assurances that the Normandy landing was a feint and the Allies still had fifty divisions available for a main attack at Pas-de-Calais. Jodl and Hitler read the message, and its contents reinforced their decision not to send the Pas-de-Calais panzer units to Normandy.

For his perceived contribution to their war efforts, the Germans awarded Garbo their Iron Cross. The British also awarded Garbo the Member of the Order of the British Empire (MBE), likely making him the only person to be recognized by both sides in the war.

German indecision continued for weeks after D-Day, far longer than the Allies could have hoped. On July 17, German army senior staff in France reported that "a large-scale landing in the sector of Fifteenth Army [Pas-de-Calais] . . . must be expected."[38] At Hitler's daily military briefing on July 31, he reminded his staff to remain vigilant for another Allied landing "either in the West, in Italian territory, or in Brittany or further north, which would be even more tragic."[39] It was not until August 5 that the Germans accepted that Normandy was the only invasion, with a Berlin radio broadcast declaring, "Large scale landing operations by the Allies need no longer be reckoned with." Incredibly, the announcement explained, "The intentions of the Allies are now quite clear, and that is an advantage to the Germans."[40] The head-scratching proclamation came sixty days after D-Day, by which time more than one and a half million Allied troops were firmly ashore in Normandy.

German sluggishness to recognize that Normandy was the invasion defied military logic and a degree of common sense. Even if the German high command remained deceived for weeks after D-Day that the Allies still had several dozen more army divisions waiting to deploy from England, possessing additional divisions did not necessarily mean the Allies would open a second invasion site. Once the Allies established a solid beachhead, why deploy their additional divisions at a new invasion site when they could just continue unloading troops in Normandy?

This obvious question apparently remained absent from German minds until late in the game. On July 23, Rommel's chief of staff belatedly speculated, "In view of the continuing movement of forces to the Normandy front a far distant landing operation is becoming less probable, . . . The more and the faster [British general] Montgomery is gaining ground from the bridgehead [Normandy] towards the south, the less probable becomes a landing on a new spot by the forces still in England."[41]

Six years after the war, one US general wrote in his memoir, "In devising this cover plan, we had hoped for no more than a modest delay, a week or two at most, until we had sufficient divisions ashore to secure the Normandy landing. Even now, I cannot understand why the enemy believed for so long in so transparent a hoax. For once we landed in

Normandy, only a fool could have thought us capable of duplicating so gigantic an effort elsewhere."[42]

While Hitler and his commanders anxiously watched the horizon for weeks after D-Day waiting for a second Allied invasion, German divisions and tanks idled far from Normandy. Of the nearly sixty German divisions stationed in western Europe at the start of Operation Overlord, ultimately only half participated in combat against the Allies by mid-August. By then, the Germans had lost the Battle of Normandy, their forces shattered and in retreat toward Paris. Masterful Allied deception combined with the Germans' leadership failure to pursue their critical success factor limited the Germans to fighting the decisive western European battle of the war with one hand tied behind their back.

||||||||||||||||||||||||||||||||||||||||||||||||||||||||||||||||||||||||||||||||||

Those Damned Hedgerows

ADAPTING TO A CHANGING LANDSCAPE

"Every success story is a tale of constant adaption, revision, and change."
—Sir Richard Branson, co-founder of the Virgin Group

"We were flabbergasted by the bocage."
—US General Pete Quesada, commander of the 9th Tactical
Air Command during Operation Overlord

In preparation for D-Day, Allied military leaders and strategists spent two years planning the invasion, keenly focused on how their forces would break through the heavily defended beaches at Normandy. By the afternoon of D-Day, the combined American, British, and Canadian forces had taken the beaches, although at great cost.

However, as Allied troops moved inland off the sands and into the Norman countryside, in some places the landscape changed into a terrain that shocked senior commanders and rank-and-file soldiers alike. Allied equipment, training, and tactics—carefully developed and practiced in the massive preparations leading up to D-Day—suddenly proved ineffective. Watching their carefully choreographed offensive slow to a crawl and casualties soar, Allied senior leaders realized they had no immediate answers for how to advance in this unexpectedly challenging environment.

Then and now, armies must adapt to topography and terrain to achieve strategic and tactical objectives. Business organizations also exist within complex and dynamic landscapes, albeit shaped more by economic, competitive, technological, market, and cultural features.

This case study explores how Allied top military commanders neglected to prepare for a changing terrain after D-Day, and consequently how it was up to mid-level leaders to recognize the challenges and innovate solutions. The Allied armies' experiences in the Norman countryside serve as an excellent proxy for the importance today's business leaders must place on embracing change and adaptation.

As you read the case study, keep in mind the following leadership questions:

- How do effective business leaders balance focusing on today's issues and challenges while not ignoring or overlooking oncoming changes?

- Does our team or organization place emphasis on adaptability as a desired cultural value?

- Are creativity and innovation routinely praised within our organization?

The Case Study: Those Damned Hedgerows

British Prime Minister Winston Churchill called them "hateful."[1] A US Army regimental history observed after the war that they were a "nightmarish hell."[2] One American soldier referred to them as "little boxes of terror."[3] Most everybody else just called them "those damned hedgerows."

In the mid-twentieth century, hedgerows covered huge swaths of the Norman countryside in northwest France.[4] The Normans called this distinctive patchwork of small fields surrounded by tall, thick hedges and served by sunken dirt paths the *bocage*. The bocage was the product of a multigenerational cooperative effort between humans and nature. Beginning in feudal times, Norman farmers built earthen and stone walls around the perimeters of their pastures and orchards, and then encouraged trees and thorny shrubs to grow up and through these embankments, making sure to leave a narrow opening in one or two corners to permit entrance and exit. These quasi-organic walls demarcated property boundaries, shielded crops from harmful winds, and sheltered livestock. Over centuries, the hedgerows grew taller and thickened with undergrowth, some exceeding fifteen feet (almost five meters) in height and stretching half as wide at their base. Because most farmers worked modest, irregularly shaped plots, Normandy's landscape compartmentalized into hundreds of thousands of randomly arranged, closely concentrated hedgerow-lined fields.[5]

While the hedgerows made for centuries of happy Norman neighbors, in June of 1944 as US troops moved off the D-Day beach and advanced inland, almost immediately they encountered their first Norman hedgerows, and the German defenders hidden within. The opaque, thick hedges afforded German troops ideal cover and concealment, arguably even better defensive terrain than the static concrete pillboxes they had constructed and occupied on D-Day's beaches. Simultaneously, the tall, impenetrable hedges frustrated the Americans' ability to see, shoot, and move—requisite actions for an army on the offensive.

For You History Buffs: The Americans and the Bocage

The bocage dominated western Normandy and the base of the Cotentin Peninsula, behind Utah and Omaha Beaches, where US forces landed on D-Day. British and Canadian troops to the east faced less dense bocage country in their areas of operations. (However, the British and Canadians

continued

> battled most of the German tank forces in the Battle of Normandy.) Because the Americans encountered the greater share of bocage country, this case study largely focuses on their experiences.

Initially, US infantry rushed each hedgerow through the narrow corner openings. This proved futile and fatal, for the Germans anticipated this and zeroed in their weapons on these gaps. The next logical move for the American GIs was to push through the hedges, but neither infantry nor tanks could breach the dense walls of earth, root, and stone. Tanks could drive up and over the embankments, but the cresting tank would then expose its thinly armored belly to German fire, with cruel consequences for vehicle and crew. Predictably, American tanks funneled into the heavily worn cart trails between the hedgerows, driving into German traps formed from felled trees and minefields, where the tanks proved easy targets for the Germans' pre-positioned anti-tank guns.

For You History Buffs: Where Did "GI" Come From?

The origin of "GI" is murky but is most understood to mean "Government Issue." During World War II, American soldiers took to sarcastically calling themselves "GI" to reflect they were nothing more than the mass-produced products of the US government.

Blinded by the Bocage

The bocage nullified the Americans' primary combat advantages of superior firepower and mobility. Restricted observation lines and cramped spaces deprived the American GIs of supporting air strikes and naval bombardment from Allied warships patrolling off Normandy's coast. The bocage's mishmash lines offered few reference points by which to direct American artillery fire. Furthermore, the proximity of hedgerow combat—opposing forces often clashed within a hundred yards (about ninety meters) or less—created a constant risk of friendly fire. The indistinguishable checkerboard landscape swallowed up entire formations of US troops, unable to determine their direction or position on a map.

In addition, tanks and infantry struggled to communicate and coordinate their efforts. Conventional offensive tactics and formations proved useless. Interlocked hedgerows could not be outflanked or bypassed. With "nothing but hedgerows, a few swamps, small villages, and more hedgerows" in sight for hundreds of miles, the advancing Americans had no choice but to push blindly ahead into the little boxes of terror.[6]

German defenders, many of whom were veterans of years of combat against Soviet Russia, transformed each occupied hedgerow into a kill zone. German infantry dug foxholes and trenches into the base of hedgerows to maximize cover. Camouflaged snipers secreted in the dense foliage, tying themselves to branches high in the treetops, picking off unwary Americans, many of whom were in combat for their first time. Defenders wielding *panzerfaust*—handheld rocket launchers modeled on the American bazooka but with superior power and range—ambushed US vehicles at ranges so close it was difficult to miss. German artillery fired at targets cross-referenced against previously plotted map coordinates, a benefit from having occupied the land for the past four years. They also made masterful use of mortars—small, portable artillery tubes that could accurately lob grenade-sized bombs into the bocage's tight spaces.

However, the terrible ruler of the hedgerows was the German MG42 machine gun. This inky-black automatic weapon fired more than twenty rounds per second—double the rate of Allied equivalents, each bullet leaving the barrel at twice the speed of sound. Its distinctive ripping noise and fearsome lethality earned it the gloomy nickname "Hitler's buzz saw." The German army possessed them in prodigious quantity. One MG42 manned by a handful of half-trained German soldiers hidden in a hedgerow's corner could hold up a company of GIs, some two hundred soldiers. Several MG42s concealed in a network of hedgerows, interconnected by radio wires, could stop a US battalion—some eight hundred soldiers.

"Every hedgerow can become a strong point," Churchill wrote in a postwar memoir. "This is a murderous game, for the line of march is cut every few hundred yards by a deep bank of earth flanked with trees and bushes. Each of these is an ambush. . . . Troops caught in the open have a choice: they can charge, or they can run away and die. Tanks are useless. It is costly ground and hateful."[7] When US troops finally overwhelmed a hedgerow-encased field and dislodged its defenders, the surviving Germans melted away, pulling out and occupying defensive positions prepared in another hedgerow behind, leaving mines and booby traps in their wake.

The hedgerow troubles quickly drew attention from America's top military leaders. Shortly into the battle, General Dwight D. Eisenhower, supreme commander of Operation Overlord, wired his boss General George C. Marshall, chief of staff of the US Army, on his forces' struggles in Normandy. "The going is extremely tough," Ike explained, due to "the nature of the country. Our whole attack has to fight its way out of narrow bottlenecks flanked by marshes and against an enemy who has a double hedgerow and an intervening ditch almost every fifty yards as ready-made strong points."[8]

American media quickly picked up on the arduous battles in the bocage. War correspondent and future television news icon Andy Rooney remarked about the bocage that "all the military genius of every West Point graduate there ever was could hardly have designed a fortress more difficult to penetrate."[9] Pulitzer Prize–winning *New York Times* journalist Hanson Baldwin penned the headline "NORMANDY BATTLE AMONG TOUGHEST; Every Hedgerow Is Miniature Campaign and Conquest Is Hard and Costly."[10]

Baldwin reported accurately. Fighting in the bocage produced some of the bloodiest combat during the Normandy campaign. The US 83rd Infantry Division's tragic experiences provide evidence. An inexperienced unit disembarking in France in mid-June several weeks after D-Day, the

83rd launched an attack on July 4 against German defenders embedded in the bocage. One day later the battered division ground to a halt, having advanced about 1,600 yards (about 1,450 meters) at the cost of more than 2,100 casualties—one American killed or wounded for every two feet of ground gained.[11] In a report prepared shortly after the war, a company commander recorded that "there were days when the regiment was lucky to gain two hedgerows. During one operation, the 3rd Battalion attacked for three days to capture a single orchard which was held by a die-hard unit of the 17th SS Panzer Division."[12]

Allied Advantage Fades

The juggernaut that mightily broke through Germany's vaunted beach defenses on D-Day slowed to a vicious field-by-field crawl, setting back the meticulous pre-invasion timetable by weeks. Casualties skyrocketed. Between D-Day on June 6 and the end of July, the US Army in Normandy suffered almost 100,000 killed, wounded, or captured, the disproportionate share among soldiers fighting in the bocage. Morale plummeted.

While all combat is terrifying, bocage fighting struck particular horror for the GIs who incessantly crept forward into the labyrinthian hedges, unable to see the fanatical enemy to their front and prone to losing sight of their fellow GIs to the sides and rear.

Nations worried. The American and British public, observing on a map their armies' scant forward progress,[13] murmured about a possible stalemate in France, triggering frightful World War I memories of millions of soldiers fighting and dying in unchanging and unending trench warfare. The possibility of stalemate panicked those nations' leaders too. Deadlock in Normandy would hand Hitler an immense political victory, potentially blocking any prospect for Allied victory in western Europe.[14]

The bocage caught Allied top leaders off guard, but not for lack of foreknowledge. Overlord planning documents routinely mentioned the bocage. The Allies possessed detailed aerial reconnaissance photographs showing the patchwork countryside. Many British and Free French military leaders knew the bocage firsthand, either from prewar travels or from combat experience earlier in the war. At the top of this list, Britain's most powerful military officer, Field Marshal Alan Brooke, chief of the Imperial General Staff and top advisor to Churchill, had spent his childhood summers vacationing in Normandy. Earlier in the war, in 1940, he led Anglo-French forces through the Norman bocage as they retreated from the German blitzkrieg.

Brooke seems to have been the lone senior Allied commander who voiced concerns about the bocage. Almost a year before D-Day, Brooke queried General Frederick Morgan, the author of the original Operation Overlord plan, about the bocage. Morgan acknowledged the terrain's distinct characteristics but equivocated about whether it would benefit the Allies or the Germans, depending on who occupied it. In his postwar memoir, Morgan wrote that "the side which could first occupy the bocage with sufficient strength would score a most decided advantage."[15] As long as the Allies gained the bocage before Germany's expected counterattacks against the invasion site, then the inhospitable terrain would aid the Allied defense. But in Morgan's analysis, if the Germans occupied the bocage first—as actually occurred—the Allies would be in serious trouble.

Morgan's pre-D-Day ambiguity failed to placate Brooke, who continued to express concerns. As late as several weeks before D-Day, Eisenhower noted that "Brooke had been extremely pessimistic at all times about our prospect of fighting through bocage country."[16] Despite Brooke's top leadership role and firsthand bocage experience, his apprehensions went unheeded, without any explanation in the historical records.

Brooke may have been the only Allied leader prior to D-Day worried about the bocage, but others recognized that the terrain at least created questions. For example, in a briefing paper written two months prior to the invasion, one of Eisenhower's closest aides observed that "it is difficult to judge whether such terrain favors defending or attacking infantry," and advised that combat operations in the bocage "should be given considerable study."[17] But it appears that nobody studied the issue. The bocage stunned senior Allied commanders in Normandy (other than Brooke) not because of lack of foreknowledge, but because of a breakdown in leadership.

In planning and preparing for Operation Overlord, American and British leaders were hyper-focused on getting and staying ashore.[18] Invasion planning staffs numbering in the thousands scrutinized a dazzling list of issues associated with attacking and securing the invasion beachhead, studying coastal fortifications, tidal and lunar cycles, weather patterns, rail and river transportation networks, shipping capacities, the layout of Norman towns and roadways, and of course the position and strength of German military forces. But the Allies ignored the bocage.

Consequently, once their troops entered the bocage the terrain confounded American commanders. General Omar Bradley, leading all US ground forces in Operation Overlord, exclaimed, "I couldn't imagine the bocage until I saw it." It was "the damnedest country I've ever seen."[19] General J. Lawton "Lightning Joe" Collins, a senior Army officer in Normandy, noted the bocage reminded him of the tropical jungles in Guadalcanal, where earlier in the war he had led US forces in combat against the Japanese. General Pete Quesada, commander of the largest US tactical air force in Operation Overlord, later admitted, "We were flabbergasted by the bocage."[20] General James M. Gavin, leader of the famed 82nd Airborne Division, wrote after the battle, "Although there had been some talk in the UK before D-Day about the hedgerows, none of us had really appreciated how difficult they would turn out to be."[21]

Allies' Incorrect Assumptions Cost Them Dearly

Compounding their myopic focus on the beaches, on the few occasions Allied leadership paused to consider the bocage, in varying degrees they made two incorrect assumptions, both of which validated their belief that there was no need to give the bocage serious pre-invasion consideration.

First, some Allied leaders, including English General Bernard "Monty" Montgomery, the overall commander of Allied ground forces on D-Day, assumed the Germans would not fight in the bocage. Once the Allies landed at Normandy and secured the beachhead against the inevitable German panzer counterattack,[22] Monty and others believed Hitler would prudently pull back German forces out of Normandy and closer to Paris, to establish defensive lines on the other side of the Seine River. This was a flawed assumption. After the invasion started, Hitler, perceiving the battle in Normandy to be an existential contest for his Nazi regime, ordered that Germany not surrender one inch of occupied French land and dig into the bocage.[23]

The Allies' second erroneous assumption was that the hedgerows found in Normandy were comparable to the English version, and therefore their pre-invasion training exercises conducted in the British countryside adequately prepared troops for the bocage. In one typical example, a top-secret US Army intelligence report prepared several months before D-Day described the terrain behind the invasion beaches: "Hedges and earth fences abound and are similar to those in southern England."[24] In fact, Normandy's typical hedgerows were considerably taller, denser, more tightly spaced compared to the English version, and thus more disruptive to seeing, shooting, and moving.

Allied armies conducted no specialized hedgerow combat training in England prior to the invasion because they wrongly assumed there was no need for it. In one incident, an American officer with the 357th Infantry Regiment recalled a visit from General Bradley to their camp several weeks prior to D-Day, during which the general asked what training was being conducted for hedgerow fighting. Not much, was the junior officer's answer: "Because the hedgerows of central England were very similar to those encountered in the United States and the fields were rather larger, the hedgerows did not leave the impression of being a difficult problem."[25] This officer and his regiment sadly learned otherwise, like so many others in Normandy. In the 357th Regiment's first four days in the bocage, more than seven hundred of its three thousand soldiers were wounded or killed.[26]

Another US Army field commander wrote after the Normandy battle that "we rehearsed endlessly for attacking beach defenses but not one day was given to the terrain behind the beaches, which was no less difficult and deadly."[27] Because the generals failed to anticipate the changing terrain's implications and prepare a suitable response, their subordinates leading regiments, battalions, companies, and platoons marched off the beaches and blindly entered the hateful hedgerows. The pre-D-Day conversation between Bradley and the 357th regimental officer was an anomaly; a postwar study revealed that only one percent of US Army officers in Normandy had heard of the bocage prior to the invasion.[28]

The Allied leadership's lack of investigation and preparation for the bocage is even more jarring when one examines the depth and breadth of ingenious efforts applied to study, assess, and plan for attacking the beaches:

- Allied D-Day planners broadcast a request asking civilians to turn over postcards and family photographs from prewar vacations on European beaches. Eventually, ten million were collected and Oxford University cartographers incorporated 150,000 into maps of the French coastline.[29]

- Reconnaissance aircraft flying at altitudes from thirty thousand feet (about nine thousand meters) down to wavetop height photographed the invasion beaches through oblique, stereoscopic, and panoramic lenses. The Allies took care to image the entire European coastline from the Netherlands to the French border with Spain to avoid tipping off the Germans on the actual invasion targets.

- Fifty-foot-long (sixteen-meter) British midget submarines called X-craft secreted ashore commandos to collect soil samples (stored in condoms) from the invasion sites to test how well the beaches would support heavy vehicles such as landing ships and tanks.

- French Resistance agents smuggled via carrier pigeon intelligence reports detailing German coastal defenses in Normandy, including the width of concrete walls in beachfront pillboxes, the name and number of German military units stationed in the invasion area, and the diameter of coastal artillery cannons.

- The Allies held elaborate dress rehearsals with code names such as Duck, Beaver, Fox, and Tiger to test and perfect amphibious equipment, tactics, and training. The live gunfire rehearsals featured tens of thousands of soldiers storming English beaches at Slapton Sands, Bracklesham Bay, Hayling Island, and Littlehampton, each selected for their resemblance to a specific D-Day beach.[30]

- The British invented a series of modifications to tanks to increase the vehicles' firepower and utility against coastal pillboxes, minefields, and anti-tank ditches. The equipment included a flame-throwing tank called the Crocodile, a mine-clearing tank called the Crab, and a swimming tank called the DD (Duplex Drive).[31]

Little of this devious data-gathering, intense training, and technical innovation was directed beyond the beach. When comparing the massive effort invested into taking the beaches against the near-total absence of anticipating the terrain that followed, one can only conclude that the top Allied leaders were tragically shortsighted.

Mid-Level Leaders React Quickly and Creatively

Senior American leaders' myopia is half of this story. The second element is how mid-level American military leaders responded to the hedgerow challenge and invented, tested, and deployed a wide variety of adaptations to restore seeing, shooting, and moving in the bocage. Their decentralized efforts occurred in parallel and in different places, for these mid-level commanders realized two things. First, their equipment, tactics, and pre-invasion training were ill suited for combat in the bocage. Second, the flabbergasted top brass had no answers. Solutions had to be found quickly, for each day GIs were dying or being wounded at tragic and unsustainable rates.

Some initial experiments were less effective. In an effort to see over the hedgerows, brave GIs scaled ladders extended above the dense foliage to visually locate enemy positions and radio for artillery fire. Unfortunately, German snipers quickly cooled enthusiasm for this tactic. However, some help came from the air. With the German air force cleared from the skies over Normandy, the US could fly over the battlefield L-4 Piper Cub and L-5 Stinson Sentinel light aircraft, collectively called the Grasshopper Fleet due to their slight size and green color. These spotter planes carried an observer to locate and radio the position and disposition of German forces hiding in the hedges. Slow, small, and vulnerable to ground fire as they loitered overhead, the Grasshoppers received little glory, but they helped restore the US Army's ability to see and shoot—when the Grasshoppers could fly. One of the stormiest Normandy summers in recent memory frequently kept these diminutive aircraft grounded.

Other efforts focused on increasing firepower in the bocage. Some gains could be had by retraining GIs to fire their existing weapons more vigorously, even at unseen enemies in the foliage. In an Army training pamphlet released a month after D-Day, a fictitious character unimaginatively named Sergeant Infantry presented the new rules of bocage warfare in a piece called "Notes from Normandy." The sergeant reported to his GI audience that since landing in Normandy, "We were taught only to shoot what we see, and in the desert [North Africa and Sicily] it worked out fine. But here all you see is hedges. So we're shooting into whatever area we want to move into—we spray it with plenty of lead."[32]

The US needed more than just rapidly firing riflemen. The M1919 standard American light machine gun was poorly suited to hedgerow combat. Its tripod mount proved too tall and cumbersome, and when the gun barrel overheated, a GI could not hold the weapon to shoot and advance at the same time in an offensive tactic called marching fire. After considering the issue, Lieutenant Daniel L. Donnelly from the US 90th Infantry Division invented a "spike mount" to resolve the gun's limitations.[33] The single-legged stand was easier to position, provided a new handhold separate from the barrel, and increased ammunition storage. Two hundred spike mounts were quickly manufactured and adopted for use in his unit.

Innovating Scalable Solutions—The Rhino Tank

While these efforts helped, the Americans' greatest need was getting their tanks freely moving through hedgerow country. Tanks provide firepower, protection, and mobility—exactly what US forces desperately needed. The US Army discovered it already possessed a potential solution in the form of dozer-tanks, a tank paired with a hydraulically operated bulldozer blade. Dozer-tanks had been invented to help on D-Day to demolish German beach defenses and expand egress lanes off the sands.

The Americans discovered dozer-tanks also could easily plow through a section of hedgerow. However, there were too few of these hybrids to go around—initially only four were assigned to a tank battalion,[34] and some had been lost in combat on the beaches. An urgent order was placed for 278 dozer blades, but installing the equipment in England, shipping the dozer-tanks to Normandy, and conducting the requisite crew training would take weeks. The limited number of available dozer-tanks were put to use in the bocage, but in the meantime the Americans needed a rapidly scalable solution.

Multiple American outfits took up the problem of getting regular tanks moving through the hedges. At the 29th Infantry Division, lead engineer Lieutenant Colonel Roger R. Ploger and his team discovered that two fifty-pound (twenty-two-kilogram) canvas bags of TNT placed ten feet apart at the base of a hedgerow blasted a gap wide enough for tanks. However, scaling this tactic demanded prodigious quantities of explosives; Ploger calculated seventeen tons of explosives per day.[35] Further experimentation revealed that burying the dynamite at the hedgerow's base increased the blast effects and reduced the required explosives by seventy percent. But digging blast holes into a hedge's packed earth and interlocked roots took time and alerted the German defenders. Once the explosives blew a gap, the ready Germans immediately fired every available gun on that location.

Ploger's experiments drew the attention of Lieutenant Colonel Stuart G. Fries, commander of the 747th Tank Battalion. As an alternative to digging blast holes in the hedgerows, Fries's tankers welded two four-foot-long (more than one meter) metal pipes to the front of a tank hull, protruding forward like prongs on a fork. As their test tank charged into a hedge, the prongs punctured the thick base, instantly boring two holes. After the tank withdrew, engineers rushed forward, shoved explosive charges formed from repurposed artillery shells into the cavities, and blew up the hedge. The process eliminated hand-digging holes, but still tipped off German defenders and required a steady supply of engineers and explosives. And the tanks' prongs easily bent or broke. But the prongs could puncture a hedge, hinting that the GIs were on to something.

The Americans needed a means to get tanks freely moving through the hedgerows, without forfeiting the element of surprise or demanding an impossibly large supply of TNT. While the Ploger-Fries ad hoc team worked with prongs, other groups pursued their own ideas. Several weeks into the battle, Captain James G. Depew with the 102nd Cavalry Reconnaissance Squadron stood at attention while General Leonard Gerow, one of the top Army commanders in Normandy, pointedly asked Depew if he and his unit had a solution to the hedgerow problem. Depew admitted they did not, and Gerow ordered him to get on it.[36]

That evening, Captain Depew met with his squadron to discuss the challenge. During their deliberations, twenty-nine-year-old Staff Sergeant Curtis "Bud" Culin theorized that several stiff metal blades welded to the tank's lower front hull might chew through a hedgerow, like large metal teeth. The rest of the men in the meeting laughed, but an intrigued Depew asked maintenance officer Lieutenant Steve Litton to fabricate a prototype. In two days Litton and his mechanics designed and installed a set of teeth on the front hull of a Sherman tank. The modified tank was soon munching through hedges with ease. Somebody imagined the blades resembled horns more than teeth, and the altered tank earned the nickname "Rhino."

Depew and his team demonstrated the Rhino to Gerow, who immediately wired his boss General Bradley to come see "something that will knock your eyes out."[37] In mid-July, Bradley, Gerow, and other top Army brass watched in amazement as the Rhino sped by and burst through hedgerows, sending earth, roots, and branches hurling through the air. The solution proved "so absurdly simple that it had baffled an army for more than five weeks," Bradley later recorded.[38]

Rhinos could rapidly penetrate the hedges from any quarter, without requiring explosives, complex equipment, or specialized crew training. The remaining challenge was immediately sourcing an extensive supply of large, flat, metal plates from which to fabricate the horns. In one of World War II's great ironies, the Americans located the answer right behind them, back on D-Day's beaches. They fabricated Rhino horns by repurposing the countless heavy steel anti-tank obstacles that the Germans had installed in the surf to rip open the thin-skinned hulls of Allied amphibious landing craft.

The Allies rounded up nearly every welder and oxygen acetylene cylinder in England and flew them to Normandy to establish an assembly line. Rhino tanks were created by the hundreds, such that soon about sixty percent of American tanks were so converted. Although it was a team collaboration,[39] the US Army's public relations team singled out Culin and turned him into an instant celebrity with the American public.[40]

Allies Revitalize Communications and Combined Arms Operations

While these teams focused on getting tanks moving through the hedgerows, others explored overcoming the bocage's stifling effects on communications and teamwork, particularly between tank crews and accompanying infantry. Tanks and infantry possess complementary capabilities. While tanks provide protection, mobility, and firepower, tank crews suffer severely limited visibility in combat, particularly if the tank commander cannot risk riding with his head outside the turret for fear of snipers. Their restricted vision makes tank crews vulnerable to hidden enemy infantry attacking their vehicle with short-range weapons like *panzerfausts*. In contrast, infantry on foot possess no organic protection, are not highly mobile, and have limited firepower. But infantry can deal with close-in threats and see better than the tankers buttoned up in their steel vehicles. Tasking tanks and infantry to operate in close teamwork, commonly called combined arms operations, allows each force to leverage the capabilities and mitigate the weaknesses of the other.

Tank-infantry communications and coordinated movement, difficult in the best of situations, became nearly impossible in the bocage. Hand signals proved futile in the dense, confined, compartmentalized fields, especially once battle commenced and the tight spaces filled with deafening tank engines, shellfire, dust, and smoke. Infantry were forced to jump up and down in front of the tank to get the crew's attention, a risky move in the middle of combat.

Further complicating affairs, at the start of the Normandy battle most American infantry and tanks used radios operating on incompatible frequencies. Out of the seven radios issued to an infantry company, only the company commander's radio was compatible with tank radios. Conversely, in a tank platoon only the platoon leader and the platoon sergeant had radios capable of communicating with an infantry company commander's radio.[41]

After considerable experimentation, one successful improvisation involved affixing two infantry field telephones to a tank—one on the inside for the tank commander's use, and the second externally mounted on the vehicle's rear hull in an empty ammunition box. With this setup, infantry sheltering behind the tank could speak with the tank commander to compare threat information and synchronize their tactics. Later variations added a signal light to the rear-deck phone activated by the tank crew to initiate contact with nearby infantry. The early-adapters at the US 2nd Infantry Division reported the new rear-deck telephone greatly improved infantry-tank communications and practically eliminated infantry casualties due to sniper fire.

New Fighting Tactics Supported

Alongside improving firepower and communications, the Army had to rethink its tactics in this unexpected terrain. A standard US Army attack formation called for two battalions (about 800 soldiers each) to advance in line abreast on a front between 500 and 1,000 yards (450 to 900 meters) wide. In the bocage, where high hedges and sunken, tunnel-like dirt paths disrupted or channelized any line of movement, such a formation was impractical. The Army needed to learn how to conduct attacks led by a tank or two, not two battalions.

Multiple units working in parallel devised new tactics. The US 29th Infantry Division wrote a hedgerow assault plan that downsized attack formations to small infantry teams working with a single tank and supported by mortars. The mortars lobbed smoke rounds to open an assault, immediately followed by a dozer-tank or Rhino punching through the hedgerow while firing its cannon and machine guns in a precise pattern into the perimeter hedges to suppress German defenders. Finally, accompanying infantry advanced to kill or capture any remaining enemy.

Meanwhile, the 83rd Infantry Division created its own hedgerow playbook, centered around a pair of tanks advancing through the hedgerows almost in leapfrog manner, accompanied by a supporting team of infantry, engineers, and artillery. The 3rd Armored Division devised yet another plan, attacking a line of three hedge-encapsulated fields in a carefully choreographed sequence starting with the two outer fields and finishing with a convergence on the center. This pattern maximized terrain coverage while minimizing exposure to German fire.

Initially, these grassroots adaptations were decentralized and uncoordinated. However, as the various new devices and ideas were put to proof, they were shared, copied, and improved upon throughout the Army and across Normandy. US Army senior leadership, at first surprised and stymied by the bocage, threw their support and institutional resources into organizing and disseminating the most effective new tools and methods.

Army leaders wrote and distributed revised training materials complete with illustrations. Bradley hosted a four-day training program in the Norman countryside at which divisional and regimental leaders learned the new tactics and techniques, and their battalions, companies, and squads put the new resources and ideas to practice. While watching the process, one American general reflected, "What held us up at first was that we originally were organized to assault the beach, suffered a lot of casualties among key men, then hit another kind of warfare for which we were not organized. We had to assemble replacements and reorganize. Now we have had time to reorganize and give this warfare some thought."[42]

No single device, process, or tactic rewrote the rules of the bocage's murderous game back in favor of the Americans. Many of these adaptations came late in the battle, by which point the GIs had already advanced through a considerable portion of hedgerow country, if at terrible and irretrievable cost. However, ingenuity and innovation, mostly from mid-level leaders such as colonels, captains, lieutenants, and sergeants, drove adaptations, which restored the Americans' combat effectiveness in Normandy's cursed hedgerows.

Leadership Insights

Focusing on winning and keeping a Normandy beachhead was an imperative for Allied military leaders. If they could not take and hold the beaches, then the invasion of Europe would end in defeat, with cataclysmic consequences. Their intense concentration on the beaches is understandable; if the Allied leaders had to err, better to focus too much on the beaches rather than too little.

All complex operations—including military and commercial—inevitably include unknowns and baked-in assumptions. Allied leaders in Operation Overlord got most things right, as evidenced by winning the battle, to humanity's eternal gratitude. Yet with regard to the bocage, Allied leadership fell short. They knew the terrain dramatically changed after the beaches, yet they tuned out warnings from credible people who had been there, looked past their own hard evidence, and rationalized away the issue with unnecessary and ill-advised assumptions.

Their leadership error was not that they failed to solve the bocage problem prior to D-Day, but rather that they failed to anticipate that the bocage presented a potential problem. If the Allied leaders at least had embraced that the bocage presented operational uncertainties, they could have diffused much of the bocage's massive initial shock and quickened the process to adapt. Without taking their eyes off the beaches, before D-Day they could have alerted their unit leaders about the bocage and made them aware of its uncertain challenges. Alerting their forces in some manner would not have redirected time, resources, or focus away from their planning to take the beaches.

However, the Allies, particularly the Americans, entered the bocage both unaware and unprepared. A military historian may dismiss expecting Allied D-Day leaders to possess this prescience as armchair generalship; but business leaders are expected to spot and call out potential oncoming challenges, threats, or opportunities, even if their organization does not yet have the bandwidth or means to determine its response to the new terrain.

If necessity is the mother of invention, then necessity has no parent more forcible than life-and-death combat. Any nation's soldiers struggling and suffering in the bocage would have sought to invent equipment and tactics that reduced the risk of physical harm. However, the American Army in the bocage displayed a cultural agility of remarkable speed and extent, particularly among its mid-level leaders. "The Americans were getting better with each passing week, if not day," noted a prominent British military historian. "There was a willingness to learn that was endemic and equally a willingness to innovate."[43]

Adapting in a changing environment is essential for today's business executives, leaders, and managers. Business conditions and landscapes, internal and external, constantly change at a seemingly ever-increasing pace. Teams and organizations that remain static inevitably fall behind, decay, and disappear. Teams and organizations that excel at anticipating and leveraging change differentiate themselves from competitors, stay ahead of market trends, attract and retain top talent, increase their value to customers, and achieve sustained profitable growth.

Building organizations that embrace change is easier said than done. Change is messy. It causes individual and institutional discomfort and friction. To drive change, leaders must have a clear vision of the intended outcome, consistently lead and support the process, take personal risks, and nurture critical thinking and creativity. Looking back on the hedgerow case study, business leaders will find two examples of how the US Army in Normandy demonstrated a culture that valued adaptability during the hedgerow crisis: psychological safety and cross-functional collaboration.

Psychological Safety

To welcome and embrace change, leaders need to create psychological safety, an environment where individuals feel secure taking the personal risk that comes with challenging the status quo, vocalizing a dissenting point of view, or suggesting new and unprecedented ways of doing things. A Harvard Business School study explained psychological safety as "a sense of confidence that the team will not embarrass, reject or punish someone for speaking up . . . a team climate characterized by interpersonal trust and mutual respect in which people are comfortable being themselves."[44]

A 2012 internal initiative at Google called Project Aristotle concluded that psychological safety was the most important trait within highly effective teams. The project identified two team norms that foster psychological safety: "conversational turn-taking" and "social sensitivity."[45] In conversational turn-taking, all team members verbally participate and contribute in roughly equal proportion, whether that time is formally partitioned or occurs naturally. If a subset of people consistently dominates the airtime, psychological safety and effectiveness suffer measurably. The second team norm was social sensitivity, meaning how well team members use nonverbal cues to intuit how others feel in the moment. High social sensitivity enables teams to detect if any member is upset or feels left out, and in response encourage participation and inclusivity.

Leaders can implement steps to develop a psychologically safe environment:

- Celebrate employees or teams that pursue or generate innovative ideas, both successes and failures.

- Emphasize that failure is an essential part of advancement and creates opportunities for learning and growth. Share "fail fast" agile concepts with the team when pursuing new products, services, or markets. Extract and publish lessons from failures as well as successes.

- Watch and ensure team members vocally participate in discussions and exercises in approximately equal portions. Individually coach any employees who tend to dominate the group's time and encourage participation from those who defer and hold back.

- Encourage free thinking and unfiltered sharing during creative discussions. For example, when brainstorming, establish a ground rule that "There are no bad ideas during brainstorming." This mantra lessens some people's tendency to evaluate and shoot down their own ideas before sharing them, for fear of embarrassment.

While history books and documentaries often give Sergeant Culin most of the credit for the Rhino tank innovation, several moments in this story give evidence of the value the wider American Army placed on adaptability. Culin's idea was initially met with laughter. Whether the laughter was purely in good humor or contained any derision is unknown. What is certain is that Sergeant Culin, a noncommissioned officer (NCO) surrounded by higher-ranking superiors, felt sufficiently safe to suggest an idea that was novel if not downright wacky.

"In no other army in the world would the initial idea of a mere NCO be listened to, then proved and embraced so emphatically," wrote one D-Day military historian. "The US Army was truly a people's army of civilian conscripts, not constrained by regimental tradition, and that gave it a freedom to innovate in a rapidly evolving world."[46] Subsequently, Culin's squadron leader Captain Depew possessed sufficiently flexible thinking and the sense of personal security to order an experimental test without permission from a higher echelon. Finally, once the idea proved effective, senior Army leaders celebrated the ingenuity, issuing commendations to Culin and eight additional servicemen.

Promote Cross-Functional Collaboration

Innovation and adaptation are fueled by bringing together people with diverse perspectives and experiences. When leaders combine individuals or teams drawn from different areas and functions within the greater organization, they accelerate not only learning, but also identifying change opportunities and implementing desirable innovations. To promote cross-functional collaboration within your team or company, consider taking the following steps:

- Identify an issue, need, or objective that you want a cross-functional team to address. Define the desired outcomes.
- Populate the group with individuals or teams known to have diverse experiences, perspectives, and responsibilities.
- At the start, conduct exercises to help people get to know each other. Identify and communicate the organization's greater goals, and explain how each person, team, or department supports these objectives.
- Utilize tools that encourage collaboration, such as shared workspaces, online messaging and communication platforms, and project management applications.

The hedgerow struggles spontaneously birthed multiple cross-functional teams within the US Army, particularly across infantry, tank, and engineering units. The hostile and unforgiving bocage demanded that field commanders get their combined arms teams working closely and effectively. Leaders like Lieutenant Colonels Ploger from the infantry and Fries from the tank corps pooled together their teams to evaluate the specific challenges, brainstorm solutions, and test and improve upon ideas.

Their story exemplifies what was happening at the grassroots level across Normandy in the summer of 1944. As various battalions, regiments, and divisions independently devised new equipment and tactics to restore combat effectiveness in the bocage, senior American leaders such as Bradley and Gerow organized larger forums to implement the new ideas across the entire US Army in Normandy.

Leadership Exercises

The following exercises revisit and expand on the historical events associated with "Those Damned Hedgerows," and present leadership learning opportunities for individuals and teams to explore.

Exercise #1

After exiting the beaches, the Allied forces, particularly the Americans, entered an unexpected terrain that stalled their advance. With their senior commanders caught unaware and unprepared, mid-level American leaders from across the US Army organized and led grassroots efforts to innovate new equipment and tactics to adapt to the bocage. After reviewing the case study, consider the following questions:

- What was most interesting or surprising within this case study?
- What potential lessons does the case study offer our team or organization?
- How well do we embrace innovation within our team or organization?

Exercise #2

Allied planning for D-Day's initial amphibious and airborne assault was all-consuming. An Allied report written a year before D-Day instructed that "the landing-assault against the German-held coasts of Western Europe constitutes an operation of combined arms without parallel in military history. . . . From the military standpoint, the operation is so difficult and so important that every single preparatory step which facilitates it in any way must be taken."[47] Consequently, Allied leaders gave little consideration to what came next after the beaches and failed to anticipate that the bocage presented almost as much of a threat to their objectives.

- How do effective business leaders balance focusing on today's issues and challenges while not ignoring or overlooking oncoming changes?
- What are some of the ways our operating environment and external landscape may change over the next several years? What are some steps we can take to prepare for and leverage these potential changes?
- Currently, what is our most important strategic goal or project? Once that goal or project has been achieved, what comes next?

Exercise #3

Sergeant Culin felt sufficiently psychologically safe to propose his unconventional idea of installing metal teeth on the front of a tank to cut through hedgerows. A McKinsey & Company study found that psychological safety is essential to create "an agile organizational structure that empowers teams to tackle problems quickly by operating outside of bureaucratic or siloed structures."[48] Yet the same study concluded that "only a handful of business leaders often demonstrate the positive behaviors that can instill this climate."

- How can leaders foster a psychologically safe environment? How psychologically safe is our work environment?
- Do we actively foster conversational turn-taking during discussions, meetings, brainstorming exercises, etc.?
- How can socially sensitive leaders create inclusive environments? Do we readily pick up on nonverbal cues to understand other people's emotions, especially if a team member feels uncomfortable or excluded?

Exercise #4

US Army offensive tactics relied on tanks and infantry effectively working together in combined arms attacks. However, during June and much of July, combat in the bocage revealed that American infantry leaders regularly did not know how to work alongside tanks, and tank commanders did not understand how to best support infantry. An Army report written before the invasion stipulated that "the development of operational procedures and techniques between the infantry and close support tanks must not be left until the arrival in the combat zone," but that is exactly what happened.[49]

- Describe the key actions and behaviors of individuals or teams that excel at cross-functional cooperation.
- How well do our different teams or departments work together? Are there any places where our teams could better support one another?
- Currently, what are our best opportunities to increase internal cooperation and efficiency?

Exercise #5

During Operation Overlord, US Army train-the-trainer pamphlets called "Army Talks" provided combat leaders with the latest battlefield learnings and offered tips on leading group discussions on the subject matter. The pamphlets featured fictionalized conversations between soldiers to make the content approachable and actionable. The Army Talks series instructed unit leaders that group discussions "be held in all units within this command, using one hour of training time each week . . . Remember, Army Talks are for discussion."

- Do our leaders and managers deliver consistent messages to our teams and employees?
- What internal communication resources do we have for our team or company? Are we utilizing them as effectively as we can?
- Do we disseminate to employees and associates regular updates such as company performance, recent wins or losses, external market news, etc.?
- Are there any topics that we are not sufficiently discussing at this time?

Exercise #6

As the American Army realized it was ill prepared to operate in the bocage, many mid-level leaders independently went to work devising technical and tactical solutions, a testament to the value placed on adaptability within the Army's culture.

- Describe the key actions and behaviors of leaders and organizations that embrace change and comfortably adapt to new conditions.
- Do we place emphasis on adaptability as a desired cultural value?
- Are creativity and innovation routinely praised within our organization?

Epilogue

By the second half of July, the Americans had penetrated sufficiently deep into Normandy that in many places more bocage countryside lay behind them than in front of them. Additionally, their equipment modifications and tactical changes developed in response to the hedgerows were coming online. Meanwhile, Germany had suffered heavy and irreparable losses since D-Day; and although the Germans' battlefield ferocity had not waned, the size and strength of their forces in Normandy had. With the lion's share of German armored divisions still locked in combat with British and Canadian units in eastern Normandy, the conditions finally aligned to set up an American breakthrough in the west.

On July 25 near the Norman town of Saint-Lô, the US launched Operation Cobra, a massive combined arms attack involving eight infantry divisions and three armored divisions fielding 2,500 tanks and armored fighting vehicles—many equipped with Rhino horns or similar anti-hedgerow devices. After a slow start marred by poor weather and one of the most heart-rending friendly-fire incidents in the war, the American assault ultimately crashed through German lines. More than 100,000 American troops poured through a five-mile gap into the Norman countryside, finally free of the bocage.

For You History Buffs: Friendly Fire During Operation Cobra

Operation Cobra's battle plan opened with thousands of American bombers carpet-bombing German lines immediately in front of the US forces. On July 24 the scheduled start was postponed due to poor weather, but some bombers mistakenly dropped their ordnance on American positions, killing and wounding about 150 US personnel. The next day the weather improved, and Cobra finally kicked off, but continued American miscommunications led to a second and larger errant bombing, this time killing 111 US soldiers and wounding almost 500 more. The American reporter Ernie Pyle was caught in the friendly fire and called it the most horrible experience of his life.

A rout of German forces in Normandy seemed at hand, and senior Allied leaders quietly discussed the potential for Germany's collapse and defeat before Christmas. Unfortunately, those hopes proved overly optimistic, and the Battle of Normandy and D-Day story was far from over.

After the war, for GIs who fought in Normandy in the summer of 1944 the word "hedgerow" forever conjured up painful memories. In the 359th Infantry Regiment's postwar history, a veteran composed:

> Chaotic beaches and shattered villages offer
> first impressions, but very soon the hedgerows
> not only alter our impressions but our lives.
> We fight for hedgerows;
> we live in hedgerows;
> we sleep in hedgerows.[50]

‖‖

Failure at Falaise

DELEGATING AUTHORITY

"True delegating means giving up what we'd like to hold on to—the authority—and holding on to what we'd like to give up—the responsibility."
—Dr. Peter Kuriloff, University of Pennsylvania

"This is an opportunity that comes to a commander not more than once in a century. We're about to destroy an entire hostile army."
—US General Omar Bradley, commander of all American ground forces in Operation Overlord

By mid-August 1944, about ten weeks after D-Day, Allied armies managed to nearly encircle the bulk of Germany's remaining forces in Normandy, surrounding them in a "pocket" with the open end facing east near the French town of Falaise. Closing the pocket and entrapping the Germans would have produced the kind of total and decisive victory that most generals can only dream about. However, Allied leaders struggled to complete the encirclement before a nucleus of Germans escaped, leaving historians to debate if the primary headline for the events at Falaise should be that of a partial Allied victory or rather a regrettable missed opportunity.

This case study explores the importance of effective delegation of authority, without abdication of responsibility. Delegation is a critical leadership activity that requires skillfully balancing authority and responsibility between leaders and their team members. Leaders who delegate too little weaken leverage and slow individual and organizational growth. Leaders who delegate too much cross over into abdication, undermining accountability and usually leading to inferior results.

The case study centers on Allied Supreme Commander General Dwight Eisenhower's decisions and actions during the Falaise Pocket episode. With the potential in hand to encircle and destroy the remaining German forces in Normandy and dramatically shorten the war, Eisenhower's passive, hands-off leadership style contributed to the poorly coordinated Allied effort to complete the encirclement.

As you read, keep in mind the following leadership questions:

- When does delegation cross over into abdication?

- What are the signs that a business leader may be too hands-off? What are the risks and consequences should this occur?

- What steps can team leaders take to ensure everybody on the team cares about the group's objectives rather than just focusing on their individual roles or contributions?

The Case Study: Failure at Falaise
From D-Day to Late July 1944

After the Allies' initial success landing on the Normandy beaches on D-Day on June 6, their offensive crawled forward. Daily progress was often measured in yards and meters rather than miles and kilometers. In some places the Allies had advanced only a few miles from the coast. The ground gained came at a terrible cost—the Allies suffering tens of thousands of casualties due to determined and often fanatical German opposition.

On the Allied right flank (the western end of the invasion area), American troops hacked through the jungle-like hedgerows called *bocage*[1] and by late June captured the port of Cherbourg, critical to expanding the Allies' flow of supplies. However, before surrendering Cherbourg, the Germans so thoroughly destroyed the port facilities that no significant Allied shipping would unload there for months.

On the Allied left flank (the eastern end of the invasion area), British and Canadian forces, locked in combat with most of the German panzer units in Normandy,[2] captured the important crossroads town of Caen. Located less than ten miles from the invasion beaches, Caen was supposed to have been taken on D-Day. Media coverage in the Allies' home nations questioned the invasion's progress and potential outcome, with the word "stalemate" creeping into the conversation.

The Germans too had suffered massive losses in men and equipment since D-Day. Unlike the Allies, Germany's losses were irreplaceable. German casualties in Normandy included top commander Field Marshal Gerhardt von Rundstedt, who was fired, and the famous Field Marshal Erwin Rommel, wounded in an air attack.

Yet, the grinding war of attrition bought time for Germany. Dictator Adolf Hitler needed this time to commence his vengeance weapon attacks on England, featuring the V-1, the world's first cruise missile, and the V-2, the world's first ballistic missile. Hitler believed terrorizing the English civilian population would finally force Britain to negotiate a peace. With the vengeance weapons raining down on Britain's cities, the Allied military commanders in Normandy fell under added pressure to break out of their confined beachhead, advance toward Paris, and wipe out the German missile launch sites.[3]

Toward the end of July, the long-sought breakout finally occurred. After a ferocious one-week battle to capture the French town of Saint-Lô, American forces staged a massive attack called Operation Cobra. In a highly unorthodox tactic, more than 1,500 strategic bombers carpet-bombed a concentrated area immediately ahead of the American lines. Despite causing hundreds of friendly-fire casualties among American troops, the bombing and the Americans' overwhelming numerical advantage in troops and tanks finally ruptured German defensive lines. Cobra proved to be a turning point in the Normandy battle. Within days, more than 100,000 American combat troops rushed through a five-mile-wide gap (about eight kilometers) in German defenses near the French town of Avranches, the gateway from Normandy to Brittany. Anxious talk of a stalemate faded as American forces surged into the largely undefended French countryside, racing to take more territory and pursue an enemy seemingly on the ropes.

The breakout left US Army General Dwight Eisenhower—Ike—practically giddy. Ike held absolute command and responsibility for all Allied forces within Overlord, accountable for the destruction of Germany's armed forces in Normandy. However, the D-Day combined airborne-amphibious assault was too complex for one person to oversee while simultaneously commanding the ground armies. So, until the Allies were firmly established in France, Ike delegated leadership of the multinational ground armies to British Army General[4] Bernard "Monty" Montgomery. This temporary leadership arrangement put Monty in the interim role of ground forces commander-in-chief while he also commanded the British and Canadian armies operating in eastern Normandy.

Meanwhile, in western Normandy, US Army General Omar Bradley commanded the American Army forces and thus reported to Monty for as long as Monty was acting ground commander-in-chief. But once Ike took back from Monty the overall leadership of the Allied ground armies, then both Bradley and Monty would report directly to Ike and become peers.

With tens of thousands of American troops disembarking in Normandy every day and the breakout near the town of Avranches open, Bradley needed to expand the size of the US Army leadership team in Normandy. Therefore, as per the pre-invasion plan, Bradley pulled General George Patton off the bench to lead the newly activated US Third Army.[5]

August 2

Adolf Hitler ordered his new overall commander in the west, Field Marshal Gunter von Kluge, to counterattack the Allies and plug the recent American breakout. Hitler's plan, called Operation *Lüttich,* would send nine German panzer divisions westward toward the French village of Mortain with the goal of cutting the supply lines of American forces surging through the Avranches gap. Hitler warned Kluge that "the decision in the Battle of France depends on the success of the attack," and the operation represented "a unique opportunity, which will never return, to drive into an extremely exposed enemy area and thereby to change the situation completely."[6]

Kluge, whose nickname was Clever Hans, was smart enough to know Operation Lüttich could not work.[7] But Hitler was in no mood to listen to Kluge or any of his generals, for two weeks earlier an assassination attempt on his life by a group of German officers had driven Hitler's distrust in his military commanders to a twisted intensity. Hitler told Kluge to follow orders and attack "recklessly to the sea, regardless of the risk."[8] But Kluge had no reserve forces to launch Operation Lüttich and needed several days to withdraw panzer units engaged elsewhere and reposition them to implement Hitler's gamble.

For You History Buffs: Assassination Attempt on Hitler

On July 20, 1944, a group of German officers attempted to assassinate Hitler by placing a briefcase bomb under a large conference table at the dictator's feet during a staff meeting. The bomb exploded, killing and wounding several men, but Hitler improbably survived because before the bomb exploded, a German officer not involved in the plot unwittingly moved the briefcase with his foot, pushing it behind the table's bulky leg and shielding Hitler from the blast.

After the attempt on his life, Hitler ordered the conspirators be identified and prosecuted. The search grew into a witch hunt in which nearly five thousand persons were executed. The Nazis called the failed assassination attempt the July 20th Plot, but today it is more commonly known by the conspirators' code name, Operation Valkyrie.

August 6

Ike, Monty, and Bradley received secret Ultra intelligence alerting them of the brewing German counterattack. Reviewing a map, Bradley confidently saw that the German offensive created an opportunity rather than a threat. Strong American forces were already located near Mortain, the target of the Germans' attack. Additionally, a German offensive westward toward Mortain and Avranches would expose the Germans to themselves being counterattacked by the newly activated forces under Patton.

For You History Buffs: Ultra

By this point in the war, the Allied top-secret intelligence operation called Ultra was routinely intercepting and decoding German military radio messages. Allied commanders often read German communications only a few hours after the Germans who were the intended recipients. The existence of Ultra and its impact on the battle was not disclosed until the 1970s. Histories of Normandy and memoirs from various Allied commanders published prior to then omit Ultra and its importance to the campaign.

August 7

Field Marshal Kluge launched Operation Lüttich at midnight to maximize surprise and avoid Allied aircraft. Kluge remained convinced Hitler's plan could not succeed, and wrote in his diary, "I am aware, that a failure of this attack will lead to a complete collapse of the entire Normandy front, but the order is so unequivocal that it must be carried out unconditionally."[9] Kluge's panzers advanced in the dark and fog toward Mortain, a small town sometimes called the Norman Switzerland for its wooded inclines and narrow roads. The attack was weaker than Hitler had wanted; Kluge kicked off with only half the instructed number of panzer units due to fuel shortages and difficulties extracting forces away from other combat areas.

Positioned in the path of the German attack were more than a half-dozen American Army divisions, with the US 30th Infantry Division in line to receive the main blow. The 30th had come ashore at Omaha Beach five days after D-Day, and two months of combat had hardened the division into steady veterans. Fighting near and around Mortain was intense, and by noon German tanks charged past the town and penetrated six miles into American lines. They would get no further. Afternoon sunlight burned off the fog and exposed the German forces to relentless British and American air attacks. American units, initially overrun by the Germans, dug in and held their ground.

For You History Buffs: The 30th Infantry Division at Mortain

In one part of the battle at Mortain, approximately 700 American troops from the 30th Infantry Division, surrounded on a hill numbered 314 reflecting its height in meters, held off for five days against an entire German SS Panzer Division. From the hilltop, US troops repeatedly ordered artillery strikes on Germans climbing toward them, at one point radioing, "Enemy N, S, E, W."

Their defense helped halt the German advance toward Avranches. More than half of the soldiers on Hill 314 were either killed or wounded

continued

before the Germans quit. The combat around Mortain is a largely unknown story, and until recently unrecognized. It was not until March of 2020 that the 30th Infantry Division received a Presidential Unit Citation for its heroic stand at Mortain.

Meanwhile to the northeast, British General Montgomery sought a breakout for his British and Canadian units pushing past the newly captured French town of Caen. However, unlike the rapidly growing American forces in Normandy, British manpower reserves were exhausted by this stage in the war. Short of troops, Monty tapped inexperienced Canadian and Polish soldiers under Canadian General Harry Crerar to lead an attack toward the French town of Falaise.[10] But Monty had concerns about Crerar, recently having written, "I have grave fears that Harry Crerar will not be too good; however I am keeping him out of the party as long as I can."[11] The attack was optimistically christened Operation Totalize.

August 8 through 10

The Allies laid a trap for the German armies in Normandy.

After the American breakout at Avranches, most of Patton's forces surged to the south and subsequently turned to the east. Consequently, the combined Allied forces in Normandy resembled a giant letter *C* with the opening facing east, toward Paris. The ill-advised German counterattack toward Mortain in effect pushed the Germans into the open mouth of the *C*. One of the most important episodes in the war resembled on a map the popular video game character Pac-Man, as the Allied armies appeared positioned to munch and swallow the Germans rushing headlong into their mouth. (See the following Falaise Pocket map.)

Allied commanders recognized the situation and immediately reacted. On August 8, Ike and Bradley were together at Bradley's headquarters. Sensing the developing opportunity, Bradley called his temporary boss Monty to quickly formulate a plan. Monty's combined British, Canadian, and Polish units would continue their current attack southward toward Falaise, thereby forming Pac-Man's "Upper Jaw." After taking Falaise, Monty's forces would proceed to the Norman town of Argentan. Bradley's American forces, including most of Patton's Third Army, formed the "Lower Jaw" and would attack northward toward Argentan. At Argentan, the two armies were to meet and snap the Pac-Man's jaws shut in what's known in military parlance as a "pincer" move or double-envelopment. The objective was to encircle and entrap twenty German divisions, representing most of the remaining German forces in Normandy. Ike, monitoring the call between Bradley and Monty, approved the plan.

Ike, Monty, Bradley, and Patton appreciated the magnitude of the opportunity before them. Success would not only victoriously conclude the Battle of Normandy—it could hasten the end of World War II in Europe. (Eisenhower wrote shortly after the war, "The prospects of inflicting a decisive and annihilating defeat upon the [German] Seventh Army and Panzer Group West had been so good that I had no hesitation in making my decision. If their units could be shattered in Normandy, then I knew that there was no further German force in France capable of stopping us.")[12]

Bradley, eager to taste victory, told a visitor, "This is an opportunity that comes to a commander not more than once in a century. We're about to destroy an entire hostile army."[13] Patton wrote his wife that "the enemy is finished. . . . We may end this war in ten days."[14] Monty urged his forces to advance on Falaise. "This is a first priority," he urged, "and it should be done quickly."[15]

With the German attack blunted near Mortain, Germany's Kluge also detected the possibility that his forces could be encircled. He appealed to Hitler to let him extricate German forces from the potential pocket (the jaws of the Pac-Man). Instead, Hitler egotistically and foolishly instructed Kluge to keep attacking westward, pushing the German divisions even deeper into potential encirclement and playing into the Allies' hands. Kluge bitterly noted his army was "blissfully planning an attack while far behind it an enemy is busily forming a noose with which to strangle it."[16]

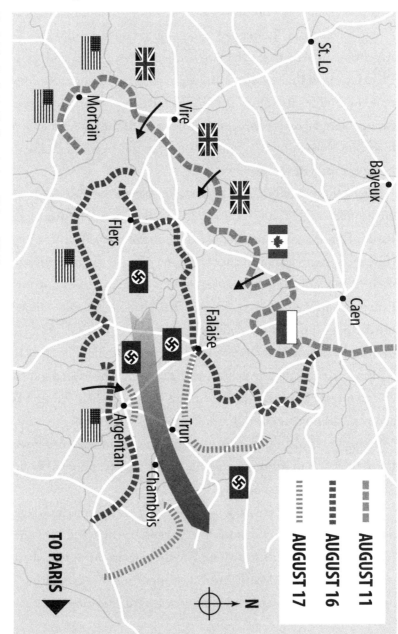

The Falaise Pocket battle lines during mid-August 1944.

August 9 through 12

The Upper Jaw

Operation Totalize, aimed at Falaise, initially gained ground, but Crerar's Canadian and Polish troops encountered strong German defenses, leading to some of the most ferocious combat of the campaign. The inexperienced Canadians' attack faltered, despite greatly outnumbering the German forces, including a ten-to-one advantage in tanks. Monty's forces remained about twenty-five miles (forty kilometers) north of Argentan, the location selected for the two jaws to come together.

The Lower Jaw

While a portion of American forces held against German attacks in the western end of the pocket near Mortain, Patton's forces advanced north against weak German opposition. They reached the outskirts of Argentan late in the evening on August 12. One half of the giant mouth was in proper position.

Inside the Pocket

Kluge's worst fears were confirmed: The Allies were attempting to encircle his army. The German field marshal tried in vain to convince Hitler to call off the attack westward toward Avranches because the Germans were only pushing themselves further into the pocket (into Pac-Man's mouth). A querulous Hitler finally agreed, but demanded that Kluge's depleted forces reverse and attack in the other direction toward Argentan.

August 12 through 14

The Lower Jaw

On August 12, Patton and the bulk of his Third Army sat idle at Argentan, waiting for Monty's forces to arrive from the north and close the pocket shut. That evening, seeing that Monty was still twenty-five miles (about forty kilometers) away and making slow progress, the ever restless Patton sent some of his reconnaissance units north to investigate closing the pocket on his own. Patton called his boss Bradley to relay this decision, perhaps expecting Bradley to applaud the initiative. Demonstrating Patton's trademark lack of tact, he rhetorically asked Bradley, "Shall we continue and drive the British into the sea for another Dunkirk?"[17]

Exactly what happened from here and over the next twenty-four hours is still intensely discussed and debated by historians, but what is clear is that Bradley sharply commanded Patton to remain at Argentan and wait for Monty, a moment historians refer to as "Bradley's halt order."

Bradley gave a stunned Patton several reasons for staying put. Most important, Bradley believed Patton's forces near Argentan were not strong enough to close the pocket and withstand the inevitable horde of Germans attempting to escape. After the war Bradley wrote, "Although Patton might have spun a line across the narrow neck, I doubted his ability to hold it. Nineteen German divisions were now stampeding to escape the trap. Meanwhile, with four divisions George [Patton] was already blocking three principal escape routes. . . . The enemy could not only have broken through, but he might have trampled Patton's position in the onrush. I much preferred a solid shoulder at Argentan to the possibility of a broken neck at Falaise."[18]

After Bradley's halt order, throughout the night and into the next morning the four Allied generals (Ike, Monty, Bradley, and Patton) and their staff officers held a flurry of calls regarding the situation. Their contemporary accounts differed, and not every conversation or communication was documented. But at some point, Patton called Bradley's headquarters again to plead for permission to move north toward Falaise. Bradley was unavailable, on his way to meet in person with Eisenhower. Bradley's chief of staff took Patton's call and said he would get back to Patton later.

Meanwhile, another member of Bradley's staff called Monty's head-quarters[19] to ask permission to shift northward the agreed-upon meeting point between the two armies from Argentan to Falaise, which would have given Patton a green light to proceed north. Monty's staff denied the request, agreeing with Bradley. Monty affirmed that Patton must stay at Argentan and remained confident that his Canadian and Polish forces would soon shut the Upper Jaw as planned.

By mid-morning the next day, Bradley arrived at Eisenhower's headquarters. Their conversation was not documented, but they discussed the "Falaise Pocket" situation. After Ike and Bradley conferred, Bradley's chief of staff returned Patton's calls and once again ordered that Patton's forces must remain at Argentan. An angry and frustrated Patton ordered his reconnaissance forces, which by that point had reached within six miles (ten kilometers) of Falaise, to pull back. An embittered Patton recorded in his diary, "I am sure that this halt is a great mistake, and I am certain the British will not close on Falaise."[20]

August 14

The Upper Jaw

After several days of preparations, Monty ordered another major attack southward toward Falaise and beyond it Argentan. Called Operation Tractable, it too ran into problems. An Allied preparatory air bombardment caused several hundred friendly-fire casualties.[21] Dust stirred up by the bombing mixed with a pre-attack smoke screen and caused attacking units to lose their sense of direction. To make matters worse, a Canadian divisional officer accidently drove into German lines and was killed. From his car the Germans recovered a copy of the Operation Tractable battle plan and positioned their defenses appropriately. Over the next day the battered but determined Canadians and Poles slowly advanced in heavy fighting to within one mile of Falaise. However, the gap between them and the Americans remained about fifteen miles (twenty-four kilometers) wide.

The Lower Jaw

At this point, six days had passed since the Allies first launched their plan to encircle the German armies, but now Allied leaders began to wonder how many Germans might still be trapped in the pocket. Top-secret Ultra decoded messages alerted the Allies that some German units were ordered to reverse and attack to the east, moving toward the mouth of the pocket. That evening, a key aide to Bradley lamented in his journal that "it is clear now that our chance to close the German army between Falaise and Argentan has vanished for reasons both clear and difficult to conceive."[22]

Patton, whom a wartime reporter once described as "a warring, roaring comet," was frantic to get his five divisions sitting idle at Argentan to attack something.[23, 24] The once-in-a-century opportunity seemed to be slipping away. Watching Monty's forces unable to make speedy progress to close the pocket, Patton called Bradley and proposed a new plan. If Bradley would not let him attack northward to meet Monty, then Patton proposed splitting his forces, leaving three divisions at Argentan and sending the other two roaring eastward toward the Seine River and Paris. Once at the Seine River, Patton believed the Allies could attempt a new effort to encircle the German armies remaining in Normandy; most of the bridges over the Seine River had been destroyed by Allied air attack, leaving the Germans trapped against the river's west bank. Patton's new plan in effect extended the lower jaw to the east in the hopes of restoring an opportunity to swallow the German armies. Patton wrote privately, "It is really a great plan, wholly my own, and I made Bradley think he thought of it. Oh, what a tangled web we weave when first we practice to deceive."[25]

Bradley, also frustrated that the pocket remained open, agreed to Patton's request. In his written orders issued the next day, Bradley stated, "Due to the delay in closing the gap between Argentan and Falaise, it is believed that many of the German divisions which were in the pocket have now escaped. . . . In order to take advantage of the confusion existing, the 3rd Army will now initiate a movement toward the east."[26] Bradley did not consult with or notify Montgomery that he had changed the battle plan.

August 15

Allied forces launched Operation Dragoon, an amphibious invasion in southern France, a long-planned supplement to the invasion of Normandy. Operation Dragoon encountered little opposition and the German hold over all of France immediately was at risk of collapsing. German Field Marshal Kluge, after meeting with one of his commanders early that morning, got into his car and disappeared for the day, out of communication until late that evening. Upon returning, he explained his car had been attacked by Allied aircraft and he spent the day huddled in a ditch. Hitler, who saw enemies and traitors everywhere, suspected Kluge snuck away to secretly negotiate a surrender to the Allies.

For You History Buffs: Operation Dragoon— The Second Invasion of France

Operation Dragoon, the Allied invasion at Provence in southern France, was originally intended to occur simultaneous to Operation Overlord in Normandy. However, insufficient shipping forced the Allies to delay this second attack. Dragoon was one of the most contentious disagreements of the war between the English, who opposed the attack, and the Americans, who ultimately insisted on it.

At one point, British General Alan Brooke, chief of the Imperial General Staff, wrote to his American counterparts: "If you insist on being damned fools, sooner than falling out with you, which would be fatal, we shall be damned fools with you."[27]

The operation had originally been code-named Anvil, but Churchill changed the name to Dragoon, allegedly to reflect the feeling he and the British had been unwillingly "dragooned" into it by the Americans.

By this time the Falaise Pocket was about forty miles (sixty-five kilometers) long and up to fifteen miles (twenty-four kilometers) wide. Despite the Allied senior leaders' assumptions that a large portion of Germans must have escaped from the pocket, in fact more than 100,000 troops remained inside under constant artillery fire and air attack. If the Allies could finally complete the encirclement, they would have captured and defeated the bulk of the German armies remaining in Normandy.

On the Allied side, Monty and Bradley convened at midday to discuss the military situation. Crerar's Canadian and Polish forces continued to doggedly advance toward Falaise while taking severe casualties. At this meeting, Monty finally learned that forty-eight hours earlier Bradley had permitted Patton to divide his forces at Argentan and send two divisions charging to the east.

August 16 through 18

The Upper Jaw

Crerar's forces entered Falaise on August 16.[28] The town had been bombed and shelled so completely that after the battle the Allies brought in bulldozers to carve new streets through the rubble.[29] Falaise was finally in Allied hands, but the pocket remained open with American units sitting at Argentan about fifteen miles (twenty-five kilometers) to the south. With German forces desperately fighting against encirclement, the Canadian and Polish units pressed toward the French villages of Trun and Chambois, located in between Falaise and Argentan, to continue their battle to close the pocket.

The Lower Jaw

Late on August 16, Monty called Bradley and, reversing his previous decision, asked that US forces advance northward toward Chambois to link up with the Canadian and Polish troops and finally close the pocket. Bradley agreed and the American forces that were halted at Argentan finally attacked northward, four days after Patton's initial attempt. In the east, Patton's rapidly advancing divisions captured several French towns including Orleans, only seventy-five miles (120 kilometers) from Paris. Unfortunately for Patton, that evening Bradley halted Patton's advance for a second time out of concern that Patton's forces were overextended. Patton fumed in a letter to his wife about Bradley's prudence. "If I were on my own," he wrote her, "I would take much bigger chances than I am now permitted to take."[30]

Inside the Pocket

With German forces running low on fuel and ammunition, and under constant artillery and air bombardment, Hitler finally authorized Kluge's repeated requests to completely retreat to the east out of the Falaise Pocket, more than a week after the first threat of encirclement. A day later, Kluge was relieved of command.[31] Ordered to return to Germany to likely face charges or execution on suspicion that he somehow participated in the recent failed assassination attempt on Hitler's life, Kluge instead drove to an empty field, sat against a tree, and committed suicide by swallowing a potassium cyanide capsule.

The Allied Commanders

Meanwhile, Allied commanders demonstrated remarkably inconsistent assessments of the status of the Falaise Pocket. Late in the evening on August 17, Monty inaccurately wrote to the British Imperial Staff that "the gap has now been closed," and also to British Prime Minister Winston Churchill that "the enemy cannot escape us."[32] Simultaneously, Ike wired his bosses in Washington that "due to the extraordinary measures taken by the enemy north of Falaise [Monty's operational area] and which have taken us so long to puncture, it is possible that our total bag of prisoners will not be so great as I first anticipated."[33] As Monty and Ike sent these cables, the gap between the Upper and Lower Jaw was still approximately ten miles (fifteen kilometers) wide.

August 19 through 21

During the afternoon of August 19, Monty and Bradley met to discuss future operations beyond the Seine River. Their attention had shifted east toward Paris and Germany, and they did not discuss the ferocious battle that still raged around the mouth of the pocket near the small villages of Chambois, Trun, and Saint-Lambert.

At 7:20 p.m. on August 19, a US rifle company from the 90th Infantry Division shook hands with Polish soldiers from the 10th Dragoons in the middle of the burning village of Chambois. The encirclement was complete and the pocket closed. However, the seal remained porous, for too few Allied troops occupied the mouth of the Falaise Pocket. Combat continued for two additional days in a desperate every-man-for-himself melee, some of the most vicious and violent fighting during the Normandy campaign, before the last German troops were either killed or captured. Sealing the pocket in many ways represented the closing act of Operation Overlord, launched seventy-six days earlier on June 6, D-Day.

For You History Buffs: Polish Heroics on Hill 262

On Mount Ormel near the French village of Coudehard, also referred to as Hill 262 due to its height in meters on Allied wartime maps, about 1,500 Polish troops withstood two days of savage German attacks while radioing in artillery strikes on the retreating Germans. The Polish forces suffered over 350 killed and wounded but inflicted several thousand German casualties and severely disrupted the Germans' retreat from the pocket. Today, a memorial occupies the summit of Mount Ormel and provides visitors with a commanding view of the Falaise Pocket below.

On August 21, Monty published a message to all Allied troops in Normandy, claiming that "the German armies in north-west France have suffered a decisive defeat; the destruction of enemy personnel and equipment in and about the so called 'Normandy pocket' has been terrific. . . . The victory has been definite, complete, and decisive. . . . The end of the war is in sight."[34]

Montgomery's proclamation was both inaccurate and premature. While fifty thousand Germans were captured inside the pocket and about ten thousand killed, many tens of thousands managed to escape. Those who got away would soon form the core of a reconstituted Nazi German army in western Europe that fanatically fought on, prolonging the war for eight more months at the cost of millions of additional lives.

Leadership Insights

Finger-pointing and second-guessing about the Falaise Pocket began even before the last German soldier slipped through the Allies' fingers. The debate continues to this day, as historians wrestle with questions such as—

- Should Bradley have issued the halt order, stopping Patton's advance?
- Who holds more blame—Bradley for halting Patton at Argentan, or Montgomery for not agreeing sooner to move northward the jaws' meeting point from Argentan to Falaise?
- Should Montgomery have used the inexperienced Canadians and Polish troops in the crucial attacks toward Falaise?

For business leaders, the Falaise Pocket story creates a different set of questions, perhaps most important: Why and how did the Allied leadership team fail to capitalize on the once-in-a-century opportunity and secure a complete victory?

Most military historians agree that the key reason the pocket remained open too long was the slow rate of advance by Monty's inexperienced Canadian and Polish units, despite having an overwhelming advantage in tanks and complete command of the sky. Inadequate performance from inexperienced units was not unusual in Normandy—several green American and British units displayed similar struggles during the Overlord campaign.[35] Plus, the Canadian and Polish troops' struggles could not have surprised Monty—he had supervised their pre-invasion training in

England. Monty also knew their commander Crerar's limitations. Early in the Normandy battle, Monty had written a curt report about Crerar, stating, "I fear [Crerar] thinks he is a great soldier, and he was determined to show it the moment he took over command at 1200 on 23 July. He made his first mistake at 1205 hours and his second after lunch."[36]

Raw troops and lackluster generals may operationally explain why the Allies failed to quickly close the pocket, but it does not answer the leadership questions. For that, one needs to look at the decisions and actions of Monty, Bradley, and Eisenhower.

General Montgomery's Failures

Monty put the Canadians and Polish troops in the lead of the attack toward Falaise, bowing to his nation's dwindling manpower reserves. Yet why did Montgomery keep Crerar's forces in the lead despite their repeated inability to make progress toward the potential war-winning objective of closing the pocket? Monty's well-documented ego and narcissistic personality certainly played a role.[37] Elaborate, carefully planned operations like Totalize and Tractable were his specialty, and Monty had never lost a battle that he commanded (a fact he would share in conversations). Removing the Canadians and Poles would have come too close to admitting he had made a mistake in assigning them to the attack.

On top of his personal pride, national hubris likely played a role too. Monty may have sought to avoid tarnishing British honor by allowing the Americans to close the pocket when his British-led forces could not.

General Bradley's Failures

While Monty's personality shortcomings played a part in the leadership breakdown, business leaders and managers must expand the lens to include Bradley's conduct too. Bradley reported to Monty at this stage of the battle, and the two generals regularly communicated through phone calls, messages relayed between aides, and occasional in-person meetings. However, on critical occasions during those mid-August days, these two leaders failed to act as a unified team focused on closing the Falaise Pocket.

The events around Bradley's halt order present a clear example of muddled leadership. Bradley had sound operational reasoning for stopping Patton from continuing north beyond Argentan. But, with Patton's forces sitting idle at the agreed-upon location where the jaws would snap shut, and Montgomery's forces still tens of miles away and making poor progress, Bradley and Monty took no meaningful steps to address the situation and adjust their plan to seal the pocket.

In a postwar memoir, Bradley reflected on that moment and wrote, "If Monty wanted help closing the gap then let him ask us for it."[38] Bradley's churlish comment reflected the deep animosity that developed between Monty and Bradley after the Normandy battle; at the time of the Falaise Pocket events, their relationship was largely intact. However, Bradley's comments revealed that during the Falaise Pocket episode he and Monty were two team members assigned the same objective but not operating from the same page. As soon as Patton's forces reached Argentan, one does not need stars on their shoulders to see that Bradley and Monty could have immediately conferred, reassessed the situation, and adjusted plans and actions as needed. Instead, they continued to independently pursue a joint objective while collectively failing to get the job done.

Another example of Bradley's inadequate leadership occurred shortly after the halt-order incident. Patton, itching to do something other than sit still at Argentan, convinced Bradley to let him send about half of his forces surging to the east toward the Seine River. By agreeing to Patton's request, Bradley reduced the US forces available to close the pocket at Falaise, altering his own plan that he had convinced Monty to approve. Whether or not Bradley's decision was militarily correct, he authorized Patton's maneuver without consulting or promptly notifying Monty, who was both Bradley's commander and partner in the attempted encirclement.

General Eisenhower's Failures

Monty's and Bradleys' fingerprints can be found on the leadership short-comings in the Falaise Pocket story, but business leaders and managers must consider Eisenhower's role too. Ike was the top commander of Allied forces during the Normandy battle. However, at multiple points in this story, Eisenhower remained remarkably detached, abdicating responsibility for a strategic objective that was his alone.

Eisenhower knew that Monty's choice to stick with the Canadian and Polish troops despite their slow progress toward Falaise and Argentan was ruining the opportunity to close the pocket. Writing after the war, Bradley recalled that "if Monty's tactics mystified me, they dismayed Eisenhower even more."[39] But despite being dismayed by Monty's methods, Ike went no further than radioing his subordinate occasional pep talks urging more speed. As one historian noted, "Although Eisenhower was in Normandy much of the time, he took no active role in the affairs leading to and culminating at Falaise. . . . Eisenhower scrupulously refrained from meddling . . . he visited his subordinates, listened to them, encouraged them, but never interfered."[40]

Eisenhower was known as a hands-off leader. He would not have circumvented the military chain of command and directed Monty or any subordinate specifically how to lead their teams. However, many business leaders are familiar with the situation that Ike found himself in—he had delegated to his team an important objective, but the team's performance was on pace to come up short. In that circumstance, when does re-engaging with the team to address a lagging effort rise to the level of meddling? At some point does remaining hands-off in the face of inadequate performance cross over into a leader abdicating responsibility?

Historical records do not contain every conversation or communication between Eisenhower and Montgomery during this period, but there is no indication that Ike initiated a discussion midway through the operation to identify root causes for the failing pace, nor asked Monty to propose corrective actions. Ike failed to maintain sufficient involvement during the situation and consequently surrendered his influence over the outcome.

Hands-Off Leadership

Throughout the war Eisenhower gave his subordinate commanders wide latitude. During Operation Overlord the American and British/Canadian forces largely fought two separate land battles. They landed in Normandy on the same day, but at different beaches many miles apart. After the D-Day landings, the two attacks proceeded inland in different directions and in pursuit of different targets. Monty and Bradley, commanding the two different advances, only broadly coordinated efforts with one another.

However, when the opportunity presented itself to encircle the main body of German units in Normandy, the two Allied teams needed to come together, rapidly and with precision. Instead, they plodded and stumbled, and consequently a sizable number of Germans escaped Falaise. "Large operations of encirclement are extremely difficult to execute," as one military historian has noted, "but the Allies let the chance for an overwhelming victory slip through their fingers. . . . The Germans themselves had foolishly pushed their heads into a noose, and the Allies had been unable to pull the string shut."[41]

Eisenhower held those strings in his hand. Despite seeing that his two teams were not closing the pocket quickly and tightly, he took no significant action. A likely partial explanation was Ike's hesitance to directly confront Monty, with whom Ike struggled to maintain an effective working relationship (as did many others), and out of respect for Monty's near legendary status with the British people.[42]

Eisenhower's permissive leadership style with his subordinates extended beyond Monty and was generally true during the war. Business leaders must ask if Ike could have taken steps without compromising his hands-off style or interfering with his subordinates' prerogatives. Few operating environments are as fluid and unpredictable as a battlefield; would it have been meddling to convene his top two army commanders and periodically reassess their progress toward an objective that might accelerate a rapid end to the war?

Delegation without Abdication

Under the D-Day command structure, Eisenhower had delegated authority of the ground forces to Monty, but leaders cannot delegate away their responsibility—that is abdication and an abandonment of accountability. Ike was responsible for winning the battle, but with a potential war-winning opportunity in front of him, Ike never demanded that his team apply the necessary focus, coordination, and follow-through to achieve the objective, nor did he maintain sufficient oversight regarding their efforts or take meaningful corrective action.

Eisenhower is not usually praised as a military genius. He is universally lauded as the leadership glue who brilliantly held together a challenging and often divisive multinational military coalition.[43] Ike's team stayed together and won the war in western Europe. In that paramount sense, Eisenhower's leadership methods ultimately must be deemed successful. But holding a team together and holding a team on task are not the same thing. At Falaise, Ike's team did not stay on task toward his singularly most important responsibility—defeating the German army. Superior leadership at Falaise may have ended the war sooner, reducing bloodshed and suffering.

Effective delegation fuels company growth. A Gallup survey showed that companies with CEOs who are skilled delegators grow faster and larger than companies with CEOs who are less effective delegators.[44] Delegation requires the balance of assigning authority to others to pursue and accomplish an objective while maintaining oversight and responsibility. Under-delegating stifles individual and team development, creates a culture of micromanagement, and dulls adaptation and responsiveness. Over-delegation dilutes focus and undermines accountability.

To achieve the desired balance, when delegating objectives, leaders and managers must be effective at these eight steps:

1. Clearly communicate the objective(s) and priorities.

2. Share relevant contextual information.

3. Define any important deadlines, considerations, guidelines, or boundaries.

4. Ensure the team has the ability, resources, and decision-making autonomy to accomplish the objectives.

5. Maintain continuous communication and feedback.

6. Regularly monitor their team's progress.

7. Provide assistance if the team's efforts and/or progress is insufficient.

8. Reinsert themselves directly into the situation if the team is in danger of falling short of meeting the stated objectives.

Leadership Exercises

The following exercises revisit and expand on the historical events associated with "Failure at Falaise," and present leadership learning opportunities for individuals and teams to explore.

Exercise #1

In the Falaise Pocket case study, Allied leaders failed to focus and coordinate efforts to complete an encirclement of German forces in Normandy, while Eisenhower maintained only distant oversight and arguably fell short of his responsibilities.

- What was most interesting or surprising within this case study?
- What potential lessons does the case study offer our team or organization?
- Within the eight steps identified previously, where do I or we excel? Where do I or we have potential areas for improvement?

Exercise #2

Once the Allies committed to pursuing an encirclement of the German armies in Normandy, Monty's battle orders and communications to his forces stated their operational goal was to take Falaise. In contrast, at the same time Patton's orders specifically stated, "The purpose of the operation is to surround and destroy the German army west of the Seine."[45]

- How important is communicating consistent objectives within a leadership or management team?
- What are the signs that a team is either well aligned or misaligned?
- When assigning objectives or tasks, how can business leaders verify that their people or teams fully understand the mission or objective and are working from shared priorities?

Exercise #3

After the war, Bradley wrote that "I have often asked myself, if I should not have done Monty's work, and if we should not have closed the gap ourselves."[46]

- Does Bradley's comment suggest anything about his views on teamwork?
- What steps can team leaders take to create a culture where everybody on the team cares about the overall objective rather than just focusing on their individual roles or contributions?

Exercise #4

Between D-Day and the Falaise Pocket episode, Eisenhower issued no direct commands to his two primary ground forces subordinates, Monty and Bradley. Rather, he limited his role largely to approving their recommendations and cheerleading their efforts, even when his subordinates were failing to decisively close the pocket. Yet, one of Eisenhower's closest aides during the war later said, "General Eisenhower, as Supreme Commander of the Allied Expeditionary Force, was responsible for each decision his subordinates made . . . if a subordinate commander fails, it is the Supreme Commander who is at fault for having placed him in a position of command."[47]

- What are the signs that a business leader may be too hands-off? What are the risks and consequences should this occur?
- When an individual or team is struggling to perform, what steps can leaders and managers consider taking? What is the difference between managing and meddling?
- Within our team or company, do we have a culture or tendency to be too hands-off or manage too tightly?

Exercise #5

On August 8, Bradley called Monty and proposed a plan to encircle the German armies and close the trap at Falaise. Eisenhower, already at Bradley's headquarters for another purpose, overheard the discussion and approved the idea, but did not participate in the call. During the crucial mid-August days, these three top commanders did not speak as a group.

- What can happen if some members of a team miss important conversations and discussions? How can leaders minimize gaps in communications?
- With today's technology providing a wide variety of communication methods and resources, are there circumstances when teams still must come together for a live discussion? Does your team or organization have too many or too few group discussions?
- Do you see opportunities for improving communications and discussions within your team(s)?

Exercise #6

Eisenhower strove to maintain a working relationship with the insufferable Monty, but the underlying discord contributed to the leadership shortcomings at Falaise Pocket. Monty was careful to maintain outward professional appearances, but he seethed about Ike in his private communications. On August 14, as the Allies were in the throes of attempts to close the pocket, Monty wrote a member of the British General Staff that Ike's "ignorance as to how to run a war is absolute and complete. . . . One thing I am very firm about, he is never allowed a meeting between me and my Army Commanders and Bradley!"[48]

- All business leaders and managers face personality differences within their teams and organizations. What are the warning signs that personality differences or conflicts are negatively impacting individual, team, or organizational performance?

- When do the needs of the greater team or company outweigh the need to tolerate friction caused by one person or a small group of people?
- How do you promote healthy interpersonal relationships within your team or company? Do you see opportunities for additional improvement?

Epilogue

Despite the Allies' leadership lapses, eventually they closed the Falaise Pocket and achieved an important victory. In their defeat at Falaise, the Germans suffered an estimated 10,000 killed and 50,000 captured and lost about 2,500 pieces of heavy equipment including tanks, vehicles, and artillery. The German armies in and around the pocket had been decimated in the savage fighting. As Eisenhower reported after the war, "The lovely, wooded countryside west of Argentan had become the graveyard of the army which, three months earlier, had confidently waited to smash the Allied invasion on the Normandy beaches."[49] On August 25, four days after the pocket was finally sealed, the Allies took Paris. (General Dietrich von Choltitz, the German military governor of Paris, disobeyed Hitler's orders to destroy the city and instead surrendered Paris to protect it from destruction.) The Battle of Normandy, launched on D-Day, June 6, 1944, had officially concluded.

However, the Allied victory was not complete. The Germans would replace their lost equipment; ironically, August of 1944 marked the peak month of German armaments production. Tens of thousands of German troops escaped entrapment, with historical estimates ranging widely between 20,000 to as many as 200,000 successfully fleeing the pocket. Equally troubling was not how many got away, but who. Most of the senior German field commanders inside the pocket eluded capture. "Five

German corps commanders had been inside the pocket; only one was taken prisoner. Of fifteen German division commanders present, merely three were captured."[50]

The Allies would soon confront these same Germans—and suffer for it. Less than one month after closing the pocket, the Allies attempted an audacious combined airborne and ground attack called Operation Market Garden but were defeated by some of the same German forces that had escaped Normandy. In December of 1944, ten German panzer divisions launched a surprise attack against American lines in what became known as the Battle of the Bulge—nine of those divisions were reconstituted from the veterans of the Falaise Pocket.

For You History Buffs: Operation Market Garden

Operation Market Garden was an Allied attack featuring more than forty thousand paratroopers dropped into German-occupied Netherlands with the objective of simultaneously seizing nine bridges across key rivers, paving the way for Allied ground forces to rapidly advance into northern Germany. The attack was ill-conceived and poorly planned from the start, and ultimately failed.

Market Garden became the subject of Cornelius Ryan's 1974 book *A Bridge Too Far*, and a 1977 epic war movie of the same name. The phrase "a bridge too far" has come to mean an objective that is too ambitious and beyond reach.

On August 8, when Allied leaders such as Ike, Monty, and Bradley first hatched the plan for encircling the Germans, they were giddy with anticipation of a rapid end to the war. They may have been overoptimistic in the moment, but a faster and complete encirclement of the Germans at Falaise would have helped speed the Allied victory. The greatest tragedy of the squandered opportunity at Falaise was the loss of life that might have been avoided. The Western Allies suffered about 750,000 combat casualties (killed and wounded) between D-Day and the surrender of Germany on May 7, 1945, two-thirds of which occurred after the events at Falaise. Any shortening of the war would have lessened Allied combat casualties by the thousands and saved countless more civilians. After the war, Bradley wrote that the outcome at Falaise was "a shattering disappointment—one of my greatest of the war. A golden opportunity had truly been lost."[51]

||||||||||||||||||||||||||||||||||||||||||||||||||||||||||||||

Paying the Price of Victory

Freeing Normandy from German occupation came at great cost. During the Battle of Normandy's nearly three months of combat, daily casualty rates approached those of the hellish warfare raging in the east between Germany and Soviet Russia. Between D-Day and when the last German troops fled Normandy across the Seine River toward Paris, Germany suffered nearly 250,000 dead and wounded and another 200,000 taken prisoner. Western Allied losses were comparable. The US killed and wounded exceeded 130,000 soldiers, sailors, and aircrew. The combined British, Canadian, and Polish forces sustained over 90,000 casualties as well.

Suffering was not limited to combatants. Between the pre-invasion aerial bombings and the battles fought on Norman soil, an estimated 20,000 to 30,000 French civilians died and many tens of thousands more were wounded or left homeless. Dozens of Norman towns and villages were razed by bombings and shellfire. Where the opposing armies had clashed, scores of dead soldiers, pack horses, and livestock lay rotting in Norman fields. Burnt-out tanks and trucks clogged country lanes. Trenches, craters, mines, and unexploded ordnance defiled farms and orchards. Normandy's lands would not return to their prewar pastoral beauty for years. And of course, the dead would never return.

Once Normandy fell to the Western Allies, Germany's defeat was assured. All that remained was the price that would be paid to complete the eradication of the Nazi regime and its armies. Initially, it seemed the tab might come in lower than expected. The collapse of German forces in Normandy in mid-August, culminating at the Falaise Pocket, opened the gates for a surge of Allied advances. Paris fell to combined American and Free French forces on August 25. Patton's divisions raced across the Meuse River on August 31 and the next day stood at the gates of Metz in northeastern France, barely thirty miles (forty-five kilometers) from the German border. Allied forces liberated Belgium in early September. A growing sense within the Allied leadership and the public back home was that German resistance would soon collapse, allowing British and American soldiers, sailors, and aircrew to return home by Christmas.

But this was not to be. A combination of Allied supply chain woes and Germany's herculean efforts to reconstitute its armies brought the rapid Allied progress to a halt. Under Hitler's maniacal control, Germany redoubled its manufacturing efforts in 1944 to pump out deadly new tanks and artillery, and refilled its divisions by putting uniforms on increasingly younger boys, increasingly older men, and an expanding variety of conscripts drawn from ethnic groups and countries outside the profile of the master Aryan race. (By the closing stages of the war, as much as one-third of the ultra-nationalist and racist *Waffen SS* consisted of non-Germans.)

Fighting in Europe would continue for eight agonizing months, until May of 1945. After paying the price for victory in Normandy, the Western Allies would add to their costs at many more battles to come, including Operation Market Garden, the Battle of the Bulge, the Hurtgen Forest, and the Ruhr Pocket.

Meanwhile, in the east the Soviet Union's colossal struggle against the lion's share of German forces continued. As the combined western Allied and Soviet armies surrounded Germany and pushed toward Berlin, the price of victory rose at an accelerating pace. During the final four months of the war, between the start of 1945 and Victory-Europe (VE) Day on May 8, an average of 650,000 soldiers died in combat each month, more than double the monthly rate during 1944. Appallingly, the number of civilian deaths and wounded followed the same catastrophic upward trajectory.

However, the Allied leadership and populations at home largely remained committed to paying the price and fighting till the bitter end. History too has largely agreed that the price needed to be paid. Some have labeled World War II a "good war," reflecting the war's moral imperative to eradicate grotesque regimes including Nazi Germany and Imperial Japan that murdered, raped, and tortured humans by the millions.

Wars are never good, only sometimes necessary. Human conflict and warfare are inevitable in a world where some use violence against others out of hatred, racism, or the desire to dominate. The price to defeat World War II's aggressors had to be paid, for if those regimes had not been toppled, the mid-twentieth-century world risked falling into "the abyss of a new Dark Age" as Churchill warned.[1]

The most effective leaders are lifelong learners. And successful leadership demands the ability to understand and positively influence human nature, beliefs, and behavior. For these reasons, history in general and warfare in particular offer compelling leadership laboratories for all leaders, including today's business owners, executives, and teams.

War brings out extreme beliefs, decisions, and actions in individuals and societies. To examine war is to encounter the entire spectrum from abhorrent and barbaric up to heroic and selfless. It is this contrast and complexity that both repulses us and commands our attention.

Some people shun the study of warfare for fear that examining it is the same as glorifying it. Just as we are not glorifying crime when we praise a police officer who rescues a civilian from a violent assault, we are not glorifying war when we acknowledge and honor those who, having found themselves thrust into the conflict, demonstrated courage, sacrifice, or wisdom.

It is possible to condemn warfare and seek all possible means to avoid it, and simultaneously study events such as D-Day and Operation Overlord to gain lessons and insights that we can apply to better ourselves as persons, voters, leaders, and members of society. Because war impacts practically every aspect of human experience and existence—family life, politics, demographics, economics, culture, etc.—war can produce lessons relevant to every human activity and endeavor.

By extracting and incorporating those lessons into our personal lives and professional roles and responsibilities, we are applying and enjoying the freedom that was purchased for us by those who went before us.

Selected Reading List

One could fill a small library or bookstore with books related to D-Day. If you are interested in an excellent telling of the broad story, the following titles offer engaging and approachable historical accounts of Operation Overlord.

- Atkinson, Rick. *The Guns at Last Light*. Henry Holt & Co., 2013.
- Beevor, Anthony. *D-Day: The Battle of Normandy*. Penguin Books, 2010.
- Caddick-Adams, Peter. *Sand & Steel: The D-Day Invasion and the Liberation of France*. Oxford University Press, 2019.
- D'Este, Carlo. *Decision in Normandy*. Diversion Books, 1983.
- Hastings, Max. *Overlord*. Simon & Schuster, 1984.

Notes

Introduction

1. Stearns, Peter. 1998. "Why Study History?" American Historical Association. https://www.historians.org/resource/why-study-history-1998/.

2. Atkinson, Rick. 2020. "Projecting Power in a World War," YouTube, December 21, 2020. https://www.youtube.com/watch?v=KCc2SOGm8yo.

3. Allied wartime convention capitalized code names. British Prime Minister Winston Churchill fixated on code names and insisted on personally selecting names for major operations. He replaced D-Day's original randomly generated code name of Roundhammer with Overlord to emphasize the operation's scale and importance.

4. Among them was Sergeant Waverly Woodson, from the 320th Barrage Balloon Battalion, the only African American combat unit to land on D-Day. In 1942, Woodson dropped out of premed studies and voluntarily enlisted in the Army. After being denied a post in the artillery due to his race, Woodson became a medic. On D-Day, he landed on Omaha Beach in the third wave, but before reaching shore the twenty-year-old Woodson was hit by shrapnel in the back and groin when a German shell exploded inside his landing craft. After receiving aid on the beach, Woodson joined a field dressing station, and for thirty consecutive hours without rest he recovered and triaged wounded soldiers. Woodson saved dozens of soldiers' lives—some accounts credit him with rescuing as many as two hundred. For his D-Day exploits he was initially awarded a Bronze Star and Purple Heart, but many believe Woodson would have received higher honors had he been white. After the war, Woodson was denied entry into medical school due to his race, but ultimately earned a degree in biology and worked for the National Naval Medical Center and National Institutes of Health. He was buried with full honors in Arlington National Cemetery after his death in 2005. In June of 2024, eighty years after D-Day, Waverly Woodson was posthumously awarded the Distinguished Service Cross.

5. Eber, Karen. 2023. *The Perfect Story*. Harper Horizon. Page 15.

6. Balkoski, Joseph. 2006. *Omaha Beach*. Stackpole Books. Page 576. Everand.

7. History proved him correct, although the split did not occur until after World War II. It became the Cold War.

8. Called Operation Jubilee, the raid on Dieppe involved an amphibious landing of about six thousand mostly Canadian and British soldiers. It was a fiasco. The Allied invaders retreated into the sea after losing more than half of their troops as killed or captured.

9. In World War II, Germany, Italy, and Japan were the primary "Axis" powers aligned against the "Allies" led by Britian, the United States, Soviet Russia, and China. Dozens of additional nations participated in the war on both sides.

10. Military historians vigorously debate to what extent the German army was superior to Allied armies, if at all. Regardless, in mid-1944, Allied military personnel from top commanders down to rank-and-file soldiers widely respected the combat capabilities and ferocity of the German soldier.

11. One can safely assume that General Dwight D. Eisenhower would not have been elected the 34th president of the United States if the D-Day invasion had failed under his command.

12. Ambrose, Stephen E. 1999. *D-Day, June 6, 1944*. G. K. Hall. Page 129.

13. Throughout this book, military titles and ranks are usually condensed. For example, US Army officers holding the rank of brigadier general, major general, or lieutenant general are all referred to simply as "general" in the text. Because some leaders experienced promotions in rank during the events covered in this book, and with different nations and different service branches using a variety of terminology, the military ranks used here are simplified for non-military readers.

14. Ambrose, page 89.

15. Grint, Keith. 2008. *Leadership, Management and Command*. Palgrave MacMillan. Page 34.

16. Rommel, Erwin. 1953. *The Rommel Papers*. Edited by B.H. Liddell Hart. Harcourt Brace. Page 466.

17. Barr, Niall. 2015. *Eisenhower's Armies*. Simon and Schuster. Page 328.

18. The invasion plan for the US Ninth Air Force, just one of several Allied air forces supporting the D-Day operation, ran to 847,000 words printed on both sides of nearly 1,400 pages of legal-sized paper.

19. Hastings, Max. 1984. *Overlord*. Simon and Schuster. Page 34.

Case Study One: Readying the Big Red One

1. In addition to his regular command over the US 1st Infantry Division, General Huebner had additional units assigned to him on D-Day specifically for the assault on Omaha Beach. These included two regiments from the US 29th Infantry Division, several battalions of US Army Rangers, and other supporting forces.

2. Rogers, R. J. 1965. "A Study of the Leadership in the First Infantry Division During World War II: Terry de la Mesa Allen and Clarence Huebner." Thesis presented to the US Army Command and General Staff College. Page 8.

3. Astor, Gerald. 2008. *Terrible Terry Allen*. Presidio Press. Pages 72–73.

4. In mid-1939 the US Army contained less than 200,000 soldiers and enlisted men, making it smaller than the armies of seventeen other nations, including Romania and Portugal.

5. Johnson, Richard. 2009. "Investigation into the Reliefs of Generals Orlando Ward and Terry Allen." School of Advanced Military Studies, US Army Command and General Staff College. Page 27.

6. Atkinson, Rick. 2002. *An Army at Dawn: The War in North Africa, 1942–1943*. Henry Holt. Page 135. Everand.

7. After Germany defeated France in the summer of 1940, the French nation was administratively split in half. Germany occupied northern and coastal France, while a quasi-fascist rump state called Vichy France governed the southern half of the country and French colonies, including Morocco, Algeria, and Tunisia in North Africa.

8. Atkinson, page 701.

9. McManus, John C. 2013. *The Americans at Normandy*. Forge Books. Page 22. Kindle.

10. Holden, Walter. 2018. "Who Fired Terry Allen and Ted Roosevelt, Jr., the Best Combat Generals?" *World War II History* 17, no. 2. February 2018. Page 39.

11. Kingseed, Cole C. 2013. "The Big Red One Loses Its Commander." *Army*. November 2013. Page 45.

12. Downs, Kenneth T. 1946. "Nothing Stopped the Timberwolves." *The Saturday Evening Post*. August 17, 1946.

13. During World War II, about eight million personnel served in the US Army. About three million served in the Army Air Corps (the forerunner of the independent US Air Force,) four and a half million served in the US Navy, and more than six hundred thousand served with the Marine Corps. In total, more than sixteen million American men and women served in uniform during the war, drawn from a total US population of about one hundred thirty million people.

14. Bradley, Omar. 1951. *A Soldier's Story*. Henry Holt. Page 37.

15. Ibid., page 154.

16. Hughes, General Everett S., deputy theater commander, "Letter to Omar Bradley, 12 June 1943" (AWCL, Bradley Papers, Correspondence with Major Historical Figures, 1936–1960).

17. Astor, page 190.

18. Bradley, page 110.

19. Atkinson, page 821.

20. Ibid.

21. Kingseed, page 49.

22. Astor, page 185.

23. Ibid., page 186.

24. Dawson, W. Forrest. 1946. *Saga of the All American*. Love. Page 27.

25. Patton had problems of his own at this time. In early August on two separate occasions Patton berated and struck a hospitalized American solider suffering from "battle fatigue," accusing each man of cowardice. (Coincidentally, both soldiers were from the 1st Division.) Eisenhower quietly reprimanded Patton, but news of the incidents spread, causing considerable public outcry in the US. In response, Eisenhower benched Patton and later promoted Bradley over Patton to lead all US ground forces in Operation Overlord.

26. Kingseed, page 48.

27. Astor, page 219.

28. McManus, page 19.

29. By early 1944, the US had more than twenty Army divisions readying for the invasion of western Europe. Of those, only four had been in combat, one of which was the Big Red One. Of those four, only the 1st Division had experience conducting an amphibious assault against a contested shore.

30. Bradley, page 275.

31. Flaig, Steven. 2006. "Clarence R. Huebner: An American Military Story of Achievement." Thesis paper, University of North Texas. May 2006. Page 100.

32. McManus, page 28.

33. Ibid., page 38.

34. Rogers, page 63.

35. Chaitt, Arthur. 1973. "Clarence R. Huebner Lieutenant General USA (Retired) 1888–1972." *Bridgehead Sentinel*. Spring 1973. Page 4.

36. Balkoski, Joseph. 2006. *Omaha Beach*. Stackpole Books. Page 71. Everand.

37. McManus, page 30.

38. Chaitt, page 14.

39. Ibid., page 8.

40. Ibid., page 5.

41. McManus, page 34.

42. Chaitt, page 7.

43. Combat engineers played a crucial role in the invasion—about twenty-five percent of the troops landed on D-Day were engineers of some type. Their initial role in the attack was to demolish and clear beach obstacles and defenses. Once the beach was secured, engineers established communication systems, set up fuel and supply dumps, and built roads exiting the beach.

44. See Case Study Four: Ike's Call for further discussion.

45. Chaitt, page 6.

46. Ibid., page 10.

47. Ibid., page 5.

48. Rogers, page 68.

49. The Distinguished Service Cross (DSC) is the second-highest military decoration that can be awarded to a member of the United States Army.

50. The navigational error proved fortuitous, for they landed on a stretch of Utah Beach with significantly weaker defenses.

51. Roosevelt's exploits on D-Day are dramatized in the 1962 epic film *The Longest Day*, in which he is played by American actor Henry Fonda. Roosevelt was universally respected as a combat leader of the highest bravery.

52. Jim Collins, "Level 5 Leadership," video transcript, accessed December 13, 2024, https://www.jimcollins.com/media_topics/Level-5-Leadership.html.

53. In World War II, a US Army Corps typically contained two to five divisions under its command.

54. Rogers, page 84.

55. Rogers, page 81.

Case Study Two: Where to Put the Panzers

1. Some German units consisted of men who shared a common physical aliment, such as "stomach battalions" populated with men suffering from gastrointestinal issues.

2. In 1943, German panzer counterattacks had come close to successfully defeating Allied landings at Sicily and Salerno.

3. Hitler, Directive 51. The Fuehrer directives were a series of seventy-four memos issued by Hitler during the war covering a range of military and governance topics. The directives were considered laws and Hitler expected them to be implemented to the letter.

4. Hitler, Directive 51.

5. The number of panzer divisions deployed to western Europe fluctuated prior to D-Day. Hitler shuffled these units back and forth across the continent in an increasingly desperate attempt to hold back the armies surrounding Germany. On D-Day, there were ten panzer divisions deployed in western Europe.

6. D'Este, Carlo. 1983. *Decision in Normandy*. Diversion Books. Page 116.

7. Rommel, Erwin. 1953. *The Rommel Papers*. Edited by B.H. Liddell Hart. Harcourt Brace. Page 468.

8. The two men were already acquainted, Rommel having served under Rundstedt during the German conquest of France in 1940.

9. Messenger, Charles. 2018. *The Last Prussian: A Biography of Field Marshal Gerd von Rundstedt, 1875–1953*. Pen & Sword Military. Page 311. Everand.

10. Geyr survived World War II, was captured, and was extensively interviewed by the US Army. Fluent in English, well-spoken, and unabashed about sharing his point of view, Geyr's commentary was colorful, insightful, and biased.

11. Geyr von Schweppenburg, Leo. 1954. "B-466 Panzer Group West (Mid 1943–5 July 1944)." US Army Foreign Military Studies Historical Division. Page 8.

12. Ibid., page 6.

13. Ibid., page 19.

14. Ruge, Friedrich. 1954. MS#A-982: "Rommel and the Atlantic Wall (December 1943–July 1944)." US Army Foreign Military Studies Historical Division. Page 8.

15. Rommel, pages 469–470.

16. Ambrose, Stephen E. 1999. *D-Day, June 6, 1944*. G. K. Hall. Page 113.

17. Geyr, page 8.

18. Mitcham, Samuel W. 2019. *Desert Fox*. Simon and Schuster. Page 356. Scribd.

19. The invitation-only General Staff constituted the senior group of German military leaders responsible for studying and preparing the country's strategic war plans and operations.

20. Wilt, Alan F. 1975. "An Addendum to the Rommell-Rundstedt Controversy." *Military Affairs*, vol. 39, no. 4. December 1975. Page 180.

21. Mitcham, page 357.

22. Rommel, page 468.

23. Overy, Richard. 1995. *Why the Allies Won*. Pimlico. Pages 155–156.

24. Hammond, William. 2019. *Normandy: 6 June 1944–24 July 1944*. US Army Center of Military History. Page 21.

25. Liddell Hart, B.H. 1948. *The German Generals Talk*. W. Morrow. Page 145.

26. See Case Study Six: Hitler Snoozes for further discussion.

27. See Case Study Four: Ike's Call for further discussion.

28. Knesebeck, Goetz von dem. 1954. "B-019 Report of von Geyr." US Army Foreign Military Studies Historical Division. Page 19.

29. Caddick-Adams, Peter. 2019. *Sand and Steel: The D-Day Invasions and the Liberation of France*. Oxford University Press. Page 693. Kindle.

30. Speidel, Hans. 1954. MS#B-720: "Rommel's Views (1 April–May 1944)." US Army Foreign Military Studies Historical Division. Page 18.

Case Study Three: The Battle for the Bombers

1. Hastings, Max. 1984. *Overlord*. Simon and Schuster. Page 39.

2. The Allies' greatest shipping challenge was a lack of sufficient "landing ship, tanks" (LSTs). These 300-foot specialized cargo ships featured flat bottoms and clamshell bow doors, allowing them to steam onto a beach and unload vehicles, troops, and cargo. While these unsung vessels helped achieve Allied victory at Normandy and elsewhere during the war, troops reinterpreted LST to mean "large slow target," given their lack of speed, poor sea-handling qualities, and vulnerability to enemy attack.

3. See Case Study Two: Where to Put the Panzers for further discussion.

4. French Resistance forces sabotaged German transportation and communication facilities before and after D-Day, significantly contributing to the interdiction of German forces in Normandy.

5. Italian General Giulio Douhet is often considered the godfather of strategic bombing, having published his influential book *The Command of the Air* in 1921.

6. In 1939, the United States manufactured 921 aircraft. In 1944, the US produced 96,318 aircraft. (Source: *Smithsonian* magazine, May 2007.)

7. Earlier in life, Spaatz had legally changed his surname's spelling, adding an extra "a" to encourage proper pronunciation as "spots" rather than "spats."

8. Davis, Richard G. 1993. *Carl A. Spaatz and the Air War in Europe*. Department of the Air Force. Page 328.

9. Morrison, Wilbur H. 1986. *Fortress without a Roof: The Allied Bombing of the Third Reich*. St. Martin's Press. Page 37.

10. By this point in the war the British conducted their strategic bombing missions largely at night. Earlier in the war the British had conducted daytime raids but suffered immense losses from German fighter aircraft and anti-aircraft guns, and thus switched to night bombing to gain the cover of darkness. The Americans conducted their missions during the day to maximize accuracy, confident that their bombers and fighter aircraft escorts could overcome German defenses. The different British and American tactics proved complementary, resulting in round-the-clock bombing that stressed Germany's ability to defend its airspace against continuous attacks.

11. Carver, Michael. 2005. *The War Lords: Military Commanders of the Twentieth Century*. Pen & Sword Military Classics. Page 983. Everand.

12. Ambrose, Stephen E. 2014. *Eisenhower: Soldier and President*. Simon & Schuster. Page 121.

13. The German army depended heavily on horse-drawn transportation throughout the war, harnessing almost three million horses to haul supply wagons, mobile kitchens, ambulances, and artillery pieces. Hitler instructed German photographers and film crews to mask this dependency. Thus, the wartime photographs and film contributed to the myth of a highly modern and mechanized German military.

14. Davis, page 330.

15. Allied dominance in the air eventually became so absolute during Operation Overlord that German foot soldiers in Normandy joked that "British aircraft are green, American aircraft are silver, and German aircraft are invisible."

16. American strategic bombers had been haphazardly sent against a range of industrial targets including manufacturers of aircraft, rubber, and ball-bearings, as well as U-boat bases.

17. Davis, page 348.

18. Veeder, Timothy. 1997. "An Evaluation of the Aerial Interdiction Campaign Known as the Transportation Plan for the D-Day Invasion, Early January 1944 to Late June 1944." Research paper presented to Air Command and Staff College, Maxwell Air Force Base. Page 10.

19. Grant, Rebecca. 2007. "The War on the Rails." *Air & Space Forces Magazine*. August 1, 2007.

20. Hastings, Max. 2013. *Bomber Command*. Zenith Press. Page 219. Everand.

21. Caddick-Adams, Peter. 2019. *Sand and Steel: The D-Day Invasions and the Liberation of France*. Oxford University Press. Page 294. Kindle.

22. Dwight D. Eisenhower to George C. Marshall, December 25, 1943. *The Papers of Dwight D. Eisenhower, Volume 3*. Edited by Alfred D. Chandler. Johns Hopkins University Press. Page 1612.

23. Caddick-Adams, page 121.

24. On the first day of the war, Bomber Command launched a ten-aircraft raid against the German naval base at Wilhelmshaven. Seven bombers were shot down with no significant damage accomplished.

25. Atkinson, Rick. 2013. *The Guns at Last Light: The War in Western Europe, 1944–1945*. Henry Holt. Page 17.

26. Most of Eisenhower's senior team was assigned to him, in some cases over his opposition. Because Ike was American, to maintain a desired balance between the Allies, his principal subordinate commanders in air, land, and sea forces were all British: Leigh-Mallory was the air commander-in-chief, Admiral Bertram H. Ramsay the naval commander-in-chief, and General Bernard Montgomery initially would lead the invasion's ground troops.

27. Rawson, Andrew, Dwight D Eisenhower, and George C Marshall. 2012. *Eyes Only: The Top Secret Correspondence between Marshall and Eisenhower 1943–45*. Stroud: History. Page 30. Everand.

28. Hastings, *Overlord*, page 44.

29. Mark, Eduard. 1995. *Aerial Interdiction*. Diane Publishing. Page 226.

30. Ibid., page 230.

31. Rawson, page 64.

32. Butcher, Harry C. 1946. *My Three Years with Eisenhower*. Simon and Schuster. Page 474.

33. Tedder, Arthur. 1966. *With Prejudice*. Little, Brown. Page 508.

34. Davis, page 334.

35. Ibid., page 337.

36. Eisenhower, Dwight D. 1944–1969. *The Eisenhower Papers, Volume 3*. Johns Hopkins University Press. Page 1758.

37. Butcher, page 499.

38. In November 1943 at a conference in Tehran between Roosevelt, Churchill, and Stalin, the Soviet dictator learned that the Western Allies had not yet selected a leader for Operation Overlord. Incredulous, he accused the US and British of not being committed to the invasion. The following month Roosevelt appointed Ike, and FDR subsequently scribbled on notepaper a single-sentence telegram for Stalin—"The immediate appointment of General Eisenhower in command of OVERLORD operation has been decided upon. Roosevelt." Marshall kept the message and gave it to Eisenhower as a memento.

39. During 1943 the British and Americans lost around 60,000 men killed in combat fighting the Germans, while the Soviet Russians experienced around 2.3 million combat deaths and millions more civilians killed.

40. Tedder, page 510.

41. Davis, page 344.

42. Ibid., page 348.

43. Ibid., page 341.

44. Eisenhower, *The Eisenhower Papers, Volume 3*, pages 1766–1767.

45. Butcher, page 498.

46. Rawson, page 110.

47. Davis, page 349.

48. Ibid., page 338.

49. Hastings, *Overlord*, page 40.

50. Hastings, *Bomber Command*, page 454.

51. Rostow, W.W. 1981. *Pre-Invasion Bombing Strategy*. Gower. Page 90.

52. Ibid., page 91.

53. Ibid., page 92.

54. Davis, page 353.

55. Rostow, page 93.

56. Ibid., page 94.

57. Davis, page 338.

58. Carver, page 912.

59. Hastings, *Bomber Command*, page 415.

60. Ibid., page 789.

61. Tedder, page 527.

62. Davis, page 352.

63. Eisenhower, John S.D. 1982. *Allies: From Pearl Harbor to D-Day*. Doubleday. Page 448.

64. Darlow, Stephen, and Shanda Brown. 2010. *D-Day Bombers*. Stackpole Books. Page 254. Everand.

65. Craven, W.F., and J.L. Cate. 1983. *Europe: Argument to V-E Day, January 1944 to May 1945*. Office of Air Force History. Pages 161–162.

66. Operation Chattanooga Choo-Choo in late May sent more than one thousand Allied fighter bombers sweeping across western Europe strafing and bombing train locomotives. By D-Day more than five hundred were destroyed or damaged. As Zuckerman predicted, many damaged locomotives went unrepaired because the railroad service yards were largely bombed out by the Transportation Plan strategic bombing missions.

67. The 2nd SS Panzer Division would have presented a serious threat to the invasion if it had arrived earlier. Attacks by French Resistance partisans contributed to the division's delays, including one operation where several French teenagers drained the axle grease from the railcars and replaced it with an abrasive powder secretly parachuted to them by British special operations forces. Other tactics included placing fake mines on the roads by turning soup dishes upside down, as well as real mines disguised as cow patties. In reprisal for these attacks, the 2nd SS Panzer Division rounded up and murdered hundreds of French civilians.

Case Study Four: Ike's Call

1. High winds and rough seas severely interfered with and endangered the Allied amphibious and airborne invasion of Sicily in the summer of 1943, known as Operation Husky.

2. Atkinson, Rick. 2013. *The Guns at Last Light: The War in Western Europe, 1944–1945*. Henry Holt. Pages 31–32.

3. Initially the invasion was to occur in May, but shortages in amphibious shipping pushed the invasion date back to June.

4. Grint, Keith. 2008. *Leadership, Management and Command*. Palgrave MacMillan. Page 54.

5. Beevor, Antony. 2014. *D-Day: The Battle for Normandy*. Penguin Books. Page 11.

6. Hogben, Lawrence. 1994. "The Most Important Weather Forecast in the History of the World." *London Review of Books*, vol. 16, no. 10. May 26, 1994. https://www.lrb.co.uk/the-paper/v16/n10/lawrence-hogben/diary.

7. D'Este, Carlo. 2003. *Eisenhower: A Soldier's Life*. Holt Paperbacks. Page 856. Everand.

8. Ibid., page 518.

9. Ibid., page 518.

10. Atkinson, page 31.

11. Ross, John. 2014. *Forecast for D-Day*. Rowman & Littlefield. Page 188. Kindle.

12. Beevor, page 12.

13. Major General Henry J.F. Miller, after his indiscreet remarks in a bar at London's famous Claridge's Hotel, was reduced in rank to lieutenant colonel by Ike and given twenty-four hours to return to the United States.

14. Miller, Merle. 1988. *Ike the Soldier: As They Knew Him*. Putnam. Page 612.

15. Ryan, Cornelius. 1959. *The Longest Day: D-Day, June 6, 1944*. Simon and Schuster. Page 61.

16. Beevor, page 21.

17. Atkinson, page 35.

18. Ambrose, Stephen E. 2014. *Eisenhower: Soldier and President*. Simon & Schuster. Page 187.

19. D'Este, page 522.

20. Ambrose, page 187.

21. Ibid., page 187.

22. D'Este, page 862.

23. Ross, page 204.

24. CBS Reports. 1964. "D-Day Plus 20 Years—Eisenhower Returns to Normandy." YouTube Video. (10:53), https://youtu.be/vNaxTXfjfXk?si=c_D4bf1ncin31hRT.

25. CBS Reports, "D-Day Plus 20 Years—Eisenhower Returns to Normandy" (12:15).

26. Stagg, James Martin. 1971. *Forecast for Overlord, June 6, 1994*. Ian Allen. Page 29.

27. Wilmot, Chester. 2003. *The Struggle for Europe*. Wordsworth Editions. Page 237.

28. Larson, Erik. 2016. "A Checklist for Making Faster, Better Decisions." *Harvard Business Review*. March 7, 2016. https://hbr.org/2016/03/a-checklist-for-making-faster-better-decisions.

29.　See Case Study Five: The Tanks that Sank off Omaha for further discussion.

30.　See Case Study Six: Hitler Snoozes for further discussion.

31.　Ross, page 213.

32.　Caddick-Adams, Peter. 2019. *Sand and Steel: The D-Day Invasions and the Liberation of France*. Oxford University Press. Page 339. Kindle.

Case Study Five: The Tanks That Sank off Omaha

1.　Weiner, Alan. 1987. "The First Wave." *American Heritage*, vol. 38, issue 4. May/June 1987.

2.　The primary defense contractor was Firestone Tire and Rubber Company in Ohio, although several subcontractors were also involved. Workers at the plants were sworn to secrecy and assembly areas restricted. Completed DD tanks were shipped in sealed plywood crates.

3.　The tally varies across different historical sources, with some sources reporting 240 total DD tanks.

4.　See Case Study Four: Ike's Call for further discussion.

5.　The Beaufort wind scale is a measure of wind speed and accompanying sea conditions. First created by Francis Beaufort of the Royal Navy in 1806, the scale measures sea state and wind speed from 0 (calm) to 12 (hurricane).

6.　US Navy, DD LCT Unit Commander, Lieutenant Dean L. Rockwell. "Memorandum for Commander, Eleventh Amphibious Force." April 30, 1944. (2, RG 407, Box 24377, File 659, NA II.)

7.　Connor, Joseph. 2019. "The Courageous General Who Led the Way to D-Day's First Successful Assault." HistoryNet, April 3, 2019. https://www.historynet.com/man-on-a-mission-the-courageous-general-who-led-the-way-to-d-days-first-successful-assault/.

8.　Normandy lies along the 49th parallel north, roughly the same latitude as much of the border between the lower forty-eight US states and Canada.

9.　Harkey, R. L. "Record of Events Concerning DD Launching LCT 602." June 16, 1944. Eisenhower Center Peter Kalikow WWII-Era Collection, at the National WWII Museum, New Orleans, LA. Page 3.

10.　US Navy, DD LCT Unit Commander, Lieutenant Dean L. Rockwell. "Memorandum for Commander-in-Chief, United States Fleet." July 14, 1944. Page 3. (2, RG 407, Box 24377, File 659, NA II.)

11.　US Army. "741st Tank Battalion after Action Report." July 19, 1944. Page 1. https://8th-armored.org/aar/8aarepts.htm.

12. Barry, J.E. "Action Report, 'DD' Tanks." July 22, 1944. Eisenhower Center Peter Kalikow WWII-Era Collection, at the National WWII Museum, New Orleans, LA. Page 4.

13. MacKenzie, Donald. "Launch of DD Tanks." July 5, 1944. Eisenhower Center Peter Kalikow WWII-Era Collection, at the National WWII Museum, New Orleans, LA. Page 3.

14. Sullivan, Henry. "Launching of Tanks for the Assault on D-Day, 6 June 1944." June 15, 1944. Eisenhower Center Peter Kalikow WWII-Era Collection, at the National WWII Museum, New Orleans, LA. Page 4.

15. Metcalf, J.A. "Launching—Report of." June 17, 1944. Eisenhower Center Peter Kalikow WWII-Era Collection, at the National WWII Museum, New Orleans, LA. Page 2.

16. Harkey, page 3.

17. Three of the four 741st DD tanks aboard LCT 600 did not launch at sea. Executing the order to launch, the first tank immediately sank. As this occurred, the second tank in line, free of its chain lashings, lurched after a strong wave and bumped into the third tank, which in turn collided with the fourth. The thin shrouds on the three tanks tore, and consequently the LCT officer-in-charge took these DDs and their crews directly to the shore. Two of those DD tanks are visible in Robert Capa's "Magnificent Eleven" D-Day morning photographs.

18. McManus, John C. 2013. *The Americans at Normandy*. Forge Books. Page 337. Kindle.

19. Harkey, page 5.

20. In the epic Omaha Beach combat scene in *Saving Private Ryan*, the central character Captain John Miller, played by Tom Hanks, comments in the middle of the chaotic battle that "all the armor's foundering in the channel" (12:30) and then later, "No armor has made it ashore. We got no DD tanks on the beach" (14:00).

21. US Army. "First United States Army, General Omar Bradley, Memorandum for Naval Commander Western Task Force." May 7, 1944. (2, RG 407, Box 24377, File 659, NA II.)

22. US Navy. "Operational Plan No. 2-44 of the Western Naval Task Force." May 29, 1944. Annex F.

23. Ibid., Annex F.

24. US Navy. Eleventh Amphibious Force, "Commander Assault Force 'O,' Action Report of DD Tanks in Assault on Coleville-Vierville Sector." July 14, 1944. Page 1.

25. Ibid., page 2.

26. Barry, page 5.

27. US Army. "743rd Tank Battalion After Action Report." July 19, 1944. Page 1. https://8th-armored.org/aar/8aarepts.htm.

28. Rockwell, "Memorandum for Commander-in-Chief, United States Fleet," page 1.

29. Caddick-Adams, Peter. 2019. *Sand and Steel: The D-Day Invasions and the Liberation of France*. Oxford University Press. Page 644. Kindle.

Case Study Six: Hitler Snoozes

1. Zetterling, Niklas. 2000. *Normandy 1944*. J. J. Fedorowicz. Page 27.

2. Ruge, Friedrich. 1954. MS#A-982: "Rommel and the Atlantic Wall (December 1943–July 1944)." US Army Foreign Military Studies Historical Division. Page 8.

3. Hiter, Fuehrer Directive 51.

4. Gersdorff, Rudolph C. von. 1954. "A-895 Critique of the Defense Against Invasion." US Army Foreign Military Studies Historical Division. Page 6.

5. Hitler, Fuehrer Directive 51.

6. Reardon, Mark J. 2002. *Victory at Mortain: Stopping Hitler's Panzer Counteroffensive*. University of Kansas. Page 21.

7. The Allies did plan to capture a port near the invasion site, but their initial objective was Cherbourg, not Antwerp.

8. Latimer, John, 2001. *Deception in War*. Overlook Press. Page 238.

9. The code words came from a popular French poem called "Autumn Song" published by Paul Verlaine in 1886. On June 1, the Allies broadcast the opening lines of the poem, "Long sobs of autumn violins," to alert French Resistance that the invasion would start within two weeks. On the evening of June 5, the next set of lines, "Wound my heart with a monotonous languor," indicated that the invasion would start within forty-eight hours. The message alerted French Resistance forces to commence sabotage efforts against rail and communication targets.

10. Caddick-Adams, Peter. 2019. *Sand and Steel: The D-Day Invasions and the Liberation of France*. Oxford University Press. Page 376. Kindle.

11. Allied paratroopers contributed to German confusion. Instructed to disrupt German communication after landing in France, throughout the early morning hours on D-Day, paratroopers cut phone lines with knives and demolished telephone poles with grenades.

12. Three Allied airborne divisions attacked on the night of June 5–6: the American 82nd and 101st and the British 6th.

13. Pemsel, Max-Joseph. 1954. "B-763 Seventh Army (6 Jun-29 Jul 1944)." US Army Foreign Military Studies Historical Division. Page 1.

14. To continue playing on the Germans' assumptions that Normandy was a diversionary invasion preceding the main attack, on D-Day Allied political and military leaders were instructed to announce to the press that the Normandy assault was the first in a series of landings. However, Free French leader General Charles de Gaulle, whom US President Roosevelt once described as an "apprentice dictator," broke from the script and declared to media that the invasion of Normandy was "the supreme battle." An irate Churchill ordered de Gaulle be arrested and deported from England but changed his mind later that same day.

15. Anticipating the Allied invasion, the Germans had created a set of plans arranging for the reinforcement of specific coastal areas upon an attack at that location. The plan providing for an attack along the Channel coast was called Blume 1, and the Normandy site was labeled Event Three.

16. Blumentritt, Guenther. 1954. "B-283 Evaluation of German Command and Troops." US Army Foreign Military Studies Historical Division. Page 97.

17. Radar data available to Rundstedt was spotty. In the weeks leading up to D-Day, Allied signal tracking stations in England named Ping Pongs had triangulated and identified ninety-two German radar sites along the coast, and hundreds of air strikes subsequently damaged or destroyed most of them.

18. Carrell, Paul. 1963. *Invasion! They're Coming!* Dutton. Page 39.

19. The two panzer divisions were the 12th SS Panzer Division and the Panzer Lehr Division. Together at full strength these elite units could bring close to four hundred tanks and armored fighting vehicles to the battle.

20. Rundstedt held a dim assessment of the Atlantic Wall, calling it an "enormous bluff."

21. Canadian Army Headquarters Historical Section. 1951. Report #40: "The Campaign in Northwest Europe." Appendix. Page 8.

22. The high command of the German Armed Forces, commonly abbreviated as the OKW (*Oberkommando der Wehrmacht*).

23. Canadian Army Headquarters Historical Section, page 33.

24. See Case Study Two: Where to Put the Panzers for further discussion.

25. Many historical accounts give slightly different times for the various events on D-Day, and often do not specify the local time zone. Most of the times in this narrative are approximate.

26. Shirer, William L., and Ron Rosenbaum. 1960. *The Rise and Fall of the Third Reich: A History of Nazi Germany*. Simon & Schuster. Page 1851. Everand.

27. Pemsel, page 122.

28. Margaritis, Peter. 2019. *Countdown to D-Day: The German Perspective*. Casemate. Page 755. Everand.

29. Canadian Army Headquarters Historical Section, page 111.

30. The 84th (or LXXXIV) Army Corps of the German army was stationed at the D-Day invasion area and was one of the first major German headquarters to respond to the invasion.

31. Carell, page 64.

32. Grint, Keith. 2008. *Leadership, Management and Command*. Palgrave MacMillan. Page 112.

33. Ibid., page 112.

34. D'Este, Carlo. 1983. *Decision in Normandy*. Diversion Books. Page 118.

35. Zimmermann, Bodo. 1947. "B-801 OB-West 9 Questions (June 1944–March 1945)." US Army Foreign Military Studies Historical Division. Page 6.

36. Warlimont, Walter. 1964. *Inside Hitler's Headquarters, 1939–1945*. F.A. Praeger. Page 425.

37. Eisenhower, David. 1991. *Eisenhower: At War, 1943–1945*. Wings Books. Page 287.

38. Pemsel, page 105.

39. Heiber, Helmut. 2004. *Hitler and His Generals—Military Conferences 1942–1945*. Enigma Books. Page 454.

40. Grint, page 113.

41. Canadian Army Headquarters Historical Section, page 81.

42. Grint, page 410.

Case Study Seven: Those Damned Hedgerows

1. LeVien, Jack. 1962. *Winston Churchill: The Valiant Years*. Bernard Geis. Pages 277–278.

2. Wood, Sterling A. 1947. "History of the 313th Infantry in World War II." US Army World War Regimental Histories, Book 187. Page 83.

3. Sohl, Albert. 2004. "From Utah Beach to the Hedgerows." *Military History*, June 2004. Page 54.

4. During the second half of the twentieth century, a considerable portion of the Norman bocage was cleared to accommodate larger, modern farms and an expanding urban population.

5. For example, one eight-square-mile section of Norman countryside photographed prior to D-Day shows approximately four thousand separate hedgerow-enclosures.

6. Folsom, Charles D. 1948. "Hedgerow Fighting Near Carentan." Research paper. Page 1. https://83rdinfdivdocs.org/accounts/Capt_Folsom-Hedgerow_fighting_near_Carentan.pdf.

7. LeVien, page 277.

8. Miller, Merle. 1988. *Ike the Soldier: As They Knew Him*. Putnam. Page 656.

9. Rooney, Andrew A. 2002. *My War*. PublicAffairs. Page 166.

10. Baldwin, Hanson. 1944. "Normandy Battle Among Toughest." *The New York Times*, July 19, 1944. Page 3.

11. Doubler, Michael Dale. 1988. *Busting the Bocage*. Combat Studies Institute. Page 50.

12. Folsom, page 9.

13. While American armies struggled to advance in bocage country, to the east British and Canadian forces appeared to have stalled as well, in large part because they faced the greater concentration of veteran German armored units.

14. Churchill also worried about events to the east. Two weeks after D-Day, Soviet Russia launched a titanic attack against German lines called Operation Bagration. The Soviet offensive kicked off with more than 1.6 million combat personnel and 6,000 tanks and assault guns. The attack quickly broke through German lines, shattered more than thirty German army divisions, and produced Germany's largest defeat during World War II. With American, British, and Canadian armies seemingly stalled in Normandy, and Soviet forces rapidly advancing toward the heart of the continent, Churchill presciently worried about minimizing Soviet conquest and domination of postwar Europe.

15. Morgan, Frederick. 1950. *Overture to Overlord*. Doubleday. Page 158.

16. D'Este, Carlo. 1983. *Decision in Normandy*. Diversion Books. Page 87.

17. Atkinson, Rick. 2013. *The Guns at Last Light: The War in Western Europe, 1944–1945*. Henry Holt. Page 111.

18. See Case Study Three: The Battle for the Bombers for further discussion.

19. Beevor, Antony. 2014. *D-Day: The Battle for Normandy*. Penguin Books. Page 253.

20. Hastings, Max. 1984. *Overlord*. Simon and Schuster. Page 245.

21. Doubler, page 21.

22. See Case Study Two: Where to Put the Panzers for further discussion.

23. During the Battle of Normandy, in a meeting with his senior German army leaders, Hitler was observed to scrutinize a map of France, counting how many square kilometers his forces had lost to that point and thus would need to be reconquered.

24. US Army 1st Infantry Division. 1944. "Overlord: Tactical Study of Terrain." March 25, 1944. Page 2.

25. Ronan, Major Charles E. 1948. "The Operations of the 3rd Battalion, 357th Infantry Regiment in the Hedgerow Battle of Normandy, 8–11 June 1944." Thesis paper presented to US Army Infantry School. Page 5.

26. Ibid., page 16.

27. Atkinson, page 111.

28. Doubler, page 21.

29. Grint, Keith. 2008. *Leadership, Management and Command.* Palgrave MacMillan. Page 46.

30. One night in late April 1944, nine German torpedo boats, called E-boats by the Allies, stumbled upon Exercise Tiger, a D-Day dress rehearsal. The E-boats evaded a thin screen of convoy escorts and torpedoed multiple American ships, killing 749 American soldiers and sailors. Allied commanders kept secret the disaster until after D-Day to avoid alerting the Germans to the upcoming invasion.

31. British Major General Percy Hobart led this effort. His diverse and often bizarre adaptations came to be known as Hobart's Funnies. Most armies today still utilize modern versions of Hobart's innovations.

32. *US Army Talks Series*, vol. II, no. 27, 5 July, 1944. Page 3.

33. US Army. 1944. "90th Infantry Division After Action Report, June, 1944." Page 4.

34. A US Army tank battalion in World War II was typically equipped with about sixty to seventy tanks.

35. Doubler, page 32.

36. Gerow and other top US commanders were putting the same question to tank officers throughout Normandy, not just Depew.

37. Bradley, Omar. 1951. *A Soldier's Story*. Henry Holt. Page 161.

38. Ibid., page 162.

39. The following personnel were awarded commendations in developing and building the Rhino tanks: Arthur C. Person, James G. Depew, Stephen M. Litton, Curtis G. Culin, along with tank drivers Harmon S. McNorton and John Hughey, and welders Wesley A. Hewitt, John Jessen, and Ernest Hardcastle.

40. Culin's hometown of Cranford, New Jersey, maintains a memorial to him and his wartime invention.

41. Doubler, page 37.

42. Ibid., page 42.

43. Holland, James. 2020. *Normandy '44: D-Day and the Battle for France*. Corgi. Page 539.

44. Duhigg, Charles. 2016. "What Google Learned from Its Quest to Build the Perfect Team." *New York Times*, February 28, 2016.

45. Ibid.

46. Holland, page 539.

47. Mehlo, Noel F. 2021. *D-Day General*. Rowman & Littlefield. Page 63.

48. McKinsey & Company. 2021. "Psychological Safety and the Critical Role of Leadership Development," February 2021. https://www.mckinsey.com/capabilities/people-and-organizational-performance/our-insights/psychological-safety-and-the-critical-role-of-leadership-development#/.

49. Blumenson, Martin. 1961. *Breakout and Pursuit*. Center of Military History, US Army. Page 43.

50. United States Army. 1945 "359th Infantry—90th Division." World War Regimental Histories, book 183. Page 21.

Case Study Eight: Failure at Falaise

1. See Case Study Seven: Those Damned Hedgerows for further discussion.

2. At one point in the battle the Germans had eight panzer divisions engaged against the Allies, seven of which faced the British and Canadians.

3. More than 20,000 V-1 and V-2 weapons were fired against England, with London as the primary target. The first large-scale use of guided missiles killed about 5,000 civilians and wounded more than 20,000. Tens of thousands of British homes were destroyed. The British evacuated more than 1.2 million children from southeastern Britain during the attacks.

4. Montgomery was only promoted from general to field marshal several months after D-Day, and thus is referred to as General Montgomery in this book.

5. Patton had been in England, waiting to deploy to Normandy once American forces had sufficiently increased to warrant the new US Third Army unit. While waiting, Patton had been in command of the First United States Army Group (FUSAG), a ghost army of fictitious units the Allies created as part of the disinformation campaign to convince the Germans that the main Allied attack was not in Normandy but rather at Pas-de-Calais.

6. Blumenson, Martin. 1961. *Breakout and Pursuit.* Center of Military History, US Army. Page 460.

7. Kluge receives the nickname after a popular German horse named Clever Hans (*der kluge Hans* in German) that could supposedly perform arithmetic. Kluge was not alone in doubting Operation Lüttich. In a postwar interview, Kluge's chief of staff General Guenther Blumentritt reported that "there was not a commander on the spot who felt that this plan could succeed."

8. Atkinson, Rick. 2013. *The Guns at Last Light: The War in Western Europe, 1944–1945.* Henry Holt. Page 155.

9. Fritz, Stephen G. 2018. *The First Soldier: Hitler as Military Leader.* Yale University Press. Page 331.

10. Falaise is best known as the birthplace of William the Conqueror, likely born in 1028.

11. Blumenson, Martin. 1993. *The Battle of the Generals: The Untold Story of the Falaise Pocket—The Campaign That Should Have Won World War II.* Quill. Page 106.

12. Eisenhower, Dwight D. 1946. "Report by the Supreme Commander to the Combined Chiefs of Staff on the Operations in Europe of the Allied Expeditionary Force, 6 June 1944 to 8 May 1945." Center of Military History, US Army. Page 46.

13. Bradley, Omar. 1951. *A Soldier's Story.* Henry Holt. Page 375.

14. Blumenson, *Battle of the Generals*, page 10.

15. Atkinson, page 159.

16. Fritz, page 331.

17. Atkinson, page 160.

18. Bradley, page 377.

19. It was common for senior staff officers to communicate with one another on behalf of their commanding generals.

20. Gordon, Edward E. 2017. *Divided on D-Day*. Prometheus Books. Page 253.

21. Tragically, nobody had realized that the yellow flares used by the Canadians to indicate their own positions burned the same color that British Bomber Command used to mark its targets.

22. Blumenson, *Battle of the Generals*, page 219.

23. Atkinson, page 148.

24. To sustain the impression of always being on the offense, whenever possible Patton traveled toward the front lines by jeep or other vehicle so that troops saw him moving forward, and when traveling back to the rear he discreetly flew by utility plane.

25. Blumenson, *Battle of the Generals*, page 220.

26. Atkinson, pages 162–163.

27. Bryant, Arthur. 1959. *Triumph in the West: Completing the War Diaries of Field Marshal Viscount Alanbrooke*. Collins. Page 168.

28. Pockets of German resistance would last for several more days. About sixty teen-age soldiers of the 12th SS Hitler Youth Division would fight to the death from inside a school. Two were chosen by lot to escape on the morning of August 18 and report that Falaise had fallen.

29. Allied troops took to asking whether they were "liberating" or "ob-literating" Norman towns like Falaise.

30. Atkinson, page 159.

31. Kluge was conditionally involved in the July 20 plot against Hitler. He likely knew of the attack in advance and agreed to support the coup d'état if Hitler was killed. Upon learning that the bombing failed to kill Hitler, Kluge withdrew his support and attempted to conceal his involvement.

32. Atkinson, page 165.

33. Blumenson, *Battle of the Generals*, page 240.

34. Ibid., page 253.

35. The US 90th Infantry Division, whose soldiers linked up with Polish forces in Chambois to close the pocket, initially performed so poorly in Normandy that Bradley's staff considered disbanding the division and assigning its soldiers to other units.

36. Hastings, Max. 1984. *Overlord*. Simon and Schuster. Page 299.

37. Legend has it that some Canadian troops referred to Montgomery as "God Almonty."

38. Bradley, page 378.

39. Ibid., page 379.

40. Blumenson, *Battle of the Generals*, page 27.

41. Ibid., pages 22–23.

42. Eisenhower had not wanted Monty on the Operation Overlord senior command team but was overruled by Churchill and Monty's supporters on the British Imperial General Staff.

43. Churchill famously observed, "There is only one thing worse than fighting with allies, and that is fighting without them."

44. Bharadwaj Badal, Sangeeta. 2015. "Delegating: A Huge Management Challenge for Entrepreneurs." *Business Journal*, April 14, 2015. https://news.gallup.com/businessjournal/182414/delegating-huge-management-challenge-entrepreneurs.aspx.

45. Gordon, page 249.

46. Ibid., page 270.

47. Miller, Merle. 1988. *Ike the Soldier: As They Knew Him*. Putnam. Page 589.

48. Gordon, page 273.

49. Eisenhower, page 45.

50. Blumenson, *Battle of the Generals*, page 21.

51. Bradley, page 299.

Conclusion: Paying the Price of Victory

1. Balkoski, Joseph. 2006. *Omaha Beach*. Stackpole Books. Page 576. Everand.

ELEVATE YOUR LEADERSHIP.
LEARN FROM HISTORY.
LEAD WITH IMPACT.

Top business organizations trust Patrick Ungashick to build strong leaders and successful companies. Vistage, EO, and industry groups rely on his expertise to drive growth and lasting success.

VISIT **WWW.PATRICKUNGASHICK.COM**
TO LEARN MORE ABOUT:

CONSULTING　　**SPEAKING**　　**BOOKS**　　**FREE RESOURCES**

An award-winning author and dynamic speaker, Ungashick has led 500+ powerful workshops, helping businesses maximize value and navigate seamless leadership transitions.

Ready to elevate your company?
Contact Patrick Ungashick today!

Acknowledgments

Writing this book relied on the generous input and influence of many people, too numerous to list. My passion for history was stoked at an early age by my parents and teachers and my practice of the craft of business leadership has been guided by multiple role models. But one must begin somewhere, and so I first wish to thank my business partners: Stephen Griner, Michael Murray, Trey Prophater, Chris Rowen, Andy Mason, and Gordon Watt. Sharing ownership in a privately held company can be tricky, as I know from firsthand experience as well as my work advising hundreds of other business partnerships. I am deeply thankful to have not just one but a half-dozen partners whom I respect and appreciate. Their talents and accomplishments within our companies permit me the freedom to pursue projects such as this book.

I also wish to acknowledge Larry Hart, my former business coach at Vistage International for nearly fifteen years. Within the wisdom he gave me, many years ago during a sushi lunch he challenged me to write my first book, which became *Dance in the End Zone*. I have been writing something ever since.

A Day for Leadership demanded considerable research, more than I originally anticipated. During that effort, these people courteously offered their time and assistance: US Army Lieutenant Colonel (Retired) Charles R. Herrick; Toni Kiser, senior registrar and director of collections management with the US National World War II Museum; Andrew E. Woods, research historian with the First Division Museum at Cantigny

Park; and Claudia Rivers, head of the Special Collections Department at the University of Texas El Paso Library. The perspective they provided or documents they located—in some cases unpublished materials that I had not known existed—enriched this book's stories.

Dozens of business leaders, including clients, colleagues, friends, and friends-of-friends, provided invaluable aid by reading a few early chapters (including some uncomfortably rough drafts) or a prerelease manuscript. Without their feedback, suggestions, and encouragements, this book would remain an unfinished, lifeless project buried three-file-levels deep on my computer.

Thank you to the team at Greenleaf Book Group. They have brought to this project experience, creativity, and a genuine spirit of collaboration.

Finally, and most importantly, I wish to thank my wife, Maggie. Her wise counsel, limitless support, and passion for our shared journey made this book as much ours as mine.

About the Author

For most of his career, Patrick Ungashick has built and led companies that provide advisory services to business owners and leadership teams. An entrepreneur himself, he has been a founder or leader in a half dozen companies, in industries including sales training, wealth management, investment banking, private equity, and exit strategy consulting.

In addition to *A Day for Leadership*, Patrick is the author of two books helping business owners and entrepreneurs achieve successful exits, *Dance in the End Zone* and *A Tale of Two Owners*. An award-winning author and speaker, he has conducted more than five hundred workshops for business owners and teams on how to maximize company value and achieve successful exits and leadership successions.

Patrick has three sons, and he and his wife, Maggie, enjoy travel, boating, and wine. And, of course, Patrick is an avid student of history.

Engagement Opportunities

For more information about Patrick's books, consulting services, and speaking engagements, please visit www.patrickungashick.com.